Conversations with Ken Kesey

Literary Conversations Series
Peggy Whitman Prenshaw
General Editor

Conversations
with Ken Kesey

Edited by Scott F. Parker

University Press of Mississippi   *Jackson*

Books by Ken Kesey

One Flew Over the Cuckoo's Nest, Viking, 1962.

Sometimes a Great Notion, Viking, 1964.

Kesey's Garage Sale, Viking, 1973.

Kesey, Northwest Review of Books, 1977 (Edited by Michael Strelow).

The Day After Superman Died, Lord John Press, 1980.

Demon Box, Viking, 1986.

The Further Inquiry, Viking, 1990.

Caverns (by O. U. Levon, a joint pseudonym for Ken Kesey, Robert Bluckner, Ben Bochner, James Finley, Jeff Forester, Bennett Huffman, Lynn Jeffress, Neil Lindstrom, H. Highwater Powers, Jane Sather, Charles Varani, Meredith Wadley, Lidia Yukman, and Ken Zimmerman), Penguin, 1990.

Little Tricker the Squirrel Meets Big Double the Bear, Viking, 1990.

The Sea Lion, Viking, 1991.

Sailor Song, Viking, 1992.

Last Go Round: A Real Western, (with Ken Babbs), Viking, 1994.

*Kesey's Jail Journal: Cut the M*********** Loose*, Viking, 2003.

www.upress.state.ms.us

The University Press of Mississippi is a member of the Association of American University Presses.

First printing 2014

∞

Library of Congress Cataloging-in-Publication Data

Kesey, Ken.
Conversations with Ken Kesey / edited by Scott F. Parker.
pages cm. — (Literary conversations series)
Includes index.
ISBN 978-1-61703-970-6 (cloth : alk. paper) — ISBN 978-1-61703-982-9 (pbk. : alk. paper) —
ISBN 978-1-61703-971-3 (ebook) 1. Kesey, Ken—Interviews. 2. Novelists, American—20th century—Interviews. I. Parker, Scott F. editor of compilation. II. Title.
PS3561.E667Z46 2014
813'.54—dc23
[B]   2013035940

British Library Cataloging-in-Publication Data available

Contents

Introduction

Though he made his reputation as a writer, it is as a psychedelic guru that Ken Kesey's reputation largely maintains—and how one assesses Kesey as a cultural figure tends to have much to do with the amount and kind of value one recognizes in the psychedelic movement. Was it a noble experiment, regardless of its outcomes? Was it a lifestyle of radical self-indulgence? Surely, any honest reading of the '60s must comprise both extremes and find its center of gravity somewhere between, but it's easier to think in binary of poles, so Kesey—as the public face of acid and the unmoved mover of the psychedelic movement—gets read as a personification of the decade and therefore becomes equally polarized: either he was an unprecedented visionary whose ambitions couldn't be contained by mere literature or he was a talented but undisciplined writer who got swept up in the times.

Kesey's two great novels, *One Flew Over the Cuckoo's Nest* and *Sometimes a Great Notion*, were published in 1962 and 1964, respectively, while he was still in his twenties. When he turned away from writing after his second book it was to turn toward film and the idea of making from his life a living work of art. Film he considered a better medium than writing for capturing the texture of contemporary life, often repeating a version of "If Shakespeare were alive today, he wouldn't be using the quill pen." The idea that Kesey would "rather be a lightning rod than a seismograph" was due as much to Neal Cassady, whose influence on Kesey probably cannot be overstated, as it was to the drugs. The hiatus from writing lasted into the '70s, but after settling on a farm in Pleasant Hill, Oregon, with his family, Kesey found himself returning to writing, explaining to Paul Krassner in an interview: "I was counting on the millennium. Now I guess I'm tired of waiting." Kesey continued to write and publish, however irregularly, over the remainder of his life, but it's still for his early novels that he's known as an author.

And yet, resonate in the culture as those books—especially *Cuckoo's Nest*, thanks to its film adaptation—do, it is primarily for what happened in the mid-'60s after the publication of *Sometimes a Great Notion* that Kesey continues to hold a central place in our cultural memory. There's no talking about Kesey—or talking with Kesey—without talking drugs.

Marijuana and hallucinogens were central to Kesey's writing as early as *Cuckoo's Nest*. He'd been involved in drug experiments at the Menlo Park Veterans Hospital for years already when the book was published and stated that its first pages and the idea for Bromden, the Indian narrator, came to him on peyote. In an interview with Gordon Lish he compares the benefits of drugs for him to those James Joyce gained from his eyeglasses. But after *Sometimes a Great Notion* writing stopped seeming like an adequate means of expression for Kesey, and he began to think of the bus Furthur as his primary *artistic* product. It's with Cassady at the wheel, a refrigerator full of acid-infused orange juice in the back, and the whole country in front him, that Kesey says, "Novels are a dime a dozen, but there's only one bus Furthur."

Not everyone will agree, of course, that a psychedelic bus trip is worth more than the books that were presumably sacrificed to it, but if we take seriously Kesey's idea that Furthur was an artistic enterprise, not just a recreational one, then we can entertain the possibility that Kesey, not Tom Wolfe, is the author of the accompanying Kesey persona, even if it was primarily Wolfe's *The Electric Kool-Aid Acid Test* in 1968 that made Kesey's escapades and charisma known to the public. Kesey, then, by "authoring" the bus and his role as lightning rod to Wolfe's seismograph, can be seen to have produced a work of art that won't conform to the dimensions of a book. But in transgressing any boundary to his work, he made his creation, his "self," into one of our last writer-heroes. The irony is that he was a hero mostly insofar as he stopped being known as a writer: or, the character overtook its creator, and from that time on the author struggled to be anything but his persona.

Kesey's publications after *Great Notion* were in part different kinds of attempts to get out from under the persona. He called the persona Devlin Deboree and dumped what he hoped was all of it in *Demon Box*; he tried co-writing novels with students and friends; he turned to performance and storytelling and children's writing; and, twenty-eight years after *Great Notion*, he published one more big novel, *Sailor Song*, an attempt to return to an old-fashioned, story-based book.

In a 1993 interview with Dan McCue, Kesey said that he "wouldn't have let Tom Wolfe do [*Kool-Aid*] if I had known what I know now." But however we divide responsibility for the aftermath of *Kool-Aid*, it was Kesey alone who suffered under it. In the later interviews it's palpable how much the history weighs on Kesey, as he alternates between celebration and the suggestion of regret.

* * *

Despite the tolls of fame and drugs on Kesey, these interviews reveal an author, an artist, a person, of utmost intelligence and compassion, deeply engaged with and committed to the world around him. No matter the occasion, he speaks or writes playfully in parables full of the folksy wisdom he cultivated in Oregon coming of age amidst a storytelling family.

I have attempted to collect here interviews that represent the full range of Kesey's time in the public eye: from his first major interview with Gordon Lish between the publication of his two early novels (in which we see Kesey at his most writerly) to his last interview reminiscing about the Grateful Dead; from short newspaper pieces to long, in-depth portraits.

For someone who claimed to the *Ann Arbor Argus* that he hated interviews, Kesey gave a lot of them. In addition to major interviews (*Genesis West, Realist, Paris Review*) and interview-like pieces, Kesey gave dozens of interviews to underground papers (*Good Times, Dupree's Diamond News*), to TV shows (*Tomorrow Coast to Coast, Later with Bob Costas),* to radio shows (*Fresh Air, Chris Comer*), and even to strangers. Because he answered so many requests, there are some interviews I could not track down and many that I excluded for their repetitions of answers from interviews selected for this book.

It is possible to appreciate Kesey's magnetism just by noting how hard some of the interviewers try to impress him; talking to him falls second only to taking acid with him in conferring upon a person the rebellious status real rebels don't seek. It's nice to see Kesey chide these interviewers, just as it is sad in later interviews to hear Kesey's excessive name-dropping, which comes to sound like a claim at regaining his former relevance. In the best interviews, such as in Linda Gaboriau's or Carolyn Knox-Quinn's, we see a real effort to make the interview about Kesey rather than about the interviewer's experience with Kesey.

Alongside the interviews in this book are two distinctly non-interview pieces. One is a transcription of Kesey's first "trip" at the Menlo Park VA. This is mostly Kesey describing his experience to a tape recorder with some prompting from a nurse. But it's central to representing and understanding Kesey's interests as a writer. We hear in his voice some of the language that he will soon write into *Cuckoo's Nest* (e.g., "cogs and gears") as well as the incipient notions of what will become the acid tests and our need for a "messiah." The recording serves as a kind of preview of his entire career.

The other non-interview is a 1965 lecture sponsored by the National Defense Education Act that Kesey gave at the Institute for Teachers of

Writing. I include this lecture because it's the best articulation of Kesey's decision to turn away from writing at this time and it comes in a period when we have no other interviews except what's in Wolfe's book. We also get a taste in this talk of the Kesey we read about in *Kool-Aid*, spurring people on to the present moment, a different way of living and being; a guru, becoming the messiah he called for on his first "trip."

* * *

I have silently streamlined certain variant spellings (e.g., DayGlo and '60s) and introduced the serial comma for clarity. Otherwise, the only editing was to elide "ums" and other verbal ticks from the audio interviews and to omit extraneous material in select cases.

I would like to thank the copyright holders in general and a few in particular: Rob Elder and Linda Gaboriau were exceedingly generous with their time and assistance on this project; Zane Kesey answered many emails and allowed me to transcribe the Menlo Park recording for the first time. Additional thanks to M. J. Fitzgerald for helping to arrange the time I needed to assemble this book.

SFP

Chronology

1935   Born September 17 Ken Elton Kesey in La Junta, Colorado, to Frederick A. Kesey and Geneva Kesey.

1946   Moves to Springfield, Oregon.

1956   Marries Norma "Faye" Haxby.

1957   Graduates from University of Oregon with a major in speech and communications, having won awards for acting and wrestling, and having spent time in Hollywood trying to break into the movies.

1958   Matriculates at Stanford on a Woodrow Wilson Fellowship to study creative writing under Wallace Stegner and Malcolm Crowley. Classmates include Ken Babbs, Larry McMurtry, Wendell Berry, Ed McClanahan, Gurney Norman, and Robert Stone. Writes *End of Autumn*, an unpublished novel about college sports.

1959   Volunteers for CIA-financed drug experiments at Menlo Park VA, where he will later work as an aide. Writes *Zoo*, an unpublished novel about the beats in North Beach, San Francisco.

1960   Competes at the Olympic Trials in wrestling but fails to qualify for team.

1962   *One Flew Over the Cuckoo's Nest* is published—within ten years it will sell over a million copies and become the most assigned contemporary novel in American universities.

1963   Broadway version of *One Flew Over the Cuckoo's Nest* opens, starring Kirk Douglas as McMurphy. Kesey attends opening.

1964   *Sometimes a Great Notion* is published. Kesey travels across country on the bus Furthur with the Merry Pranksters to be in New York for the publication and the World's Fair. Along the way they film "The Movie."

1965   Arrested in April for possession of marijuana. The first of the Acid Tests takes place in November. The Warlocks, later known as the Grateful Dead, will play regularly at these events over the course of the next year.

1966   Arrested in January for possession of marijuana, fakes suicide, and flees to Mexico—which is later recounted in the screenplay *Over the Border* in *Kesey's Garage Sale*. Arrested upon return to Bay Area in late fall. The final Acid Test, the Graduation, is held on Halloween in San Francisco.

1967   Convicted of drug possession, Kesey spends six months in the San Mateo County Jail and the San Mateo County Sheriff's Honor Camp.

1968   Moves to Pleasant Hill, Oregon, just outside Springfield. Tom Wolfe's *The Electric Kool-Aid Acid Test* is published.

1970   Film version of *Sometimes a Great Notion* is released.

1971   Coedits *The Last Supplement to the Whole Earth Catalog* with Paul Krassner.

1973   *Kesey's Garage Sale* is published. In addition to the screenplay *Over the Border*, it contains essays, drawings, letters, interviews, and fiction.

1974   The first volume of Kesey's magazine *Spit in the Ocean* is published. Each volume contains an excerpt from Kesey's novel in progress, *Seven Prayers by Grandma Whittier*, as well as other work.

1975   Film version of *One Flew Over the Cuckoo's Nest* is released. The movie sweeps the major Academy Awards.

1976   *Spit in the Ocean*, no. 2.

1977   *Spit in the Ocean*, no. 3. *Kesey*, a collection of Kesey's notes, manuscripts, and drawings, is published by Northwest Review Books.

1978   *Spit in the Ocean*, no. 4.

1979   *Spit in the Ocean*, no. 5.

1980   *The Day After Superman Died*, a fictional account of Neal Cassady's death, is published. It will appear later in *Demon Box*.

1981   *Spit in the Ocean*, no. 6.

1984   Kesey's son Jed dies from a bus accident traveling with his University of Oregon wrestling team.

1986   *Demon Box*, a collection of fiction and nonfiction pieces, is published.

1989   *Caverns*, a novel co-written with his University of Oregon graduate students, is published by "O. U. Levon."

1990   *The Further Inquiry*, a screenplay that has the Merry Pranksters on trial, is published. Children's book *Little Tricker the Squirrel Meets Big Double the Bear* is published.

1991   Children's book *The Sea Lion* is published.

1992   *Sailor Song*, a novel based around the filming of *The Seal Lion* in Alaska, is published. Kesey develops diabetes.

1994   *Last Go Round: A Real Western* co-written with Ken Babbs is published.

1997   Suffers stroke.

1999   Play *Twister: A Ritual Reality in Three Quarters Plus Overtime If Necessary*, based on *The Wizard of Oz*, is performed with Kesey playing the Wizard.

2001   Dies of complications from surgery to remove liver tumor.

2003   *Kesey's Jail Journal: Cut the M*********** Loose*, which he was consolidating at the time of his death, is published.

2010   Film *Magic Trip* is released, making available some of the footage from "The Movie."

Conversations with Ken Kesey

Ken Kesey's First "Trip"

Menlo Park Veterans Hospital / 1959

Reprinted by permission of the Ken Kesey Estate.

Nurse: Do you have any anxiety? Or do you feel kind of excited about the idea? Could you tell me where you are?
Kesey: I feel more excited than I do anxious. I don't feel anxious because I think the whole atmosphere pretty well stops any anxiety that you might try to bring into it. It's not the atmosphere you get just before you're wheeled into an operating room.

Nurse: You feel pretty good about the whole thing and kind of open and just waiting to see what happens?
Kesey: That's right.

Nurse: Sounds very good. Sounds like a good experiment.

[tape off]

Kesey: The thing is I find it a good deal more difficult to talk into a tape than I do if I sit here with a pencil in my hand and just wrote it onto the paper, because when you're doing it with a paper it's between you and *something* and the paper begins to represent a person like Faye or like Vik,[1] who is going to be the reciprocate of it. The paper has something of me, whereas the machine here to my left is all cogs and gears and electricity. I keep thinking that I should hear from it not cogs and gears and electricity noises but my true story sounds from down the hall. And I wonder on these drugs what they do to keep you from just slipping into sleep. Because the first

---

1 Vik Lovell, the friend who led Kesey to the Menlo Park psychedelic tests, and to whom Kesey would later dedicate *One Flew Over the Cuckoo's Nest*.

thing that seems to happen is sleep becomes a very desirable state. [Yawn.] Even when I talk about it I begin to yawn. [Yawn.]

And I can still hear [unintelligible] sounds. And then you begin to think perhaps all this is a placebo thing and they've been administering to make you think, "I'm under drugs. How should I act under this drug?" And so you begin to fabricate certain things, thinking it's a placebo and you—Stop!

And, oh wait, it's five minutes after eleven. We must have injected this thought. Keeping my mind up on the tourniquet around my wrist—the tourniquet of time, which is not a bad phrase.

Anyway, to the placebo idea of the drugs: placebo may even be more of a drug than anything they could possibly give you because all the placebo does—it releases the . . . it releases . . . I'm beginning to get halty. I can rally all my thoughts and bring myself through it, and we won't do it, we won't ramble anymore—that Wollensak [the tape recorder], a woolen sack, what a thought. See the trouble with the tape recorder is you begin to think, "I'm rambling for rambling's sake," like I would not have said "woolen sack" under ordinary circumstances. [Yawn.] Or to have even taken the trouble with the pencil and paper.

Now let me think . . . what is there in this congenial high that is different from other highs? I feel fairly drunk like I'm lying on my back with the whirlies, and it's pleasanter than that because I don't think that at any moment I'm going to roll over and be sick. [Yawn.] I continue to yawn. [Yawn.] The dim light at the top of the room is like a great eye to which the optic nerve's leading to all the walls. And I guess this would be right because it's coming down the side here. Your optic nerve. This would be a much better situation if the tape recorder was really a person to sit here. Now if Faye was here or Vik was here or Chloe. [Yawn.] . . . I wonder if they took into account me not getting to bed till two o'clock last night. . . . Anyway, god, it's only five after eleven, it's only five minutes from eleven. It seems like, wow, can't even imagine it's been five minutes since the time I realized it was five minutes. It's gonna be years before Faye comes down here to pick me up. Years.

[tape off]

They make this tape recorder a god-devilishly hard thing to turn on. Oh, and why I turned it back on was all of a sudden maybe one of these eggs that were inside would now hatch because *wing*. [Yawn.] It was just [unintelligible]. [Yawn.] It's like being kicked right in the back of the neck. That's why I thought I might check the watch. The watch only says ten after eleven. It's like being kicked in the back of the neck. That's too much. So heretofore turn the tape recorder off, wait I've been kicked again.

[tape off]

And I thought I had the tape recorder off for a long, long time, but it's still only ten after eleven. The tape recorder now is better than the papers down there because I lie here and look at it really becomes this great beast, this toad-like thing, [yawning] all hunkered down listening, not only listening but sucking it in probably better than most people do. It's actually to you and this whole high and the thing that pumped you for tape recorder was to ah—let you know that I was just thinking of a thing that Vik, man, there was another one of those egg things popped. Vik says about it being a fine high and going to waste. I just realized a great truth: that if it's a *fine* high it does not go to waste. You know what I mean?

I can hear the people. That's the thing here I wish I could do. I never confide in paper. Or I couldn't confide in tape recorder either or maybe it's because you only confide in yourself, truly. I couldn't confide in paper because I know that eventually this paper is going to be read around, like the nurse who was in here. I couldn't confide in what I really felt about her because you never can tell when that sort of thing might get back to the nurse. And make her feel very bad. I remember saying a saggy white-dressed nurse came in and that wasn't the nurse at all. Let's take another look at her. Why is she saggy? She's wearing this sheet-style costume probably because the belly around her middle is beginning to be blue and overhanging and she has to cover it up and she's got a slip between that belly and her cloth and I'm beginning to think at this point of this horrible blue, rolly flesh. Just what some great psychologist will do, making this *"ah-ah, rolly flesh."* It's like looking at Rorschach and seeing mashed testicles.

I keep hearing these babbling people outside. . . .

Also, the trouble with you. And this being a sort of a trouble-finding time, with you as a tape recorder, you waiting toad, you big listening toad, is you are not really patient. You would think that a tape recorder would be the most patient thing in the world, but look at you there, you make this tiny little humming sound. It's not a patient thing at all. . . . And in fact it's very impatient. You don't realize how much you look like this toad. . . .

I could lie here the rest of the day and just feel perfectly happy with my high. The thing I'm worrying about now is pretty quick that doctor's going to come in here and he's going to have to make his money. And he's going to have ideas of his own that he's got to build up and he's going to say, "Here we are. Now, this drug you've got in your belly cost, oh, twenty bucks to the government. They gotta get twenty bucks worth a good out of it. Now we've gotta give you EEGs again and poke holes in your head and do the whole bit. So sit up here and take notice." Whereas it'd just be nice to just sit here with you the rest of the evening. And from where I lay I could see the unwinding reel that is your brain without which you don't even become a toad anymore. You're just a dead thing that needs to be reloaded with a new brain. I can see it unwinding, therefore I'm going to shut you off because we're losing too much of your brain. I'll check first with the watch. . . . I find nothing but a band on my arm. An absolute band. And it's only a [laughing] quarter after eleven. It's the most insane thing. 'Cause it was seeming like noon or thereafter. It's going to be hours.

[tape off]

I gotta tell this great thing. There's this great colored frog-of-a-man outside standing at the door at some guy's room and the guy's all teetering out of the bed there. And the guy's going "MEHN. HEY. HEY MEHN. HEY MEHN!" And then he finally tells the nurse everything's all right and goes teetering off.

[Noises of metal things being moved and dropped.] Figure out how to do this thing. Figure out how to stop it. [More noises of things being moved and dropped.]

The thing I have to remember is across the room—I gotta drag this thing—through the crack in the wall I can look in on the guy that I'll call—what would this guy's name be?—he's sure giving the nurses a hard time. Anyway, I can understand for the first time. I couldn't understand it at all why anyone would give the nurses a hard time. But the nurse is this [indecipherable]-ridden old women who stands there with eyes accusing you of all her diseases and the poor guy's lying there and it's just him and his little metal toolings, and this is all he's got between he and the wall. And I can remember this morning when we started out he says, "Wait a minute. Is this noise I'm making over here bothering you? Is the radio bothering you?" And this woman who was with me said, "No, no, go right ahead," and walked right along. He wasn't worried at all, and I knew that at the time. He wasn't worried at all about the noise bothering, what he wanted was somebody to come sit down there beside him and say, "What are you doing?" And he'd say, "Well, look here, I'm punching out the saxophone on the copper." That's what he wanted. I could see that this morning. *At the moment*, is the thing. You could really see why he had to do this, and why it's such an important thing for him to have to. I'm freezing to death! I gotta look back at the wall.

So that's what I realize is the great thing about this drug, is it enables me to—oh god, it's only twenty-five minutes after eleven—it enables me to—first I've got to pull this shade down—because—and turn out the light; how the hell do you turn the lights out?—because it enabled me to look over at these guys and their minds are really shot. You give me a chance to be on their team for a while, if I'm on their team I should be able to go out there and shoot the ball with them.

[tape off]

It's ten minutes to ten. The long length of time was taken out not just by ramblings but by people being here doing things, like the middle-aged psychologist was here with the lightning bolts through her hair. She wanted to see if I could add still, and draw lines still, and tell time still. I foxed her on the time by taking my pulse.[2]

I just realized how much the Wollensak microphone looks like a shaver and the doctor was here tapping on my legs and hitting with the rubber hammer again and making me play boxing games from my nose to his finger. Oh, this is what I was going to start to say, why I started the machine up, not just purely [Yawn.] to record. I always yawn when I get this Wollensak up in front of my face, maybe because it's a horrendous bore. . . . Oh, I realized as the doctor bent over me here I also was able to see things about the doctor and about the room that I hadn't been able to see before. Whereas my first impression of him was striding up the walk with a suitcase under one hand and dark glasses and his brisk suit. A Madison Avenue man. And now he's all of a sudden changed to a white coat and the veins coming to the surface from hard work. Just because I think this atmosphere of this hospital would do that, just the very breathing of the patients in here would suck out the veins on a person. This guy across the hall wants so much from people, wants more than people have, wants more than is his share. That's why he wanted to stop us with his metal tapping this morning. He wants more than his share. He wants to suck it out of people as much as he can.

---

2   Asked to estimate when a minute had passed, Kesey, knowing his normal resting heart rate, discretely took his pulse and counted a nearly precise minute.

Consequently people wall off. They don't give him anything. They give them maybe like [Yawn.] professional candy that they manufacture at home over the textbooks, which are cookbooks.

I do think. Oh, and what I started to say—I've got to keep my mind clear, why I started to record and not just freely associate this utter babble. [Yawning:] Which must infuriate a doctor to have to unscramble. What I started to say is that, like when tapping on the leg, perhaps a person isn't natural and then he wants to do just a little bit more of what the doctor wants him to do. Or maybe it's me, and not the rest of these patients. That could be. Maybe on the first impression this Wollensak, this toad by my side, this shaver in my hand, is no longer these things but is a psychoanalyst and he's—I'm gonna get back to what I was saying, if I can. Oh! I'm trying to *give* more, where the patients in here are trying to get more. Better keep my mind—it keeps getting away. I'm trying to give. [Yawn.]

Nurse: (from the hallway) "Are you all right in there, Mr. Nichols?"
Kesey: "Are you all right in there, Mr. Nichols?" See listen to that, that's candy from home. They're all right. Everybody's all right. The doctors can't really give any of theirselves, which is what the patients want. The doctors can't really give any of theirselves because these people are too greedy, they want too much, so they have to save theirselves for theirselves, home, family, and kids. "Are you all right in there, Mr. Nichols?" I can see where if she stuck to the door and said, "Are you all right in there, Mr. Nichols?" with concern in her voice, the patient would suck her in like this great big black vacuum.

How do you achieve a middle balance? And the other thing—this is just purely for physiological people who want to know the physiological effect of this drug: from the waist on down I'm just gnawing my legs, they writhe, they open like a stretch, a real pleasure. [Yawn.] Yes, it's a nice stretch. And I noticed another thing, it's . . . the moon [laughter] is full. . . . And I've babbled for another five minutes. I'm a ceaseless babble. Also—this is what I started to say in the first place—is I want to *give* the doctor something, knowing the doctor's going to listen to this tape and I want to give him something. I'm trying too hard. I'm not being myself. I'm not being natural. I'm not allowing myself to associate. Maybe because I'm afraid there isn't anything in here worth giving so I have to manufacture a good thing. I feel like I wanna lie here and say things about, oh, how my mother and my sister used to slip out into the woodshed together and do strange things. So I want to manufacture things, I guess, for the doctor, for Vik. For almost anyone. I can see now with the Wollensak in my hand here being my analyst, I can see where on this drug you might have great breakthroughs. And with prompting, if you can keep your goddamn mind straight, and as the doctor said, "steady as she goes," that this would be very good for analysis, this drug.

Sharing is one thing, that's a whole lot of it. Because this tape isn't just entirely for me. It's a thing to be shared, it's sharing with Faye and people an experience they were not allowed to have for two reasons: they weren't allowed to have the drug [background noise—of engine?] Jesus! Gotta see what's going on in the other room. . . .

[tape off]

It's quarter to one, and I'm high out of my mind, and I've just been down having pin cushions stuck in my head, and what before was—was not a pleasant experience, was not a pleasant man all of a sudden became these great curtains. They were cathedral walls with color, and this old guy's squeaking around in a full chorus of crepe-souled shoes: sk-sk-sk. Every time he took a step, and also if you leaned on the vent you could feel his, you could feel his—what's amazing is I seem to have a different high down there than I do up here, almost as if that machine of his was turning these color images into my mind. Wild color images. And then I keep thinking I've been here before. Also, this test that I just took. The complete little dots test, the manufacture bunny test that you used to have to do in grade school, became a great test because those angles, those angles. And they're supposed to bring me food here in just a minute, which should be a fine experience all by itself, this food. Oh man, those guys outside. What were they saying that was so funny? "How would you like a bust in the nose? That guy's just been asking for a bust in the nose. Lock him up there! Lock him up! Go on, shut the door. Keep him quiet." And somebody says, "He's been asking for it too long. It's time somebody gave him a bust in the nose." And all these cats who were eager for any sort of action in this dull place said, "Yeah, yeah, bust him in the nose." And I'd kinda like to go out there and tell them, "You're all so square. Because you're not [indecipherable]."

[tape off]

God, it's only twelve minutes—no, thirteen minutes to one. It's only been two minutes elapsed. That's amazing. Outside the window there's mad conversation going on. It's a real Burroughs scene. William S. Burroughs does exist!

He's all split-out spewing like characters out of horror movies, all of 'em. Guy over here beating a bad rhythm blues. [Singing:] *Ba-ah. Ba-ah. Ba-ah.*

[tape off]

It's five minutes to one and I'm recording something here I don't want to forget: this drug is probably one of the illegal ones that you can only get with a prescription or if you're caught with it in the compart of your car you get five years in jail. It's so wrong because it's such a good drug. And that I suddenly am filled with this great loving and understanding of people. Understanding is much [indecipherable]. I think the love was always there. This guy next door playing the blues: *do-do do-do*. And the noise of the lunchies down the hall crashing and banging with their spoons and their plates. It's a fine, fine thing. I don't say that it's a drug for every day or once week use—or maybe once a week use—but how about a high, a Friday night high in which eight or nine close, intimate friends sit around and get quietly high like this together, where we could talk and elaborate and wow? But I don't mean it for driving-home type. Nobody's going to get high on this and go out and rape somebody. They might go and take a little girl by the hand and give her a bottle of flowers, but that would be all. And the newspapers wouldn't be able to lose their minds over that. So I say public support has to get behind it. We need a huge missionary. We need a messiah to tell the people who aren't there.

[tape off]

At exactly one minute to one a question occurs to me: is it impolite to be hungry when you're high? Is this an imposition put on the high, like the high being a guest, to drop into its house and say, "Mrs. High, I've enjoyed my stay here, but I'm hungry."

[tape off]

It's now one-thirty and I've just been to see the after-image man, who is a trainee and you can tell because trainees give off an aura of traineeism and they come along here with their little eyes so wide open. They think, "I'm finding something, I'm finding something." And you could see his little ferret mind grabble at the first thing that seemed like an idea of his own. Snap snap. The after-image man. It's so symbolic.

It's one-twenty-five and in ten seconds, at the time of the tone. [Ding.] It's a fine watch. It's a self-winding Bulova. [Knock at door.] Yeah.

Nurse: How are you feeling right now? I mean is there still some effect of the drug?
Kesey: Oh yeah. A great deal of effect. I felt for the first time a little bit ago a little bit nauseous, which I hadn't felt before. I think the time the drug was at its strongest was the time I was taking the EEG, lying there with those nails driven into my head, and everything that that machine said next door scratched itself all across my mind. It was wild.

Nurse: You sort of experienced the EEG machine, the noise that it made, as sort of going across your mind?
Kesey: Into the color sensation. And those wild dreams. That man draped his own room?

Nurse: Yes, he did.
Kesey: Did he pick his own drapes?

Nurse: I think so.
Kesey: I wonder if he did it high or if he did just when he was sort of in an ordinary state.

Nurse: How did they affect you?
Kesey: The drapes? They were just fine drapes. And this time—oh, I told you about the strobe light was so great.

Nurse: What was the effect of the strobe light? Did you get that on the tape previous to this?
Kesey: I don't remember if I did or not. I don't think—

Nurse: Could you describe what the effect was?
Kesey: Ah, the strobe light, when that thing started it became like a sun, like a huge vacuous sun that sucked into it all manners of colors. Oh, no, it was like a magnetic force field because everything that went to it was concentric, going in toward the strobe light, and the faster the light would blink the faster these things would pour into it, shapes, bats, hen eggs, and everything that had been drawn with a very delicate pen-and-ink drawing cascading *into* the strobe light as it blinked.

Nurse: Were there other things? You mentioned two things: bats and hen eggs. Were there other things you could see going in?

Kesey: Well, there have been very few objects in the sense of describable objects. They're more mathematical patterns: hexagons and pentagons and nicely drawn pen-and-ink things that you might see looking through a raindrop that had fallen on the windshield of a car.

Nurse: Have you seen any of these things other than with the strobe light?

Kesey: Yeah, with the after-image man, when he was spinning this little thing. I got the same effect when the after image reached sixty cycles a minute while the alternating current of the regular lighting he was doing had a strobe effect when they corresponded, and it seemed to stop and go backwards. And I would see at one point there, I think you see first, ah, images, pictures, and then your mind makes them into things, because I saw these concentric patterns and all of them, not rectangular, but my mind made them into sort of hieroglyphical mummies and things that you might find on a pyramid wall, and so the strobe man, the after-image man, he started tapping on the—it was just something we found, and the sound was affected. He would start tapping on the thing, something, and these would begin to move and come dancing toward you. And this guy next door was playing his bad rock 'n' roll on his radio and this would have an effect of very discordant color.

Nurse: It affected the imagery.

Kesey: Mm-hmm. And the after-image man and I were wondering what would good music do? Like [Jimmy Yuke Freddy Bar??] or someone like this. Thelonious Monk. And see what kind of colors things would do.

Nurse: If you had to say just kind of off-hand what the most significant difference is between your normal state and the state you've experienced under the drug how would you describe the difference?

Kesey: Um, it seems to give you more observation and more insight. And makes you question things that you ordinarily don't question. Sounds that happen in the hall that your mind lets go in the backwash of sounds, your mind on the drug questions these sounds and becomes curious to want to look out and see what they are. At this moment I'm aware of hundreds of sounds that I'm sure I'm not aware of ordinarily. And it's not just sounds and colors but you feel at least—and it may be false—but you feel that you have a great deal of insight into the sounds and colors and into people.

Nurse: Would you say that this effect is partly that your hearing is more acute or that you attach more significance to what you hear?

Kesey: Well, both. Now, see, when you said "hearing is more acute," I just noticed it when you said the word "acute," it kinda goes *boing* and it hits the back of your mind and *spring* goes out there. And you elaborate on this with your own mind. Everything is more acute. All right, this is the first thing you realize. But you attach significance to the thing, like you—the observations make, they may be false, and you kind of question them in the moment because you realize that you're under a drug. But you still are attaching these great profound things to just squirrels dropping nuts on the sidewalk outside.

Nurse: When you close your eyes . . . Have you tried closing your eyes, and do you see any patterns?

Kesey: When I close my eyes I always see patterns. I have been doing this all the time. You just immediately see patterns as soon as your eyes are closed. They're very sharp and they're not—they're paintings, and the colors are the main things that stand out. They are done in pen and ink. They're not done with brush. Because you can see each tiny line that's used to make up any pattern. It's done with a pen and a very sharp ink. And they have certain kinds of colors. You know they call it DayGlo and Coldfire colors, these Madison Avenue greens they put on billboards to stop the cars going by. Well these you get a lot of. Especially when you get a black background like this. Immediately it's a huge scratch of lighting coming across, a great big green one. It stands out and glows by itself.

Nurse: You mentioned downstairs, either going down or coming up, the heightened significance of people or personality. Could you say something about this? Do you feel that you have greater insight into character?

Kesey: Mm-hmm. I do. I see more about people like the nurse who came in to extract the blood from my arm. Whereas before she was just a woman coming in here, suddenly she became a personality who came in here who was slipping a needle into my arm and taking blood out of it. And I was talking to her and, oh, like when she would mention that to take the urine test I was more aware of certain nuances in her voice that I hadn't been aware of before. She became a personality. She became a woman. You could see facets of her mind that I just had not allowed myself maybe to be aware of before.

Nurse: Was this, would you say, an uncomfortable or a comfortable experience.

Kesey: I think it's a good experience. I've been hoping that I can hang onto not the experience but remember that there are other things that I don't ordinarily see and therefore try to look for them. It's generally been a very good experience. Comfortable. I think any time you see more, especially if you have a basic inherent love among people, the more you see of them, of the real person, the more you like. Even these guys roaming around out here. You look at the externals of 'em and they're these old scaly warthogs, complete derelicts of humanity, and you look at 'em and you feel very great attachment to them. And warmth because you begin to understand them. You begin to see things in their personality you hadn't seen before.

Nurse: Is there anything else of significance you would like to report?

Kesey: Not that I can think of offhand.

Nurse: The time is now one-forty-five.

Kesey: The other thing I should record is that when I was lying down in the EEG room these colors that were coming to me were just piling down on me where it was almost, it was really an orgasm of perception and colors and those drapes, to where I really was sexually aroused by them, to the point of almost having a real sexual orgasm.

[tape off]

Two-thirty and I believe most of the effects of the drug have worn off. I feel now that I'd be able to get up and do just about anything I wanted to do: write, talk, read, with the same capacities I was able to do it yesterday and the day before.

What the Hell You Looking in Here for, Daisy Mae?

Gordon Lish / 1963

From *Genesis West*, Fall 1963 (Vol. 2 No. 1). © 1963 by Gordon Lish. Reprinted by permission.

Pasted on his typewriter, over the place where the maker's name would appear, there's a decalcomania that reads MOON, VIRGINIA. Under the shed which houses this typewriter and which serves as his workroom, eighteen new pups, the total offspring of two Dachshunds, raise a muted, insistent cacophony. Out over his many acres of dark woods a Sousa march screams in stereo from three hi-fi speakers fitted to the roof of the main cabin. One moves behind him, because he knows the natural hazards on this path, up the side of the hill to Barking Bug Meadow—past fimbriated mobiles hung from lateral branches—over rivulets in which enormous bottles propped against rocks hold Cool-Aid chilling in mountain water, a jigger glass capped on the cork—by extravagantly variegated paintings nailed to tree trunks—through a door that opens onto more path, more woods—past a huge pine inside whose base, hollowed-out by age or catastrophe, there rests a toy horse, the printed tin broken so that he kneels.

He has set about adorning the outlying woodland of his new home high in these California coastal mountains with the central statement of his personality: that man must cut an image of himself into the granitic indifference of this world; that he must be a maker of mysteries and legends, thereby increasing himself and diminishing the "fiercities" of a bewildering universe; that he must compete for God's attention—and wonderment.

I am talking with the novelist Ken Kesey, author of *One Flew Over the Cuckoo's Nest*, a book I regard the most perfect piece of long fiction since Salinger's *The Catcher in the Rye*. We are squatting across from each other on logs placed here so that the rump might be free of the high grass through which things crawl. We are in Barking Bug Meadow, named by his four-year-old son Zane, who once allowed as how "them damn bugs are all the time barking." This is a glade, high above the roofs of the cabins down below, and the sun is strong although the season is autumn. Between us, on the ground and nearly hidden in the long grass, is a portable midget tape-recorder.

I ask a question, and he begins to answer it, his voice very soft, almost whispering, a slow, tentative, thinking voice, bridging the pauses between phrases with hummed conjunctions, moving effortlessly from narrative to narrative, always in the dialect of the anecdote's mood. It is hours before I realize that in my absorption I have quite forgotten to turn on the recorder. Months later I will see his incredible equipment for spontaneous narration spellbinding a score of people with a carney recitation twenty minutes long, on Jonah and the Whale, or an endlessly hilarious surreal film treatment on the Woman with the Inhaling Lungs.

Writing this now, I remember here and there from what he said: a fantastic meeting he arranged between Neal Cassady (the model for Dean Moriarty in Kerouac's *On the Road*) and a dissimilar champion named Wilson—an Indian in a logger's camp suddenly crazed with the recollection of his blood and racing headlong from the mountain side to attack with his knife the grillwork of a diesel hurtling down the highway paved through his grandfather's land, dying out there bravely and badly, living again in the idea for Chief Broom Bromden, the narrator of *One Flew Over the Cuckoo's Nest*—Ginsberg arriving unannounced at his door one day and convincing him of a new truth about men—the slender fellow, at the buffet dinner, who insisted on Baldwin's enchanting elegance in a piercing, questionable voice, and who refused to argue the point until this Mr. Kesey learns to eat from a plate without holding down his meat with a thumb—volunteering himself for electric shock treatment "because a writer must work from what he knows"—agreeing to extirpate a catheterizing episode in *Cuckoo*, being sorry for it later, and not knowing its whereabouts because "some friends somewhere borrowed it"—sketching at the local museum to catch the sense of the artist/disc jockey who will narrate a novel-in-progress—and a variety of bright-colored "trips" with venison chile, Captain Marvel and Plastic Man, the nature of living, Spare-Tire, and all the many "fiercities" he is trying to name. Later, as the sun moved behind the encircling trees and the woods grew suddenly cold, I started up the recorder and made him answer questions—directly and in order. What follows are his answers, but that rare energy and imagination behind them—that came before, when I was more genuinely the listener, willing to simply talk with a man while we sat unbothered by directness and order, facing each other, in the woods.

Lish: I get a feeling of discomforting strangeness, mystery, from both *Cuckoo* and *Sometimes a Great Notion.* Even from you—as a man.

Kesey: I want that strangeness. The ordinary drifts backwards out of sight, like fenceposts along a highway. Were I able, I would wrench and distort every post along every highway—everywhere.

Lish: This sounds like the essence of a philosophy.

Kesey: Maybe it is. Right now in my life if I'm wise to anything it's only to that wish of others that I would leave their fenceposts be.

Lish: Irving Malin, the critic, had an essay in *Critique* in which he located you within an incipient movement he calls New American Gothic. He argues, as I remember it, that your characters are grotesqueries, their troubles are exaggerations, rather than amplifications, of the human complaint. Distortions, which is your word.

Kesey: Perhaps this is because I'm a parabolist, *my* word.

Lish: Which means?

Kesey: Which means, first, that I am *not* a reporter. I don't ask my reader to believe characters or situations exist anyplace other than in our minds— that there's a *possibility* for such existence in his mind and in my mind.

Lish: What's wrong with reality for a subject?

Kesey: Well, isn't it dishonest for a writer to try to convince people that things really happened as he describes them? The very act of writing, even reporting, that attempts to pass as objective, is an exercise in selection, picking and choosing *this* over *that* in order to emphasize *this* over that because the *this* suggested the deeper meaning of the scene. An artist who claims to portray life lies.

Lish: And how does this figure against conscious distortion?

Kesey: For instance, the most photographic painting of a horse is still a painting of a horse. It is not the live animal it pretends to be. It is *much* less efficient about getting a horseness than, say, a Chagall horse cavorting through a green sky. Chagall claims nothing more than a mad horse flying through the green sky of *his* painting and *his* mind. Poe understood this, for example, and for further example, Zola did not. When Zola said, "This is how it is in my world," he told a goddamned lie. A single *Batman* comic book is more honest than a whole volume of *Time* magazines.

Lish: You read comic books, don't you?
Kesey: Certainly.

Lish: Because they're honest?
Kesey: Because of their honest, open-handed bullshit.

Lish: Then you don't object to Malin's label?
Kesey: How can I? I purposefully decide to exaggerate my characters, to make them *gothic*, if you choose. A writer must practice lying for a long time before he can trust himself with anything so delicate as the truth.

Lish: Think you've had enough practice yet?
Kesey: It's coming. I'm just beginning to feel I have enough skill to attempt a character based on someone like my grandfather, for example. It'll be some time before I try someone like Faye, or my brother, or—hell, who knows—myself.

Lish: Another label occurs to me. The June issue of *Author & Journalist* carried a feature article by Gus Blaisdell in which your work is associated with something called the Neon Renaissance, which is?
Kesey: It's a name I hooked onto a thing I feel is happening nowadays. What this is I cannot say exactly, except that it's a need to find a new way to look at the world, an attempt to locate a better reality, now that the old reality is riddled with radioactive poison. I think a lot of people are working in a lot of different ways to locate this reality—Ornette Coleman in jazz, Ann Halprin in dance, the New Wave in movies, Lenny Bruce in comedy, Wally Hendrix in art, Heller, Burroughs, Rechy, Gunter Grass in writing, and those thousands of others whose names would be meaningless, either because they haven't made IT yet, or aren't working in a medium that has as its end an IT to make. But all these people are trying to find out *what* is happening, *why*, and what can be *done* with it.

Lish: What about yourself? Is your writing work or fun?
Kesey: More fun than work, and I intend to keep it that way.

Lish: That's a fairly unfashionable view. I suppose you have a reason for it.

Kesey: Something I learned when I was wrestling in the regionals for Oregon. I was matched against a guy named Barry Billington, a wrestler from U.C.L.A. who looked precisely like his name—*Big Barry Billington*, great piles of black hair all over him. He didn't train; he smoked cigarettes, and if there was a worse sin for a wrestler than smoking I sure as hell didn't know about it. Anyway, Billington generally horsed around—smiled all the time, looking over everybody and enjoying himself. Well, he just *beat* my ass, walked all over me, wound up 13-2. And one of the things I found out about Billington was that *he* was out there winning because he was having his fun. For me, it was necessary; I mean I *needed* it and I was working at it.

Lish: And this became a lesson for you?

Kesey: That's right. Whatever it is it has got to be fun. I want to love Faye and my kids not because it's a marvelous and moral thing to do but because it's fun to love them.

Lish: But your prose gives the impression of being created by a man who works himself to a fine, slim chit.

Kesey: Then that's merely an impression. I want to write a *good* novel instead of a *poor* one just because it's *fun* to write a good novel.

Lish: That kind of thinking is contrary to a vast tradition.

Kesey: I know. Our society says you're going to have to hurt a whole lot before you do *anything* good. Well, if in most cases it turns out that way, it's because it *has* to. We've just come to *believe* that it must. A guy decides to become a writer, and there's an inbred flaw in that decision. He tries to *become* a writer instead of just writing. That's work, a real pressure. He reads about Joyce or Hemingway, what they said in their letters and what they wrote. He begins to measure himself against these people—as personalities. He worries with it. Or he's out there writing and forever looking over his shoulder to see if other people are behind him. How else can he know if he's becoming a writer? That's real worry.

Lish: But I know *you* worry. You have your fiercities, or the dragons you point to in the dedication of *Cuckoo* to Vik Lovell. What are these dragons?

Kesey: Well, one of them is that thing we saw back there in the hollow of that tree. You sweat about them if they're *there* and you worry about them if they're *not.* One worry is about as bad as the other.

Lish: Yes, but that toy horse in that hole hardly explains the complexity for me.
Kesey: Okay. A dragon is a many-leveled beast, ranging from an actual, physical fiercity (the Bomb, the Big Nurses, the Barnetts, and the Barrygoldwaters of this world), through sheer fantasy ("Mommy! There's a scaly, lurky thing in the dark under my bed, and it wants to cut my *pajama string!*"), to spiritual despair ("Sugar, there ain't nothing under your bed but the dark—no dragons, no goblins, no ghosts, *nothing*."). Our lives are hung up with these dragons, either hung up that they're there or they *aren't*.

Lish: But what specific meaning did you ascribe to the dragons in the dedication?
Kesey: There I meant that Vik Lovell argued against the existence of spiritual dragons and then, quite without meaning it, led me to them.

Lish: How so?
Kesey: He arranged for me to act as a volunteer for experiments being done on most of the known psychedelic drugs.

Lish: Where was this?
Kesey: At a hospital near Stanford.

Lish: What happened?
Kesey: Another *world* happened. I took mescaline, psilocybin, IT-290, LSD, and some bad scene stuff that produces a condition intended to demonstrate to the whining neurotic how much worse off he can be. I'm grateful for this experience. It showed me scenes I'd otherwise never know. I had a tape recorder with me, free access to most of the place, and plenty of time to lie on my back watching whatever was moving around on the ceiling or the other guys who were watching their scenes. It slowly becomes evident to you that there's some awful and unique logic going on, just as real, in some ways, as your other world. It's very difficult to explain. In fact, it's taking me eight hundred pages to do it in the other book I'm preparing right now.

Lish: *Sometimes a Great Notion?*
Kesey: That one, yes. I'm fooling around with reality and what reality can be.

Lish: Is this why there are so many points of view in the book?
Kesey: Points of *view* and points of *time*. Whole bunches of ways of looking at the same event.

Lish: How many points of view?

Kesey: Nearly as many as there are people in that novel.

Lish: This sounds something like Robbe-Grillet's technique. Have you read any of his stuff?

Kesey: Tried to but I was quickly bored.

Lish: How about *Last Year at Marienbad*? Did you see it?

Kesey: Yes. That excited me as a *device* but bored me very much as a *movie*. He's lost the sense of people in his work, that's the trouble. I don't think you can veer very far from human problems and emotions and still suck the reader into turning the page. That's the writer's *first* job: suck the reader into turning the page. Otherwise, why put a ribbon in a typewriter?

Lish: Have drugs helped you in getting at these different vantage points?

Kesey: In a certain manner, yes. I've found them keys to worlds that have always existed, that *have* to be talked about. The kaleidoscopic pictures, the geometrics of humanity, that one experiences under, say, mescaline, aren't concealed in the white crystals inside the gelatin capsule. They are always in the mind. In the world. Already. The chemical *allows* the pictures to be seen. To know the world you need to see as many sides of it as possible. And this sometimes means using microscopes, telescopes, spectroscopes, even kaleidoscopes.

Lish: Has this anything to do with the lyrical and fantastic descriptions in *Cuckoo*?

Kesey: Yes, but *drugs* didn't create those descriptions any more than Joyce's *eyeglasses* created *Ulysses*. They merely help one to see the paper more clearly.

Lish: Did you do a lot of rewriting in *Cuckoo*?

Kesey: Not a whole hell of a lot. It went easier than any novel I'm likely to do.

Lish: How long did it take to bring the whole book to completion?

Kesey: About ten months.

Lish: *Great Notion*?

Kesey: Well, it's a year and three-quarters now, and I'm just finishing the final revision.

Lish: How much rewriting went into this one?
Kesey: I don't know exactly. At one point I had three different manuscripts in three different colors of paper lying around.

Lish: I saw a pretty elaborate chart stuck to the wall back there in your workroom. Has that something to do with *Great Notion*?
Kesey: It helps me keep tabs on who's where and how and who's telling you so.

Lish: Who's critical commentary was it that I found all over the manuscript for *Great Notion*?
Kesey: That's Ken Babbs. We were together in Stegner's program at Stanford.

Lish: Did he read *Cuckoo* for you, too?
Kesey: Yes, everything I do. I had to send the manuscript all the way to Vietnam so that he could go through it. He's in the Marines there.

Lish: Did you learn anything at Stanford?
Kesey: I learned a lot from Cowley.

Lish: And from Stegner?
Kesey: Just never to teach in college. You go back and read his early stuff, *On a Darkening Plain* maybe. Fine work. Then you try his later stuff and you find he's not writing to people any longer, not to the people he knows and loves, anyway. He's writing to a classroom and to his colleagues.

Lish: And that's the fault of teaching?
Kesey: Big-time teaching, yes. A man becomes *accustomed* to having two hundred people gather every day at one o'clock giving him all their attention—because he's clever, good-looking, famous, and has a beautiful voice. That can't happen without affecting a man's writing—the wrong way. And when that happens the academic life has come to the end of its usefulness for the writer.

Lish: And Cowley? What did *he* teach you?
Kesey: Well, before Cowley, I studied with James Hall at Oregon. He taught me how *good* writing can be. Cowley taught me how good a writer *I* could be.

Lish: Cowley believed in you?
Kesey: More than most.

Lish: Anybody else we should mention in this regard?
Kesey: Kerouac, I suppose. Not from what he's written but because he's shown me that the best reason for being a writer is doing what you *like* to do.

Lish: What *about* Kerouac as a novelist?
Kesey: I don't consider him one. He seems to me more a reporter. A thousand years from now when they want to know what was going on in our day, they'll have to read Kerouac. He's recorded what a great many people are doing and thinking, and with the accuracy of an historian.

Lish: You're *not* writing for posterity?
Kesey: No, I don't figure it that way. I'm writing for my brother, my dad, my mom, Faye, and the kids, the people I love and want to reach. Wait a minute. I'll add to that. I write for posterity in one kind of way that's hard to define. It's somewhere in something I remember from when I was a little kid. There was a stream that came down from the hill at our place and would have cut across our yard, but years before somebody went out there and covered this stream over with stone, mortared the stone together so that it left a hump down through the middle of this yard, as if it were left there by a seven hundred pound mole. And when the stream dried up my brother and I—he was in the third grade and I was in the fifth—we went down to the end of that tunnel and walked through it, lighting our way with torches. We found an old accordion under there. It was a *great* find, and we brought it home and tried to play it. But it wouldn't play, and we found out we could get into it by opening and opening this screw, and lifting the top off. We got into all the valves and bellows and everything, and there, stuck in a corner, we found a piece of paper, a sign, and it said, WHAT THE HELL YOU LOOKING IN HERE FOR, DAISY MAE? Well, I achieved some kind of *satori* right there—knowing that *somebody* had *sometime* a very *long* while ago *gone* in there and put that *sign* in that accordion, and he's betting all the time that *someday* somebody's going to come along and *find* it. A mystery for people to wonder about. Well, that's what I want for my books.

Lish: No more immediate audience than that?
Kesey: That's enough for me.

Lish: Putting something that normally doesn't *belong* there in a hollow of a tree?

Kesey: That's one way of saying it. Or maybe *suggesting* that something's there and letting the reader look for it and look for it until he comes to believe he's found it.

Lish: There's risk in this straining for mystery through hyperbole, isn't there?

Kesey: There *has* to be for me. Unless you get up very near that precipice where you're likely to make a *fool* of yourself, you're not showing much of how you feel. You're playing it safe—the way Hemingway did most of the time.

Lish: But many writers, great ones I think, struggled to achieve the very remoteness you decry.

Kesey: Well, we all have to go our own way, I guess.

Lish: Where are you going in *Great Notion*? What is it you're testing?

Kesey: For one thing, I want to find out which side of me really is: the woodsy, logger side—complete with homespun homilies and crackbarrel corniness, a valid side of me that I like—or its opposition. The two Stamper brothers in the novel are each one of the ways I think I am.

Lish: Has this been a problem with you?

Kesey: I tried not to let it be. But in college, for example, the guys on the wrestling team used to say, "You write? You act? What the hell you doing over there with those people?" Over in the drama or writing department they were always bugging me about associating with a gang of thumpheads. Look, I don't intend to let anybody make me live in *less* world than I'm capable of living in. Babbs once said it perfectly: *A man should have the right to be as big as he feels it's in him to be.* People are reluctant to permit this.

Lish: Your father wasn't?

Kesey: How do you mean?

Lish: You told me once about a fight, a happy fight.

Kesey: That was a scene from the Kesey family. We always competed, you see. Physically competed. Boxed, raced, wrestled, whatever needed proving.

Lish: Yes, but what about the fight?

Kesey: Well, my dad felt that a time comes when a boy has *got* to whip his father. It's a delicate business and very important. A boy has to *know* he can best his father, and his father has to present him the opportunity. It's got to be the right way and at the right time—when the boy really *needs* to make his pitch. He's got to know he can outrun, outwrestle, outlove, *outanything* his old man. My father's a wise man and he gave me the chance. Perhaps this is a father's most significant duty. I believe this, and I'm going to try to give Zane *his* chance at me, and keep giving him that chance until he can best me. Kids seldom have it anymore.

Lish: You have a new son now—Jed. With Shannon, that's three children. Are they a distraction?

Kesey: Never.

Lish: They don't deny you time you need for your writing?

Kesey: No, no. Look at this—when my writing becomes more important to me than my children, my *writing* will suffer. It's selfish of me, actually. You see, if you're writing about *people*, then they have to be *more* important than writing.

Lish: How about yourself as a child? Did you read much?

Kesey: About as much as I thought I wanted to. Lots of comic books, of course. And Zane Grey, Edgar Rice Burroughs, a bunch of science fiction. I didn't get to anything good until college.

Lish: Do any writing *before* college?

Kesey: Some poems—when I was a little kid. Not too long ago I came across some verse I wrote back in the seventh grade. I can't remember the me who wrote it, using words in a pretty silly and fancy way like that.

Lish: I can't imagine your finding anything so old. I saw manuscripts scattered all around the yard in your old home. You must lose a great deal, and you don't seem to care about it.

Kesey: When you just lose the *paper*, the stuff written on the paper, you don't lose very much. Once a guy burned a whole book in manuscript that I had sitting around on the ground outside my old workshop. He was angry with me and thought setting fire to all that paper would gain him revenge.

No, I'll start to worry when some guy destroys my faith that people *aren't* going to burn my manuscripts if I don't lock them up.

Lish: Was that the only novel you'd written before *Cuckoo* and *Great Notion*?
Kesey: No, I completed two others before *Cuckoo*. *Zoo* and *End of Autumn*, about North Beach in San Francisco and college football, respectively.

Lish: And what happened to these?
Kesey: They're around someplace. Faye would know where.

Lish: You've written a batch of short fiction, and yet you don't *publish* any. How come?
Kesey: The kick of writing is in the writing, not in the publishing. But both of them require a good deal of energy. Right now I'd like to put my energy where it belongs, in writing.

Lish: But you do, after all, publish.
Kesey: And I really dig seeing my stuff finally petrified in print. I think one of the best reasons for publishing is to see your work fixed, beyond tinkering, past playing with. That's when you can see it as what it *is*, instead of always looking at it as what it might become.

Lish: Well, how *do* you write? Does a certain set of circumstances have to obtain before you can get going?
Kesey: I seem to need to whip myself into fever. I'll try *any* method, any routine, any set of circumstances to produce this fever. And have.

Lish: Are you searching for an ultimate style of expression?
Kesey: Constantly.

Lish: How do you get a character? How do you receive his voice?
Kesey: Well, I can tell you this. I studied acting and I was taught to interpret a character by figuring out, from a detailed examination of his behavior, exactly what he *wanted*. The theory there is that everything a man does springs from his motivations. In writing, I find myself reversing the process: I know, to *start* with, what a character wants; he exists for me as a kind of abstract creature who wants a specific thing. So, by figuring out how he *gets* what he wants, I learn about the sort of man he is.

Lish: I heard about a woman who recently got what she wanted—from you. Five thousand dollars worth.

Kesey: Yes, I'm just back from New York, where we settled that. This was a girl named Gwen Davis, who decided that she was the Red Cross worker in *Cuckoo.* She convinced enough people of the likeness to collect ten thousand bucks, half from me and half from Viking. Lucky, I guess, that she didn't decide she was Big Nurse. I suspect she could have convinced the same people that she had the right qualities. And *that* would have cost me a whole hell of a lot more.

Lish: I remember once your growing angered over someone's slamming San Francisco, his saying this city was a farce, like all the other cities. I was sort of surprised by your hurried defense.

Kesey: Well, I get weary of people who use pessimism to avoid being responsible for all the problems in our culture. A man who says, we're on the road to disaster, is seldom trying to wrench the wheel away from the driver. I prefer the troublemaker. He tells them he doesn't like the way they're running the show, that he thinks he could do better, that the fact is he's going to *try*!

Lish: No major complaints with the way we're heading?

Kesey: I can't imagine another scene, another period that I'd rather be living in. I think we're living in a wild and woolly time, a time that history students will one day view in retrospect and say, "Wow! That 20th Century! Wouldn't that have been something to make!"

Lish: What would you do with the rest of your life if the power suddenly left you?

Kesey: I'll be a writer as long as I write. The only thing that could leave me would be success. Then I'd be an *un*successful writer. There are worse fates.

Lish: What are your plans for the future, when *Sometimes a Great Notion* goes to press?

Kesey: I intend to write one more book—about a place, and a lot of people that I love. Then I'll look into the possibility of conducting a massive sit-in demonstration.

Lish: Where?

Kesey: In heaven. Our generation has been discriminated against long enough.

Lish: Have you a final answer for me?
Kesey: What's the question?

Lish: Should we really tear off Big Nurse's uniform?
Kesey: That's for you to answer—for yourself.

Ken Kesey at N.D.E.A.

Pacifica Radio Archives / 1965

Recorded 1965, KPFA broadcast 28 June 1966. © 1966 by Pacifica Radio Archives. Reprinted by permission.

If you read this morning's paper, you realize that Big Nurse has again proposed a cure for which there is no disease. Fortunately, there are the Ken Keseys in this world to serve as an antidote to the Big Nurses of this world. The N.D.E.A. Summer English Institute is proud to conclude its series of lectures focused on writing with the man I consider to be the greatest novelist in America today, Ken Kesey.

First let me make it understood I'm not a writer. I haven't written anything since I finished the last drafts of *Notion*, and I don't honestly look to write anything else. I have a number of reasons for this. Mainly it's because I feel like to continue writing would mean that I would be unable to continue my work. I feel like if I wrote another few novels—I think it's impossible to do this without becoming a kind of Walter Keane. And if you look at the works of a lot of writers this is what happens. You learn to do a thing, you get so you're able to do it with some ease and some cleverness, and then you begin to do it over and over because you find that there's a market for it, a demand for it. And a lot of times there's more demand than you realize. There's a kind of panic demand, which means as soon as it gets a little tight, *hell I can knock out a novel for* Esquire, *serialize it, do it in six months and then get back to my serious work.* I don't think you ever do that. Once you realize that you're writing commercials, that's it. So I've been devoting my time to a lot more serious work like riding around on buses, exploring the inside of various jails, seeing what's going on like that.

I went back and looked over *Cuckoo's Nest* some time ago and to my surprise, as much as I still feel for the book and the situation, I recognized it as a very elaborate commercial, an advertisement. That if I remove my personal good or bad about what I like or dislike in the world and look at the bones of it it's this: it's a thing that comes in and says—like the Bayer pain ad that says, "Pain. Pain. Pain."—sells you what I think is a particular pain in the world, then goes on to sell you what I think is the particular alleviation of that pain, I've no way of knowing this is true, I didn't see it happen. I created it, I made it up. I designed, almost before I thought about it, little map points in my head, which we call "plots," and then I took the life that I was seeing out in front of me to go along and meticulously make each of those points. This is what almost all of our literature is doing, what almost all of our movies and television plays are doing right now. They go ahead, and each one picks a particular axe that that writer is trying to grind, and then the adroitness with which he conceals the grinding is how you judge his ability as a writer. Look at *Esquire* or look at *Playboy.* You can read the ads in *Playboy* and it's very obvious that they're aimed at certain audience, a certain people, to sell a certain product. You can read the short stories in this magazine the same way. Those things are designed to fit a certain length, to hit a certain audience, and to push a certain philosophy. And although it isn't soap or Mennen Skin Bracer it's still an ad man writing a very complex commercial to sell you something. And it may not have anything to do with what's going on in front of us.

When I tried more and more to break away from the usual way of plotting a story, which is you try to figure out a theme, character development. I tried to let it happen. I found that's practically impossible. We've had a system programed into us since we were this big, since we hit the ground, and we are so tightly bound by this that it's almost invisible to each one of us. It's almost impossible to talk nonsense, to hook words together, just word after word after word without making some kind of inductive sense, without following a grammatical line, because going along in front of my conversation right now, going on in front of my words is extending a kind of little number painting that I've been taught ever since I was this big, that grammar must exist in this form, that words must happen in these ways. And within this framework nothing new happens. I don't think anything really new has happened in writing for hundreds of years, with maybe the exception of Burroughs. I found that no matter how hard I would try to find new areas of my mind or of another person's mind in my writing I would be walking through a territory and see there was Shakespeare's sign, he did it, *he did it*, and we've just been doing it over and over again. He came along and set a standard. And practically everything after that time is redoing the same thing just changing the plots and the emotional interplay just a little bit.

So I found I couldn't sit down and not write. As soon as I pick up a typewriter, as soon as I begin to speak, I begin to form my words into some kind of little birthday cake to sell a particular idea to the people who are listening. When I'm talking to my kids I aim it toward them. When I'm talking to my folks I aim it toward them. We do it naturally; it's built into us. And this world that I was presenting with these words, I began to suspect might not have a whole lot to do with the world of *this* and of *this* and of *this*. So I started going out and taping with tape recorders and filming. And going back to look over what I had filmed and taped to see if people talked like they do in novels and they don't. A taped conversation typed up doesn't look like anything you read. A moment-to-moment account of what goes on doesn't look like almost any novel you've ever run across. Hollywood is the main one that I think has been doing this for some time. They have sold us an idea of what an interesting, exciting life looks like. The fabric of it, the way it should feel to us. And anything that doesn't get up to these standards is drab, is boring, so that we continually go through our lives with this number painting up here that we're trying to live up to, that we can't ever make.

I picked up the flute, started trying to play the flute. Now, I'm never going to be a great flute player, and I was playing the flute for two or three reasons. One thing, I liked the sound of it. You blow a flute long enough and you get dizzy. But I found out that no matter how hard I was trying to play this damn flute pretty soon I was trying to play "Greensleeves." I was dissatisfied with the way my flute was sounding because it didn't sound like it was coming off KPFA. I don't want to play for KPFA. All I want to do is play for myself. Even when I go out completely alone in the desert and just blow this flute for my own reasons, just blow it so that I can hear it coming into my own ear, the note as it leaves me is lost there, other than what I can extract from it for myself. I would be dissatisfied because I couldn't make it sound like *this*. I had this "Greensleeves" of the mind ahead of me, and I would always be trying to play it, and I could never get there. I could never make it. No matter how much I practice that will always be out there ahead of me. But I found another thing, that if I stopped trying to play that and just started listening to the note that was coming out of the flute, just put my ear over it like a big umbrella, pretty soon I stopped thinking about what it sounded like to another ear and just listened to the sound. And then I began to play not "Greensleeves" but something that made me feel good and made me feel close to what I think I am and what I think I'm doing. So I tried to achieve kind of the same thing in words. I've been working on this for better than a year now. How can you play the flute of language with such a "Greensleeves" of the mind ahead of us?

I've got a story I tell about a little girl who was a flower girl at our wedding. I went back up there and she's in the third grade now, and she had just done a short story for her class. They take them to the first graders and have them read 'em. There's a little folder piece of kids paper and a picture on it done in pencil that says "Blackie Takes a Trip," and it's been marked on the outside A- by the teacher in red ballpoint pen. And also written on there: "Very Good." And it starts like this: "They woke up that morning. The sun was shining. Mother and father call from downstairs. We went downstairs. I say, 'Mother, can I take Blackie along with us?' Mother says, 'No, we'll have to leave Blackie home.' Then they go outside." The teacher had gone through this and corrected these mistakes and brought them into line grammatically, making sense, tense, all that stuff. Well, what did the child learn from this experience? Not how to express oneself, but the child learned at this point that there is an accepted, correct way to express, to communicate, and that anything that veers outside of this is marked with a red ballpoint pen. And so we're locked inside of this thing, so that an ability—which means you could maybe write a novel as fast as you could read it, if it could happen; the words are all there, they're all inside of us—takes years and years of meticulous carving and carving and carving, not because that's the way I enjoy it most but because there's this person off over here with a red pen, who is going to mark A- instead of just A. So from the act of writing I found that I was being cheated. I find after you go through publishing and go through the thing running around in New York and talking to a lot of people and going down in little places and eating $1.25 hamburgers that that is a drag. You do it for a little while and that becomes very very quickly a drag. The joy in writing, anything you're to get out of this act we call writing, or painting, or dancing, or bricklaying, has to come at the moment it's happening. When we're setting down on paper here for something in the future we've lost it. We've already sold out. We're already doing a commercial.

And yet even knowing this it's practically impossible not to. You have to do something to break down these old setup standards, to break them down to where you say, "this is mine and I do entirely and only for me." It's like before coming to make this talk I have to fight myself to keep from making a bunch of notes, getting a bunch of ideas and placing them down here in an order so that I can come up here in relative safety. When you come up with absolutely nothing on your mind, you're pretty naked. And the only preparation that you've made is the preparation of thirty years up to this moment, but anything else that I'm doing I might as well run it off on mimeograph and hand it out to you at the door. I might as well not be here. The communication between one human and another doesn't exist. It means that I have a little workshop, and I retire back there to it, and I look out there and size up the people and scale the house and say, "What will go *today*?" And I begin to type this thing out and run it out on a mill, and then I bring it out and pass it out to people, and later I get it back to see what the grade is. But there's no contact. And I think this has happened in writing too. When you run across someone who is writing for entirely selfish reasons because it's what he wants to do, you get something where you begin to feel the contact. Even though you may not understand it. Bob Dylan is the best example that I can explain right now. In fact, I haven't been reading a whole hell of a lot, to tell you the truth. I feel like if I were looking back from 500 years from this time, I wouldn't look at the literature that's being turned out to see what's happening, what's going on with the people. I'd listen to the rock 'n' roll music. I'd go to the movies. I'd read the comic books and look at the papers. You read the literature here you might get a pretty good idea of what was going on 150 years ago but not right now. The art right now hasn't been slid under a glass yet, it hasn't been folded between two covers. And still I think all of our major talent is being trapped into these same old covers that say, "A sentence is this, and a novel is this, and a short story is this, and anything on either side of them we'll put in a different bag and maybe not even pay any attention to it at all."

Painting and sculpture, music, all of these other things, are breaking out of their bounds. Writing has remained the same for a god-awful long time. You can take a piece of literature, just go down and clip out paragraphs from books on the nightstand, and read the paragraphs, not read the commercial but just read the paragraphs, and you know that you've read it before over and over and over again. You recognize the situations. You do it more than you realize. I was listening to *Ben Casey* one time—I watch television and play other soundtracks to it, and that's a wild thing to do, you begin to make your own sense instead of having it made for you—and I saw the picture of this guy, he was a young guy, hair a little bit longer than mother would like, wearing glasses, and this is without the soundtrack, and I saw him and this is before the credits, *click* they showed quick still pictures and I said, "That guy is going to have an operation for brain cancer." So I turned up the television set and checked it and I was right. And that's not so strange when you stop and think about it because, how does it happen? The TV producer, he gets a script. It says in here, "One character, twenty-five to twenty-eight, has operation for brain cancer." He goes to this big book of photos and he begins to leaf through it there and unconsciously picks out the guy in there who looks like he's going to have an operation for brain cancer. And this communicates, and it's strange but what happens if you, walking the streets, also happen to look like this guy? What happens if all this stuff that's been sold us has damn near closed the door on the possibility of our doing anything new? On our doing anything except traveling on the same little circle? And if that is true, how do we break out of it?

I work on it. A lot of people work on it. But I don't have any answer. I found that I can do it sometimes and sometimes I can't. But I found that every once in a while with whatever you're doing, shooting a basketball or throwing dice or writing or running, that it's like the flute: when suddenly all the power, the attention you have comes to bear on exactly what you're doing and doesn't decide whether it's good or bad, just decides that it is, that it's already happened. The word has come out, it's already laid there in front of a person and there can't be anything done about it. It's already off your mouth and the only thing you can do is enjoy the ride. When this begins to happen, the sort of thing happens I think that happened to Vander Kelen in the Rose Bowl game two or three years ago for Wisconsin playing USC. Wisconsin's behind 37-0 at the end of the half. The guy goes in there—he's a mediocre quarterback—and he says, "What the hell? The game is shot. Let's quit worrying about whether I miss or make the passes. It's gone." And all of a sudden he comes back there and he knows it and his team knows it and pretty soon the other team knows and the whole audience and the whole TV audience. Something else has happened to this guy. Every pass is right. It falls into the hands. Every run, every way he steps is right. By some mental process that went on inside this guy he has achieved a state of grace to where what he does is as beautiful as it can possibly be, considering who he is.

And we all know that we've got this thing going in us. We've all experienced it a little bit now and then. Sometimes when you're driving or playing or talking or doing something, something clicks and the judgments stop. The catcher, which is the guy that steps back and sees you there, and another guy that steps back and sees you seeing you there and begins to put both of you down—it goes *click click click click click* and instead of a flow there's a movement like thi-thi-this and you begin to stutter mentally. This feeling, this being able to lay a pass right into the hands of an end that you barely see thirty-seven yards away, is as much as I want and I want as much of it as I can lay my hands on. I want it whether I'm writing or playing a flute or driving a car or talking in front of people. I want as much of it as I can get. And we all know that we don't always get as much of it as there is. In any given instant there's a teeny piece of stuff here and we can have from one to a hundred of it. Ordinarily we're only getting about twenty percent of it. You can see it best when you're dealing with people face to face. There's a thing that happens that I call static and it goes back to this number painting in the sky. It means that I can look at this microphone here and see it clearly. I can see every little grid in it, the way it works, see it, understand it, examine it. But when I raise that same observation to a human being something goes *ding-ding-ding-ding-ding* and I begin to think, "Well, how—What should I—I mean—Who—" I stumble. I'm missing the most important things that I'm ever to have in life. And the more intense the relationship becomes between your wife or your kid the more likely this static is to go on. Until sometimes you get so out of sync that you know that she loves you and feels you and know that you are doing the same and you both know this but there's just no contact. You're both going *wsshhh* past each other.

We can't see anymore. We can barely hear anymore. When we look, we're not looking *at* we're looking *for.* When a scientist sits down to figure something out, he's not trying to discover anymore, he's trying to prove an already existing theory that he's got going in his mind. We've reached this point of terminal existence. And I'll tell you where you can see it: go to L.A. I've just come back from L.A. I went down there to talk to some people at Universal about doing a movie about John Muir, writing the synopsis or whatever it is that you write about John Muir, trying my damnedest to sell out if somebody would just take me. It's an amazing, amazing place, Universal City. You tour through that thing, you drive through that thing for two hours, and you've got the Warsaw ghettos right up here next to a little bistro in Paris right here next to some German weenie shop. Over here right next to it is Laredo, Texas. It's all conglomerated in. We saw a band of Indians chase a cowboy through the streets of Laredo over a drawbridge and pass three tiny miniature destroyers in a moat. Hollywood has all of history. That's my knowledge of history, to tell the truth. Check back in your own mind: What color is World War II? World War I is even a better example. What color is World War I? It's black and white, whereas the Civil War is in Technicolor. I know the housing styles, the speech styles, the things that people wore, the things that people did because I've seen them in Hollywood. And we got out of this tour and there's an old P-51 Mustang sitting there, and we climbed around on this, and felt it and stuck our fingers in the bullet holes. That's history. You learn more about what was going on in World War II than in anything you can read because Hollywood is gradually gathering all the props. Four hundred acres they got down there. They can keep it all contained. They don't have to go on location anymore. They have it all right there. Eventually they won't know what's going on out here at all. They will have their own little world. In which case we can just turn it over to them. Let 'em go ahead and fight the wars. And every once in a while, every month or so, they send us a movie and we know how the world situation is. And when they finally do blow it up, you don't miss a whole lot. Anyway, watching these people run around the studios, nobody's having any fun down there. They've got all these things to play with—and I've been playing with movies—and nobody down there is having any fun. There's no joy on any face going down there. It's all very serious work. The actor doesn't get to fall off anything. . . . And looking at these people down there, instead of forming anything they're pre-forming something. The only denizens of the whole place that seem to be enjoying the thing they were going through was the dog show with the dogs jumping around and having a good time. But the actors no longer do the stuff they used to enjoy when they were William S. Hart and rode the horses because that's what they liked to do. They get somebody else to do it for them.

There's been a removal. A one-step removal, I think, from life, from our connection with life. I think it has a lot to do with movies and with writing, with the entertainment medium, the whole thing that's going on. And people are now beginning to try to make it back in a lot of weird ways, just trying to blow the flute until they pass out, trying to do something so that all of their resources are brought to bear on that one object. Imagine you're driving along and it's late and it's raining and you're playing cable and you're about half asleep and into the road runs kangaroo! Suddenly, you've got to bring all your stuff right here and miss this kangaroo. For a moment there you don't have time to plug him into any hole or try to figure him out or doing anything with him. All you can do is experience this thing. This moment becomes more and more rare because largely we're scared. We're scared to get up here and say something without having prepared it first. We're scared to do anything at any moment without having slipped back to our little workshop and put it together so we can present it.

I'll show you a thing I've been doing to try to break through this. Somebody open a book and just hand it to me. I need about three books to do this. Now, if I can do this right I do it so fast I don't know what it means: *As I get closer promising alternatives that the theories underlying the technological advance that we're expected to bear in this broom closet finds that we've become a sponge and the cigarettes create a tenseness in the air and let me slip through the door before that we're mutually appearing and racing cars down the troubled accent. Today I figure that listening to secrets of less-talented fellows will apply to the whole corpus delicti, and as the faculty runs down the freeways bothering to comb their hair there will approach them the frosted refrigerator of their youth.* [interrupted by applause]

This kind of stuff, when I discovered it, found out that I could go along speeling words down that meant nothing to me until I went back and listened to them—I found that there's something trying to say something through me. And I thought now that's a pretty crazy thought, that I'm a vehicle through which there's a greater force trying to speak. That's the sort of stuff they lock you up for, man. And so you immediately shy away from it and spend a lot of time not looking at an ability that you were marveling at just a moment ago.

We've got so that we spend most of our time not looking. When I came through Yellowstone Park with this bus, I saw this sign that said Beware of the Bear. And something clicked when I saw this and I thought *there's the problem, there's the whole hang-up that stops me from writing, stops people from singing, stops people from living.* Beware of the Bear. What did that used to mean? It used to mean be aware of the bear. Now it means be scared of him. If a bear comes out of the wings over there and I'm just being scared of him, I may turn and run crotch-first into that thing over there and get hurt a whole lot worse than I would if I'd just stay here and watch him and see what he's going to do. But we've learned instead of to be aware of something to be afraid of it as soon as it pops up. This little piece of knowledge you can plug it into any person who is being hassled by the way the world is changing. Goldwater and his bunch are scared. The people down south are scared. There's something happening that is scaring these people. Their actions are the same kind of actions of just running your crotch into the first pole, which means that something that's happening is so new around them, under their very feet, under the ground they were told was going to last, America's going to be like this. They're scared beyond any powers of reasoning. And we need in the country today some people who stop trying to sell that old, old product and just start saying, "This, as near as I can see, is what's going on, as near as I can record it. It may not make sense. It may not have a good storyline. It may not come up to certain grammatical standards that have been heretofore set by people who have come in this dusty hall before, but it still, as near as I can see with the apparatus I got, is what's happening."

And until we do this, whether it's looking at what's happening in Vietnam because we know that when *Time* looks at what's happening in Vietnam they're pushing a certain little product. And then comes along I. F. Stone and he looks at it and he pushes a certain little product. But nobody, I think, is just looking at it and saying, "I am not judging it one way or the other, I'm just trying to open up like a camera and see it clearly for a moment." Until that action begins to happen, we can't expect any of these festered places to clear up. Just like a doctor trying to cut boils away from you in the dark and all he can do is feel around wildly; he doesn't know whether he's cutting off toes or what. And talking to some of the people before this about some of the work that's been going on, I was very impressed. The guy that says, "Draw yourself," and ninety percent of the people drew their faces, figuring that's all they are, just a face and intellect. This kind of stuff goes further I think to teaching somebody how to write than any amount of study of literature or grammar. If I were to start teaching any kind of writing class, I think for the first ten weeks at least we'd have people come in, write, and as soon as they were finished with it burn it. Write it and burn it. Write it and burn it. Until finally it begins to crack through that there's no reason breaking your neck over this pencil and stuff like that unless I'm getting something out of it myself. To hell with Rust Hills and Viking and all of these other people. It's got to be first my own thing, my own enjoyment. Or I'm cheating them as well as myself. I'm giving them this half-baked product. And that, as nearly as I can come up with it right now, is why I'm no longer writing.

The Evening Standard Interview: Ken Kesey

Ray Connolly / 1969

From London *Evening Standard*, May 1969. © 1969 by *Evening Standard*. Reprinted by permission.

You don't meet too many men with the Stars and Stripes painted in enamel on their false teeth. Truth to tell Ken Kesey is the only one I know. Every time he smiles, which is pretty frequently on a good sunny day, the zip in his mouth breaks apart and his upper right incisor says a pepperminted "God Bless America" in red, white, and blue.

We're rolling and waltzing, and power jerking and swanking and feeling good behind the blue, anti-glare windscreen of his maltreated Cadillac— Kesey and me and a New York girl disciple, all doe eyes and sweeping adoration; round we go along the edges of Hampstead Heath, down the lanes and under the blossom, and Kesey's telling us how he came to be the one guy we know with an American flag printed on his tooth. And he's talking in that down-home cowboy way that he does:

"You see, I was running from the FBI when I crashed into my lawyer and wrecked my car. And somehow I caught my head, so that my tooth was hanging out by the nerves. But I had to keep hiding. So I waited in a Laundromat for a while. It's funny how you can just sit in a Laundromat and no one ever thinks of looking for you there. But the pain was terrible, so I finally made it over to a dentist I know. But he also happened to be an acid-head. And while he was fixing me, he said, 'Hey, d'you want a tooth with the Stars and Stripes on it?' and I said, 'Yeh, that'd be nice,' and so here it is. You never think these things can really happen." And he unplugs his plate with its garish token and waves it around for all to see.

Ken Kesey, the man who began the LSD fascination of hippy California, who believes he invented the word "trip," to describe the sensation, and then introduced psychedelia to provide a form of it; who turned on Hells Angels, and went on the first Magical Mystery Tour ever—years before the Beatles, is here in London, in a borrowed flat, en route for Stonehenge, the Wailing Wall, and the Great Pyramid.

Here in London with his three children, his wife Faye, his friend Spider, and now some new followers like Dilly Disciple from New York, who's sitting here with us saying how we ought to stop and get some of Dr. J. Collis Browne's Chlorodyne on account of how it has some opium extract, and rabbiting on about his trip and that trip and whatever kind of trip a man can imagine.

And then there's this other girl, too, who's staying with the Keseys, "like she's a Wasp," says Dilly Disciple, "with the hair and the turned up nose, and she's very virginal and all that." And I get the idea that there's no love lost between the Wasp and Dilly Disciple. But what a household it must be.

Kesey is thirty-three, and was born in Oregon. Faye, who is a woman of remarkable yet passive, tranquil beauty, was his childhood sweetheart, and they married in their first year of college. After college they graduated to a beat generation community, where Kesey wrote his first two novels one of which (*One Flew Over the Cuckoo's Nest*) was considered brilliant by some reviewers, and sold his body to a local clinic for their experiments into a drug called lysergic acid diethylamide—LSD. Under the surveillance of the white-coated clinic staff Ken Kesey had become the world's first acid-head guinea pig.

Soon he was turning-on everyone in his community. But when the bulldozers came to remove the community, they fixed up "an old 1939 International Harvester yellow school bus," wired it for the thousands of watts needed to play their rock and roll music, aerosolled it in DayGlo mandalas, and took themselves off on a long cross-continent acid trek of the United States.

Back in California on various narcotic charges, he faked a suicide to give the FBI the slip, slipped over the border into Mexico, and was eventually captured when, with a degree of contempt bordering on the foolhardy, he went back to San Francisco and appeared on television.

Considering the mischief he and his followers had created in the eyes of the police he was lucky to get off with six months on a work farm. But by this time he was beyond acid.

"No, I haven't taken acid in quite some time. We're now into other things. There's not a great deal of energy in dope. It's moved now to the occult or militancy," he says in his Hampstead flat, pulling on his socks, one bright red, one brighter orange, and snorting up his cold. He had come to the door just in his trousers, big as a bear, chest coated with blond curls, hair almost gone on the top but thick as a rug down the sides and round his ears. He puts on a T-shirt and the inevitable Indian token around his neck and finds a leather jacket: "I shot this elk with a bow and arrow myself. And had Mountain Girl make it up into this jacket for me," he says.

Since he first came to Britain last December with the Grateful Dead and Hells Angels and those Harley Davidsons and eggnog, he has become quite an Anglophile. England is the holiest place he's ever been, and Stonehenge is the "heaviest," he says.

"We've traced our way back right from the West Coast to the New England colonies and then back here, and Stonehenge is the oldest place we can find. We're going down there for the summer solstice, to see the sun come up between those great pillars that are as big as two Buicks.

"And then we'll get my bus over here and go off to the cathedral at Chartres and Dachau and the Wailing Wall and the Great Pyramids. I haven't seen those places, but I figure that any place that took so much in human endeavor to build must be a very heavy place to be."

He goes on rapping: "One of the troubles with all that drop-out scene was that at the same time as throwing away all of the bad things of the past and the environment, they also turned loose a lot of the good stuff too.

"But right now I think that a lot of young people are just sitting around and waiting and waiting and watching. Most people think that whatever's going to happen will be a bad thing, but I don't believe that, I think something is going to happen and it will be a good thing."

Something like the millennium, or cargo cults?

"Maybe a cataclysm that will sink California and New York by earthquakes and blow out all the old tubes," he answers.

He's also here to make a record in a spoken word series for Apple. But since their economy measures he's found himself without an office or cooperation. He's a little bitter about it, but he's carrying on with making the tapes anyway.

"I write a lot. I just haven't written anything that pleases me for a long time. Nothing I've done communicates as well as tape does for me."

He's a great Peter Pan of a fellow, quick witted and very funny, and driving around London in his cowboy hat and windcheater he looks like some leftover from Bonanza.

And later when Dilly Disciple is still on about her Dr. J. Collis Browne's Chlorodyne, we go to find a chemist's. Down Finchley Road into a side street, and there's nowhere to park. Without a moment's hesitation Kesey charges the pavement. The great Cadillac bucks and jumps on its hydraulics and down the pavement we go between shops and lamp-posts, coming to rest half on and half off the road and lodged at a forty-five degree angle to the kerb.

A little old butcher carrying a meat chopper rushes from his shop and makes insane motioning gestures toward the Cadillac's twin wafer-thin fins. "Shall I chop a bit off?" he says. And Kesey laughs. He always laughs.

Once a Great Notion

Ann Arbor Argus / 1970

From *Ann Arbor Argus*, July / August 1970. © 1970 by *Ann Arbor Argus*.

Argus: You want to do an interview?
Kesey: I hate interviews. I'll tell you about interviews. It's like, well, there's no such thing as an underground newspaper.

Argus: That's true. A revolutionary newspaper, though, how's about that?
Kesey: It's just that the whole form—every time I get in the paper, it causes trouble.

Argus: I read the thing in *Good Times* about you and it seemed to me it was pretty right on.
Kesey: I know, but it was awful—it's just awful, you don't know. I mean you can be going along, you can be moving like this and a reporter gets out there and suddenly everything is glunk.

Argus: Well, fuck it, I ain't a reporter.
Kesey: Well, I know, but you're a damn sight close to being one.

Argus: What I'm saying is . . .
Kesey: What do you want to know?

Argus: Information to give to people.
Kesey: All right, I'm willing to exchange information, but I'm warning you, I don't have much. I mean, I haven't had a new thought in years.

Argus: Well, let's go for some old ones or something.
Kesey: Old thoughts—A friend of mine says because the moon just moved

into Aquarius and we've just sent a thing to the moon that we're all under the influence of the moon more than we know. In fact, that our souls are being eaten by it and it comes to when stuff was just living around in puddles millions of years ago and the moon goes over it every twenty-eight days and until finally the crystals begin to move to it. We just came out of a Scorpio moon in Ohio, where we'd been fighting with a bunch of people.

Argus: What sign are you?
Kesey: Virgo.

Argus: How long have you been traveling with the Hog Farm buses?
Kesey: I haven't. We got a '61 Chevy that we bought in Cincinnati, and we're just trying to get back to organize just as tight as we can jump.

My brother Chuck got in a cash bind. I gotta go back, 'cause the creamery needs help. He's now making yogurt, and what it's done is that it moved him into a whole different economic thing. He's now gonna have to sell to a lot of new customers that don't quite have the money that the old customers did, but they're willing to buy newer kinds of stuff, like acidophilus yogurt. There's a piece of information. When a baby's born, there's a germ in his stomach called acidophilus germ. And it's in the stomach of every child that's born and when you shoot penicillin, it kills it. And you have to eat it again. Yogurt will almost do it, but not quite. It's the oldest bug in the world. You can get it at almost any creamery. So every time you shoot penicillin, you know, for a cold or something, eat acidophilus yogurt, and you'll be able to digest your food better.

Argus: You've sort of divorced yourself from politics.
Kesey: I've been nominated for the school board, man. Divorced myself from politics?

Argus: You going to campaign and all that?
Kesey: No, I don't think I'm going to campaign, but I think I might run. Nominated for the school board, just heard about that two days ago.

Argus: Well, listen, I'm wondering how you relate to political prisoners like John Sinclair or someone who was put away because of exactly what our culture's all about. Are you into things like getting organized to get him out of jail and stuff?
Kesey: (Singing)

When you walk the streets you will have no cares
If you walk the lines and not the squares
As you go through life, make this your goal
Watch the doughnut, not the hole.
That's where I think the revolution is.

Argus: I don't understand that at all.
Kesey: That you focus as much as you can on the positive and you try to make the world better around you as much as you can. So much of the problem has been brought about by liberals trying to do something over there.

Argus: John Sinclair is not a liberal, he's a revolutionary.
Kesey: Everybody's a revolutionary, from the first caveman that ever came out of the cave and fed a starving neighbor. Right?

Argus: No, I don't agree with that. What are you doing that's positive?
Kesey: Hmmmm. What am I doing that's positive?

Argus: What are you doing that's positive for the revolution?
Kesey: Positive for the revolution. Shit. Listen, man, the revolution—it's like this. It didn't start here and it's not going to end up here. It starts way back here and when it all finally comes to it'll go through time like that and all that stuff'll come true.

Argus: What are you doing that's positive to make people feel that?
Kesey: We took this little guy named Tony, who's a little spade without a mother, we took him downtown yesterday and bought him a pizza. What did you do?

Argus: So what you're saying is you don't relate to political prisoners or people like John Sinclair.
Kesey: I relate to people, not issues.

Argus: I'm hip, but John Sinclair would like to relate to people too, and he's in jail. It's impossible.
Kesey: Listen, the skunk cabbage in Oregon at this time of the year smells awful. I just don't know what to do about it, man. I've thought about that skunk cabbage. It just smells terrible. You know, it's down there, it smells terrible. But I'm planting flowers.

Argus: Is that some kind of metaphor about Sinclair or something?

Kesey: No, it's just that as long as there's somebody there who's going to say what about this, you can always find it. It's like a microscope looking for a dog turd. You can always find something to walk around with a protest sign to keep from having to do anything right where you are.

Argus: I don't want to have to protest anything. I want to get Bobby Seale and John Sinclair out of jail.

Kesey: I do too, but I didn't put him in jail, man. I did my six months, and I'm doing all I can to alleviate the thing in the nation that put him in jail.

Argus: How're you doing that?

Kesey: Running for school board, turning on a lot of people.

Argus: What do you turn them on to?

Kesey: Grass. You can trust grass.

Argus: Are you going to Washington for the July 4 smoke-in?

Kesey: I think so, but I'm not going to advertise it. I think it's a good thing, I think it's a damn good thing. I don't think it's revolutionary, I just think it's sensible.

Argus: You don't consider this . . .

Kesey: Listen, most of what you're talking about isn't revolutionary, it's just work. What "revolutionary" is, is to be able . . . I'll tell you a good story. There was three old Samuri swordsmen arguing about who had the sharpest swords. So they proposed a contest and they went into the woods. And this young guy, the guy who brought up the idea of the contest in the first place, he went out into the middle of the stream and he took his sword and he jammed it hilt down into the sand. And he took a piece of rice paper, and put it on the water, and let the rice paper float down on the current toward the sword. And it came to the sword like this and the sword just cut it in half. So the second guy went out there, the older guy, stuck his sword down in the thing, put the rice paper in the current. It came down, was cut in half, and then came back together on the other side of the sword. So the third guy, this very old guy, went out there, old rusty beat up sword. He jams it down into the sand, puts his rice paper up there in the water in the current, lets it float, and it floated down and came to the sword. And it went around it. And went on. Revolution, and the new revolution, is just don't take the gauntlet. I mean if you've been in jail don't let 'em push your button. Keep away from anger.

Argus: How're you going to tell that to Huey Newton or the Black Panther Party?

Kesey: Neal Cassady one time, he was driving in downtown Santa Cruz, he was just so wired, he made a U-turn in front of a bookstore. See, you're doing a thing like "Have you quit beating your wife answer yes or no." So this cop stops him, comes up and says, what are you high on? And Cassady says, "Obitrol, office, obitrol." And the cop says, "Alright, get out." So Cassady got out, and he starts to search Cassady, and Cassady reaches into his pockets and both pockets are full of pills. He grabbed the pills in his hands in the bottoms of his pockets, and pulled them out, and the change spread everywhere, and he shoved the pills back in there, and began to pick up the change and run around. Until finally he just kind of faded away. There's no sense in going against it. It's a look in your eyes and a tone in your voice, man. The revolution is getting away from that. It's getting so that whenever you go up to anybody what comes off with you is a good feeling, so that there's nothing there for them to poke against.

Argus: Do you think policemen and Richard Nixon and the rich people who run the country relate to that?

Kesey: They're people, man, and as soon as you draw the line and say they aren't people, then you . . .

Argus: Who's drawing the line? Who's putting people in jail? Who's killing people in the streets?

Kesey: What difference does it make?

Argus: You don't make any distinction between oppressor and oppressed?

Kesey: You're talking about "should," and you're talking about where things ought to be, instead of where we are as where we got to work from. It's where we are.

Argus: Don't you have any vision?

Kesey: You ask me if I've got any vision. I've got three kids. I mean, I'm invested in this world. I prune my trees even though I'm not going to have fruit for two years in a row. Because I'm doing all I can to try and build a better world. All the time.

Argus: I can dig it but the thing that means . . .
Kesey: The thing that you want is something that you're going to have to go to somebody else to get it from, because I can't give it to you.

Argus: I ain't asking for it from you, I'm asking . . .
Kesey: You're damn near demanding it.

Argus: I'm demanding answers, because I think you have information, and I think people can relate to that. And I think that personal liberation is fine, but it has to be related to liberating everybody on the planet.
Kesey: No, listen, what this country needs is sanity. Individual sanity—individual sanity, and all the rest will come true.

Argus: Bullshit.
Kesey: You can't do it any other way. You work from the heart out, you don't work from the issue down.

Argus: You don't think it's a heartfelt thing, making a revolution. You don't think that means anything?
Kesey: Not when it tightens your stomach like that.

Argus: I can dig that we shouldn't have tight stomachs, man, but who's giving us a tight stomach?
Kesey: I had to spend six months in jail, taking all the stuff that you're talking about, firsthand, over and over, until you realize that what they want you to do is what you're doing. You're going for the fried ice cream, as they call it. And as long as you're doing that, as long as that action is taking place, as long as you take the gauntlet, you'll have somebody there to slap you.

Argus: To make an analogy, John Sinclair, when he started out in 1964, was all peace and love, good vibes, one of the first hippies in Detroit. He didn't want to slap anybody down.
Kesey: Cassady served eighteen months for two joints. He never mentioned it. There was no bitterness. There was no complaint about it at all. It was unjust and everybody knew that and accepted it and just worked from there.

Argus: You see, Sinclair's in jail right now and he's gonna be there for ten years. To get back to the original thing I was trying to say, because I really want to get something out of it. That's all that happened, he was peace, love, and good vibes, and what happened is they jumped on him immediately for that.

Kesey: That's the way it's been for thousands of years. I mean . . .

Argus: So how do you change it?

Kesey: Just the way he's doing it.

Argus: By being in jail?

Kesey: No, but being in jail, sometimes that is what happens to you. Nobody guaranteed you it was going to be easy.

Argus: So we should do nothing to get him out? We should just leave him in there and just let it run its course?

Kesey: I didn't say nothing to get him out. It's karma. You just look into people's eyes and you ask yourself is their karma going up or down. And you look around, and for a while the karma of the nation was going down. But you look now more and more people—you look into their eyes and they're on to it. They're on to what's going on. And they say all right, you just don't kick a dog every day, every second. Where you are, you don't suddenly get wrapped up in the media issue. Keep away from the media, man, cause that's what done it.

Argus: All right . . .

Kesey: But as soon as he loses that audience, he loses his most valuable thing. And you see those later pic . . .

Argus: Keep away from the media?

Kesey: The media's what's done it. It's that thing right there (pointing to the microphone) what's done it. I'll tell you. I know because I've been on the end of it so much. The media does a thing it's like this.

Argus: How about making your own media?

Kesey: That's what we try to do. That's what the underground usually is, but as soon as the media finds it and shines that light on it, then you have to move, because they've got you every time. You look at the early pictures of Hemingway, because of who he's writing to. And as he becomes famous, and you see those pictures of him, and you see those people come in with cameras and take pictures of him. And notepads and asking questions. He gradually changes so that he's not talking to his audience anymore and he begins to talk to this other thing, and he's getting the feedback from that.

Argus: All right . . .

Kesey: But as soon as he loses that audience, he loses his most valuable thing. And you see those later pictures of him, and he knows what's happening and he's trying to find it again. He's trying to find that thing he once talked to. It doesn't make any difference whether it's the underground media or the *New York Times*, it's the same trip. And because any time that you're trying to put it back into another moment, it's like you're going through life picking stuff out and what you end up with is a corpse. Every time, you leave a corpse behind you.

Argus: You see what I'm trying to do in this is not leave any corpses. What I came to get is information—the way people can make themselves stronger to go out and build the revolution.

Kesey: Well, I'm trying to tell you as much as I know about it. And one of the things is just that if we can get so that we're not distracted by that camera, 'cause as soon as someone starts takin' pictures of me, I stumble. As soon as someone takes that microphone and—try it, what did you do this morning?

Argus: I ate breakfast.

Kesey: Then what?

Argus: Then I started working on the newspaper, because we have an issue coming out soon.

Kesey: And tell me how it relates to the revolution.

Argus: Well, what we're trying to do is put down essential information for people to do and it takes a lot of time and struggle and effort but we think it's worth it because when it comes out people can dig what's there.

Kesey: Has John Sinclair heard about it?

Argus: John Sinclair was one of the founders of the *Argus*, and of what the paper represents, the White Panther Party.

Kesey: Okay, now you see what I mean, you felt it there.

Argus: Well, I don't know.

Kesey: You did feel it, man, you popped to it, and you felt it. That's what I'm talking about, it's human. Just keep human. As long as we're human, we're all right. (Gestures with mike) It's this thing, once we got that in between us, we're talking through a filter that dehumanizes.

Argus: Well, you see, not everybody in the world can come here and listen to you talking right now.

Kesey: You can't talk to everybody in the world. There's nothing I have to say to everybody in the world.

Argus: There should be something you have to say to everybody in our culture that wants to try to relate to you.

Kesey: There was a wise man who lived up in the mountains and all these people wanted him to drop into the mosque and give 'em the word on Sunday, so he said all right. He showed up on Sunday, there was this huge crowd of people and he got up there and he says, "Good people, do you know what I'm going to talk to you about?" and they all shouted NO and he says, "Ignorant people!" and he turns around and he leaves. And so they go back up and say, "Wait a minute, man, you came through too fast for us, drop in again next Sunday . . ." and he says all right. So next Sunday he's down there and he starts, "Good people, do you know what I'm going to talk to you about?" and this time they're ready for him and they all yell YES and he says GOOD! and he turns around and leaves. And so finally they say, "Look, man, just one more time, 'cause somehow it's slipping past us." So he comes down and the third time he starts up there, "Good people!" and this time they're ready for him, "Some of us do and some of us don't." "Good! Let those who do communicate their knowledge with those who do not."

Argus: Well, let's do that. Communicate your knowledge with those who do not.

Kesey: I just did. It's true, man, it's all I've got, I mean, I know more about my brother's creamery than I do about the revolution. You can't expect me to know stuff about—I do not know about that stuff. I live out there in a little tiny town. My wife goes into the school twice a week. She's a librarian. We have a team of Springfield Creamery Jugs. It started out and it was the laughingstock of the basketball league because there's all those long-haired freaks and spades with afro cuts who were getting called by the ref. And when the ref calls, too much of his fascism shows for him to be comfortable about it. He points his finger and then he realizes he's held his finger out there too long and all the spades see it and everybody sees it and as soon as they go against him and play against him, they get their good game, but as soon as they get ahead they fold. It's 'cause it's like a covenant, as soon as you go against the wrong thing. Matthew says, "Resist not evil." As soon as you resist evil, as soon as it's gone, you fold. Because it's what you're based on. Finally, the spades realized that the ref wasn't just calling the fouls on them but on the whole team, on the whole idea of the team, on the way we moved. Every time we'd get out there and play these guys who were against us and we played against them in their own style of game, you know. It has to do with the way a person stands and the way he moves, instead of just bopping out there in the field, on the court. As soon as that movement took place out there in the court, we'd win. But when we got angry, and got against them, they were better at it than we were. The guys that you're opposing in this revolution thing, it's not a revolution, it's ancient.

Argus: If you resent it, and you think it limits you so much, why did you let Wolfe write the book (*The Electric Kool-Aid Acid Test*)? Did that inhibit you at all, because obviously that turned on millions of other people who otherwise wouldn't have heard about it.

Kesey: I'll tell you a little story. Wolfe was there, and this was toward the end of the time he was hanging around. We were up at my brother's farm, Spaceheater House, and we were moving this statue up onto the wall, and he had painted it with pigment. He had not used the right stuff, so the paint had never dried. Tom Wolfe was out there, and he had his note pad, and me and Ramrod were trying to move this thing up on the wall, and obviously we needed help. And there was only three of us, and Tom Wolfe was out there, and he was dressed the way he always dresses, in his blue suit, and we finally says, "Goddammit, Tom, give us a hand." So he put his note pad down, and he went to put it up there, and he got this huge swatch of red on the side of his coat, of oil pigment. We stood there, in this moment of realization, and I told him, "You just can't expect to fool around with it without getting it on you." And that's the last time I ever saw Tom Wolfe. But I love him.

An Impolite Interview

Paul Krassner / 1971

From *The Realist*, Fall May/June 1971 (No. 90). © 1971 by Paul Krassner. Reprinted by permission.

Q: Okay. Let's start off with a simple one. How would you distinguish between freedom and insanity?
A: True freedom and sanity spring from the same spiritual well, already mixed, just add incentive. Insanity, on the other hand, is dependent on *material* fad and fashion, and the weave of one's prison is of that material. "But I didn't weave it," I hear you protest. "My parents, their parents, *generations* before me wove it!"

Could be, but when you're a prisoner, the task is not to shout epithets at the warden, but to *get out.*

Q: Well, specifically, when you were in East Palo Alto, sitting in the back yard of the only white family in a black area, and there was a police helicopter hovering above you, and you wanted to shoot it down—now, even though you may not have meant that literally, can you stretch the fantasy enough to consider the possibility that you were being dogmatic when you chided Tim Leary for being Another Nut with a Gun?
A: Yes.

Q: Stop hemming and hawing . . . Is there anything you want to add to that?
A: I'm sorry that I used that phrase in my letter to Tim. I intended to be emphatic, not dogmatic, because I've had enough dealings with both ends of guns to feel qualified in making strong statements. I've shot ducks, deer, elk, geese, coyotes, and a hole in my grandfather's kitchen ceiling, and I've been shot at by farmers, cops, and federales. All of it is negative energy. When I said the thing about the helicopter, what I meant was that the men manning these abominations had better take heed of a growing impatience with this kind of bullshit. I mean I had no thirty aught six with Enfield scope handy in

the closet, but if I was, say, a black home-owner sitting out in his patio with his family, still, say, smarting from the burn of doing a hitch defending the sanctity of the American Dollar in Vietnam, and that racketing monstrosity started hanging out over my house fucking with my weekends, I might think, "Who the hell did I ever know up in a helicopter that wasn't workin' for the forces of *slavery!*"

That *then* it might cross my mind to get the gun out of the closet and clean it a little sitting out there in the sun under that motherfucking chopper, is all I was saying.

Q: It's no accident that the initials of your protagonist in *One Flew Over the Cuckoo's Nest* are R. P. M.—Revolutions Per Minute—and that you don't take that word lightly, but where is your vision of revolution in relation to both Ho Chi Minh and Charles Reich?
A: Chuck and Ho? Naturally I can't hope to under the circumstances with reference to each of their personal visions huh?

Q: I'm talking about the spectrum from Chuckie's bell-bottoms to Ho's anti-aircraft.
A: Ah. I see. Well, I think that either sticking a leg in a pair of bell-bottoms or loading a canister into an anti-aircraft weapon may or may not be a revolutionary act. This is only known at the center of the man doing the act. And *there* is where the revolution must lie, at the *seat of the act's impetus*, so that finally every action, every thought and prayer, springs from this committed center.

Q: You've said, regarding the media, that if you follow the wires, they all lead to the Bank of America. Would you expand on that?
A: When you've had a lot of microphones poked at you with questions like "Mr. Kesey, would you let your daughter take acid with a black man?" "Mr. Kesey, do you advocate the underwear of the Lennon Sisters?" "Mr. Kesey, how do you react to the findings of the FAD indicating that patchouli oil causes cortisone damage?"—you get so you can follow the wires back to their two possible sources. Perhaps one wire out of a thousand leads to one of the sources, to the heart of the man holding the microphone, while the other nine hundred and ninety-nine go through a bramble of ambition, ego, manipulation, and desire, sparking and hissing and finally joining into one great coaxial cable that leads out of this snarl and plugs straight into the Bank of America.

Q: Would you care to speculate as to the motivation of performers like Paul Newman and Country Joe McDonald in contracting to lend their graven images to advertisements for Coca-Cola?
A: They need the money.

Q: In *Sometimes a Great Notion*, you had this idealistic logger in the role of a strikebreaker, and yet now, back in real life, you're glad that the union has shut down the local paper and pulp mill. What's made the difference—ecology?
A: Women's Lib.

Q: Are you just being a smart-ass or do you mean that?
A: No, I mean Women's Lib has made us aware of our debauching of Mother Earth. The man who can peel off the Kentucky topsoil, gouge the land empty to get his money nuts off, then split for other conquests, leaving the ravished land behind to raise his bastards on welfare and fortitude . . . is different from Hugh Hefner only in that he drives his cock on diesel fuel.

Women's Lib was the real issue in *Notion*. I didn't know this when I wrote it, but think about it: It's about men matching egos and wills on the battleground of Vivian's unconsulted hide. When she leaves at the end of the book, she chooses to leave the only people she loves for a bleak and uncertain but at least *equal* future.

The earth is bucking in protest of the way she's been diddled with: is it strange that the most eloquent rendition of this protest should come from the bruised mouth of womankind?

Q: And yet, since you're against abortion, doesn't that put you in the position of saying that a girl or a woman must bear an unwanted child as punishment for ignorance or carelessness?
A: In as I feel abortions to be probably the worst worm in the revolutionary philosophy, a worm bound in time to suck the righteousness and the life from the work we are engaged in, I want to take this slowly and carefully. This is the story of Freddy Schrimpler:

As part of his training, a psychiatric aide must spend at least two weeks working the geriatric wards, or "shit pits" as they were called by the other aides. These wards are concrete barns built, not for attempted cures or even for attempted treatments of the herds of terminal humanity that would otherwise be roaming the streets, pissing and drooling and disgusting the healthy citizenry, but for nothing more than shelter and sustenance, waiting rooms where old guys spend ten, twenty, sometimes thirty years waiting for their particular opening in the earth. At eight in the morning they are herded and wheeled into showers, then to Day Rooms where they are fed a toothless goo, then are plunked into sofas ripe with decades of daily malfunctions of worn-out sphincters, then fed again, and washed again, and their temperatures taken if they're still warm enough to register, and their impacted bowels dug free in the case of sphincters worn-out in the other direction, and their hair and cheesy old fingernails clipped (the clippings swept into a little pink and gray pile), and fed again and washed again, and then usually left alone through the long afternoons.

Some of these derelicts still have a lot going and enjoy trapping flies and other such morsels in the snare of their baited hands, and some engage in contented and garrulous conversations with practically anything, and some watch TV, but most of them lie motionless on the plastic covered sofas or in gurney beds, little clots of barely breathing bones and skin under the government sheets. Even the doctors call them vegetables.

In caring for these men something becomes immediately obvious to all the young aides undergoing their first real brush with responsibility. The thought is very explicit. After the first meal squeezed into a slack mouth, or after the first diaper change or catheter taping, every one of the trainees have thought this thought, and some have spoken it.

"Without our help these guys would *die!*"

And, after the hundredth feeding and diapering and changing, the *next* thought, though never spoken, is: "Why don't we just *let* them die?"

An awful question to find in your head, because even young aides know that age can happen to anyone. "This could I someday be!" But even fear of one's own future can't stop the asking: Why *don't* we just let them die? What's wrong with letting nature take its own corpse? Why do humans feel they have the right to forestall the inevitable fate of others? Freddy Schrimpler helped me find my answer:

Freddy was seventy or eighty years old and had been on the Geriatrics Ward for close to twenty years. From morning until bedtime he lay in the dayroom in a gurney bed against the wall, on his side under a sheet, his little head covered with a faint silver gossamer that seemed too delicate to be human hair—it looked more like a fungus mycelium joining the head to the pillow—and his mouth drooling a continual puddle at his cheek. Only his eyes moved, pale and bright blue they followed the activity in the ward like little caged birds. The only sound he made was a muffled squeaking back in his throat when he had dirtied his sheets and, since his bowels were usually impacted, like most of the inmates who couldn't move, this sound was made but rarely and even then seemed to exhaust him for hours.

One afternoon, as I made my rounds to probe with rectal thermometer at the folds of wasted glutinous maximus of these gurney bed specimens— hospital policy made it clear that the temperature of anything breathing, even vegetables, had to be logged once a month—I heard this stifled squeak. I looked up; it was Freddy's squeak but since it was his temperature I was attempting to locate I knew that he hadn't shit his sheets. I resumed my probing, somewhat timidly, for the flesh of these men is without strength and a probe in the wrong direction can puncture an intestine. The squeak came again, slower, and sounding remarkably like speech! I moved closer to the pink and toothless mouth, feeling his breath at my ear.

"Makes you . . . kinda nervous . . . don't it?" he squeaked. The voice was terribly strained and faltering, but even through the distortion you could clearly make out the unmistakable tone of intelligence and awareness and, most astonishingly, humor.

In the days that followed I brought my ear to that mouth as often as the nurses let me get away with it. He told me his story. A stroke years ago had suddenly clipped all the wires leading from the brain to the body. He found that while he could hear and see perfectly, he couldn't send anything back out to the visitors that dropped by his hospital bed more and more infre-quently. Finally they sent him to the VA, to this ward where, after years of effort, he had learned to make his little squeak. Sure, the doctors and nurses knew he could talk, but they were too busy to shoot the breeze and didn't really think he should exhaust himself by speaking. So he was left on his gurney to drift alone in his rudderless vessel with his short-wave unable to send. He wasn't crazy; in fact the only difference that I could see between Freddy and Buddha was in the incline of their lotus position. As I got to know him, I spoke of the young aides' thought.

"Let a man die for his own good?" he squeaked, incredulous. "Never believe it. When a man . . . when anything . . . is ready to stop living . . . it stops. You watch . . ."

Before I left the ward, two of the vegetables died. They stopped eating and died, as though a decision of the whole being was reached and nothing man or medicine could do would turn this decision. As though the deci-sion was cellularly unanimous (I remember a friend telling me about her attempted suicide; she lay down and placed a rag soaked in carbon tetra-chloride over her face. But just before she went out completely there was a sudden clamor from all the rest of her: "Hey! Wait! What about us? Why weren't we consulted!?" And being a democratic girl at heart she rallied over mind's presumptuous choice. "Our mind has no right to kill our body," she told me after the attempt. "Not on the grounds of boredom, anyway . . .") and met with the satisfaction of all concerned.

Punishment of unwed mothers? Bullshit! Care of neither the old nor the young can be considered to be punishment for the able, not even the care of the un-dead old or the un-born young. These beings, regardless not only of race, creed, and color but as well of size, situation, or ability, must be treated as equals and their rights to life not only recognized but *defended*! Can they defend themselves?

You are you from conception, and that never changes no matter what physical changes your body takes. And the virile sport in the Mustang driving to work with his muscular forearm tanned and ready for a day's labor has *not one microgram more* right to his inalienable rights of life, liberty, and the pursuit of happiness than has the three month's fetus riding in a sack of water or the vegetable rotting for twenty years in a gurney bed. Who's to know the value or extent of another's trip? How can we assume that the world through the windshield of that Mustang is any more rich or holy or even sane than the world before those pale blue eyes? How can abortion be anything but fascism again, back as a fad in a new intellectual garb with a new, and more helpless, victim?

I swear to you, Paul, that abortions are a terrible karmic bummer, and to support them—except in cases where it is a bona fide toss-up between the child and the mother's life—is to harbor a worm of discrepancy.

Q: Well, that's really eloquent and mistypoo, but suppose Faye were raped and became pregnant in the process?
A: Nothing is changed. You don't plow under the corn because the seed was planted with a neighbor's shovel.

Q: I assume that it would be her decision, though?
A: Almost certainly. But I don't really feel right about speaking for her. Why don't you phone and ask?

[Krassner phones Faye Kesey in Oregon and reviews the dialogue. She asks: "Now, what's the question—if I were raped, would I get an abortion?" "That about sums it up." "No, I wouldn't."]

Q: But would she marry the rapist to give the child a name? . . . What would you have done in my place before abortion was legalized and someone with an unwanted pregnancy came to you for help, and you knew of a safe doctor as an alternative to some back-alley butcher?

A: I have been in your place and done what you did. I think now—not just because of religious stands but of what happened to the girls' heads as a result—that I did a great disservice because I was being asked for more than money or the name of a guy in Tijuana. In the last few years, when asked the question, I've found myself able to talk the women out of it. I could have talked them out of it back then as well. There are girls with kids coming and no old man to carry his share of the load. Women sense far better than a man what the bearing and raising of a child means in terms of a lifetime commitment. It all comes down to a pact of support. And if the man pulls out his support first, how can he blame the woman for pulling out hers? Next time you're asked to choose between hygiene and a back-alley butcher, Paul, try choosing instead against both possibilities and for life instead.

[Paul Krassner: A couple of years later, Kesey said to me, "If you're going to write about my position on abortion, I've changed, you know. It has to do with the war on drugs. The war is not on drugs, the war is on consciousness. Nobody has any right to come in and mess with your inside. They don't have any right to tell me what to do inside my head, any more than they have any right to tell women what to do inside their bodies. What's inside of us is *ours*, and we've got to fight for it."]

Q: How do you reconcile the notion of working out one's karma through succeeding reincarnations with the reality of, say, a plane crash—and you can take that on to Nazi Germany or My Lai, a flood here, a tornado there—does the common karma of all those victims simply transcend the boundaries of coincidence?

A: It's like Hell hanging in mid-air.

Q: You talk about this Thing as if it were a personal friend of yours.

A: Get off my back, Martha!

Q: What were the parts that were left out of the Tom Wolfe book?

A: The parts that might have hurt people. Tom Wolfe, as well as being a genius (he got most of that book without notes or a tape recorder; he has an astounding ability to watch and remember) is a very gentle guy. Certain passages—such as the Hells Angels gangbang—would have been stronger if he had used the real names of the real people that participated, but he very wisely made up characters instead.

Q: Jack Kerouac once stated his philosophy as: "I don't know, I don't care, and it doesn't make any difference." And yet his widow said he died a lonely man. Was he deceiving himself, or what?

A: I feel bad about Kerouac. He was a prophet and we let him die for us. He *did* know, and he *did* care, and the letters of praise that I composed in my head to him *would have* made a difference had I, and all the others who felt the same respect, mailed them. Sometimes polemics and fashion get so thick that we can't make out a clear call for help from a friend.

Q: You've referred to Neal Cassady as one of the hippest people you've ever known, and yet if it's true that he died while walking along the railroad tracks counting the ties—and his last words were "Sixty-four thousand, nine hundred twenty-eight"—it seems more compulsive than hip?

A: Long before his death Cassady had passed that point where being hip or compulsive had any relative meaning to him. His was the yoga of a man driven to the cliffedge by the grassfire of an entire nation's burning material madness. Rather than be consumed by this burn he jumped, choosing to sort things out in the fast-flying but smogfree moments of a life with no retreat. In this commitment he placed himself irrevocably beyond category. Once, when asked why he wouldn't at least *try* to be cool, he said: "Me trying to be cool would be like James Joyce trying to write like Herb Gold."

Q: How did Cassady respond the time you told him you feared you were losing your sense of humor?

A: With great concern and sympathy, as though I had told him that I had cancer of the lymphthf.

Q: How did you regain it?

A: The lymphthf? It came back of its own, after I dropped a five-gallon jar of mayonnaise on my foot.

Q: No, I mean how did you regain your sense of humor?

A: Oh, that. I never did, I guess. Rehabilitation, as my counselor up at the Sheriff's Honor Camp used to tell me, is a two-way street.

Q: How would you compare Babbs and Baba Ram Dass?

A: When one tries to come on about his best buddy it becomes too difficult to remain unbiased. So rather than risk being guilty of the "communal lie," as I guess I once called it, I'll turn the question back over to you. How would *you* compare Babbs and Baba Ram Dass?

Q: I think of Ram Dass as a sort of Johnny Carson of the future, and Babbs as his Ed McMahon . . . or maybe it's the other way around . . . they're each different sides of the same coin—Psychedelic Social Director—and they can both relate almost magically to whatever environment they find themselves in, but their styles are so different . . . What's your concept of the communal lie?

A: I remember delegates from two large communes stopping by once at my farm and negotiating in great tones of importance the trade of one crate of cantaloupes, which the southern commune had grown, for one portable shower, which the northern commune had ripped off of a junk yard. When this was over, they strutted around in an effluvium of "See? We're self-supporting."

Bullshit. A crate of melons and a ratty shower isn't enough summer's output for sixty-some people to get off behind. It was part of a lie that the entire psychedelic community, myself more than most, was participating in. When a bunch of people, in defense of their lifestyle, have to say, "Look how beautiful we were at Woodstock!" I can't help but ask, "How was your cantaloupe crop this year?" Being beautiful, or cool, or hip is too often a clean-up for not pulling weeds.

Woodstock was beautiful and historic and even perhaps Biblical, but Altamont was far more honest. Success is a great spawning ground of confidence and camaraderie; bald truth is found more often up against the wall. Bullshit is bullshit and neither the length of the hair nor the tie of the family can make it anything else.

Q: How would you compare Sonny Barger of the Hells Angels and General Patton of the Pentagon?

A: Patton, I think, must have been a madman, an occult dilettante with charisma and power and probably a stupid sex-life; Sonny is no glory hound and no madman.

Q: What's the meaning to you of the Charles Manson verdict—isn't finding him guilty the same as finding a Syndicate boss guilty of ordering murders, the only difference being that Manson didn't pay his girls?

A: When Esau, all red and hairy, preceded his twin Isaac out of the womb, he beat his brother out by, as it were, a cunt hair, winning the eldest's right to take over the leadership of the family. Years later, on his way back from helling around with the local sports on a coonhunt, Esau spies his bumpkin brother hunkered in the field eating a bowl of Cream of Wheat.

"Hey, little brother," Esau calls, "Howza bout giving a hit of that Cream of Wheat to your old brother hot back from the hunt?"

Isaac sizes up the opportunity and answers, "Tell you what, big brother, I'll trade you this bowl of Cream of Wheat for your birthright; that is, for *your right* as the *eldest of the family*."

Esau shrugs. "I, who am already dead, should give a shit for a crumby birthright? It's a deal."

As he gobbled the bowl of breakfast food, Esau didn't realize he had traded off his most precious God-given possession, for by choosing to relinquish his part in the Big Show and opting for an existential outlook he lost his *right of choice*! When the court finds Manson guilty of the power to make those girls do his will, the court is removing the girls' right of choice, our absolutely inalienable right the sanctuary of which even God cannot evade! It can only be surrendered.

Whenever someone squeals "He made me do it!" they join the distinguished ranks of the Eichmanns and Calleys, a group in hotter karmic water, really, than the Mansons and the Nixons who still have, at least, the right to be guilty.

Q: What about the beast-people for whom you see no possibility of growth?
A: These are people who have reached a terminal state, karmically and spiritually. These are the branches on the vine that have not produced and have no intention of producing and are bound for the fire and know it and *willfully defend the state*. These people are Esau again, asking again "What good is a birthright to one who is already dead?" So, it isn't that the possibility of growth and rebirth is gone—that possibility is always open, forever—it is that with some people, the *likelihood* of taking advantage of this opportunity to change is practically nonexistent. Finally, when the sea is boiling and the rock is burning and the moon is bleeding and will no longer hide them, they run to Satan and he says, "Right on! Come right in!" Then their beasthood is complete.

Q: The Bible was written when people believed that the earth was flat, that God was anthropomorphic, and that women were inferior—but if you think

of the New Testament as still in process, could you tell what I think is a contemporary parable, about that trial involving the dog?

A: I'm busted, see, for a warrant for not having acquired licenses for dogs
allegedly living on the farm with me, busted, searched, and thrown in jail
overnight for not having licensed beings which I do not consider myself the
owner of, yr honor, and I would like to call my ten-year-old daughter to the
stand as a witness:

> *Bailiff*: Shannon Kesey take the stand!
>
> *Judge*: A moment, please. [*leaning benignly down from the bench*] Shan-
> non, do you know what a lie is?
>
> *Shannon*: Yeah.
>
> *Judge*: And do you know what a truth is?
>
> *Shannon*: Yeah.
>
> *Judge*: And do you know the difference between the two?
>
> *Shannon*: Yeah.
>
> *Judge*: Then you may swear her in.
>
> *Bailiff*: ShannonKeseydoyousweartotellthetruththewholetruthandnoth-
> ingbutthetruths'helpyouGod?
>
> *Shannon*: Yeah.
>
> *Me*: Shannon, do you think of Stewart as your dog?
>
> *Shannon*: No.
>
> *Me*: Do you think of him as Jed or Zane or Mom's dog?
>
> *Shannon*: No.
>
> *Me*: Do you think of him as my dog?
>
> *Shannon*: No.

Then, based on this dramatic testimony, I advanced my argument to the
premise that, though one feeds and lives with another being, he does not
actually *possess* the being unless he is experiencing the being as a *thing* in
an I/it way, whereas I held myself to be in *relation* to Stewart and, therefore, could not be in *possession* of him. The judge's jaw dropped. The DA
turned red and sputtered under the irrefutable weight of my logic. The bai-
liff crossed himself and made a hex sign at me with his fingers, but could do
nothing to stem my argument.

"Not guilty," ruled the judge, then added, "*but*, Mr. Kesey, in as you are
not the owner—and apparently no one else is—I must tell you that it is a law
in this country that a dog *without an owner* must be put to sleep."

"You mean that by winning the case I lose the dog?"

"I'm afraid that's correct. Unless you buy a dog license."

"All right, I'll buy the license."

"And for the other dogs as well?" the DA piped up. "Or do you want them gassed?"

"I'll get a license for all the dogs."

"You are wise, Mr. Kesey," the judge said.

I watched in silence as he smiled benignly down on Shannon again and left the bench, stepping through my imagination into a reincarnate future where he is a boy being chased through Central Park by a pack of insane Pomeranians loosed after him by an organization of insane old ladies dedicated to tracking down defectors from the fifth world war. The dogs pull him down. The old ladies watch, clucking, as their highly pedigreed and thoroughly licensed pets eat away at the young man's ears, nose, crotch . . .

Q: Your favorite metaphor seems to be that the human race is involved in some sort of drama. But since there's no script, do you have any predictions as to developments in the plot?

A: The Good Guys will win. The consciousness now being forged will hang, tempered and true, in the utility closet alongside old and faithful tools like Mercy and Equality and Will Rogers. The accolades will be tremendous. Even Hitler, going through the gates only a few steps in front of Old Scratch himself, will get a terrific hand. And finally, God willing, the mortgage on this wad of woe will be fully paid off.

Q: To help bridge the gap between the Good Guys and the Bad Guys, could you talk a little about fascist humor?

A: Yeah, but first it's a little chilly in here; could we toss another Jew on the fire?

Q: I know you're not anti-Semitic, but is it possible you're a human chauvinist? I mean, I once said I don't believe that Jews are the chosen people—or that people are the chosen species—

A: I don't believe that people are the chosen species but I believe that the Jews are—or were—the Chosen People.

Q: Until?

A: When the train that pulled into the station two thousand years ago and didn't look like My Son, the Messiah, but like a beatnik in sandals and a DayGlo yarmulke, well, the train waited around a while for the Chosen to hop on board, then pulled on out. A few hobos hanging out in the yard—lazy yids and hustling goyim, mostly—slipped into the boxcars.

Q: How do you feel about the trend of rock music toward lyrics about neo-Christianity?
A: Mighty good, Paul, bein' a Christian and all; how do you feel about it?

Q: It's getting kind of quiet in here; would you toss another Christian to the lions? . . . What do you think is the meaning of a lyric like "One toke over the line, sweet Jesus . . . "?
A: I think they are singing (did you know that was the Dead backing those guys up?) about that state when you've gone and got so high that you're forced to operate mostly on faith.

Q: Would you care to elaborate a little on the relationship between dope and faith?
A: Or, what to do with your hands when the fuses blow. Sometimes we have to take steps to keep our right hand from knowing what our left hand is doing—break up their alliance and turn your palms allward and wait for the spark of creation!—and other times we need to fold our fingers in prayer. So I hearby recommend, if you feel ready to turn palms allward and spread your arms and a-gallivanting go, I recommend LSD-25 and/or psilocybin if you can be sure it's good stuff. (Where do you get this good stuff? Beats me; I don't have any. The first and best I ever got came to me by the very reliable way of the Federal Government. They gave me mine—paid me and quite a few other rats both white and black $20 a session in fact to test it for them, *started it* so to speak, then, when they caught a glimpse of what was coming down in that little room full of guinea pigs, they swatched the guinea pigs out, slammed the door, locked it, barred it, dug a ditch around it, set two guards in front of it, and gave the hapless pigs a good talking to and warned them—on threat of worse than death—to *never* go in that door again—and if you still think they should give you yours after careful examination of the rot-minded, chromosome damaged results of these little experiments begun ten years ago [check the records of Dr. Leo Hollister from early '60s file of Menlo Park and Palo Alto V.A. hospital], then I think you should demand they either give you yours or award all those poor guinea pigs the Purple Heart, the Distinguished Service Cross and full disability for them and all their offspring as well . . .) And for the times when you've had enough spoils and gallivanting, and you're weary and blistered

with the wind, I recommend let the hands join (after a little tequila, or far better, a *Dilantin*) and close your eyes and focus both the *right side of you* and *the left side of you* on the ONE BEYOND YOU . . . then drink some tea and smoke a joint and throw the *Ching* and get to work or whatever you let go to weed during your gallivant and *don't hang out*, every inch of hanging out you do past the point of knowing what needs to be done becomes more a drag, a drain, and an amalgamated lie. *Too much hanging out without a doubt will warp your spine and turn off half your mind*, the memory half, which gets tired of supplying the speech half with information squandered in rap fest *bon mots* and says, "Fuck it; if that's all he's doing with his mouth I think I'll go to sleep."

Then, after a week or so of this—"cleaning up," Cassady called it—spread those hands again and open a place for something to happen. I know of no other way to Faith; it can't be bought; it can't be learned; and it can't be muscled in. Faith doesn't come from security. It comes from survival.

Q: Do you see the legalization of grass as any sort of panacea?
A: The legalization of grass would do absolutely nothing for our standard of living, or our military supremacy, or even our problem of high school dropouts. It could do nothing for this country except mellow it, and that's not a panacea, that's downright subversive.

Q: Would you say that Christ was hindered or helped by his celibacy?
A: You gotta remember that Jesus was fathered by a celibate so he comes by it naturally. I *do*, however, think it contradicts some of the longevity claims made by the advocates of this particular crotch yoga discipline.

Q: Would you agree that sexual jealousy is essentially puritan?
A: No, I think all denominations are probably afflicted by it.

Q: Leave your cortical vigilance out of this . . . What do you think of mechanical aids to sexual stimulations, such as vibrators?
A: I've always, if you'll pardon the expression, made out quite well with the traditional equipment, thank you.

Q: Would you go so far as to say that orgies derive out of boredom?
A: All the orgies in my meager experience derived not from boredom—in fact far from boredom—but from effort, ingenuity, and a good deal of horniness.

Q: Unlike Tim Leary and his magic embrace, you don't seem to be physically demonstrative—do you attach any significance to that?
A: My dad, a Texan, raised me on good ole Amurcan handshakes; I reckon folks just does what comes natural to them. Sometimes I hug people, but it's usually when I'm interested in the configuration of their pectoral region.

Q: Did you have to overcome any homosexual defenses when you were a wrestler?
A: Just one, and he was terrific.

Q: Do you have as much faith in sports as you once did?
A: No. I played and loved sports, but I'm not going to steer my sons into them the way my father did me. I don't like the heavy fascist hit I get off the pro heroes, and I don't like the Little League consciousness that forces a kid to knuckle under a father's fading, and ill-proportioned, values. I'm afraid the old "builds a boy's character and self-confidence" argument is just an earlier version of the Marine recruiter shuck.

Q: How did you dodge the draft, by the way?
A: The dodge I had in mind was going to New Bedford to the Coast Guard Academy, so I went ahead to my exam with that in mind and when I came to the part on the exam that says "Have you ever had a separated shoulder?" it just so happened that I had separated my left shoulder a couple of years before in the PCI Wrestling tournament in San Luis Obispo when I experienced the worst trouncing of my life in the finals, so I mark, "Yeah, I have had my shoulder separated" and went on the next day to wrestle to third place in another tournament, re-separating the same shoulder, and that Monday there was a notice to return for further examination and X-ray where the doctor concluded that my shoulder (which hadn't bothered me much until the re-separation) was "slopping around in the socket like an eyeball in a quart jar of snot" and awarded me a big old 4F for my troubles.
Who says athletic training makes a lad militaristic?

Q: Would you tell about the rise and fall of our American flag tooth?
A: Ah, the tooth. This was a period of penance I did for my momentary patriotic faltering when I split to Mexico, returned, was eluding the FBI by following Rohan out toward the San Rafael bridge to a hideout, hit the brakes, nothing, hit Rohan stopped at a red light in front of me, spun across the oncoming lane and hit a white Imperial, bounced across the divider into

the field and hit a pole and finally hit the steering wheel with my mouth and cracked my front tooth off at the gums.

After a miserable night in a Berkeley hotel taking aspirin and listening to the FBI tiptoe up and down the halls I finally made my way to Santa Cruz where Dick Smith, the mad dentist, suggested replacing it with a flag partial. I flew this banner from the mast of my mouth for almost four years before I sneezed one day by the goose pond where my brother was feeding cottage cheese to the geese and to my surprise found a hole where this flag had flown. Chuck had seen something fly into a cottage cheese after my sneeze but hadn't got a good look at it. A goose had eaten it. Which goose? He didn't know so we locked all four in the chicken yard and examined the droppings for a couple of days. We found nothing out of the ordinary and my grandfather told us that the tooth would likely have been ground up in the craw anyway. It seemed to be the end of the penance. Now, as much as I love it, I would like to see Old Glory hauled down everywhere.

Q: Would you fly anything in its place?
A: The flag of the United Nations. Think about it; assuming we still have to have a Man at the Top would you rather serve under Richard Nixon or U Thant?

Q: What was your reaction to being searched by the Black Panthers before we could get into the Grateful Dead benefit?
A: A kind of holding-real-still reaction. What was yours?

Q: Somehow I wanted to communicate that my attitude was different from when I had been searched by the police in Chicago because now I was attempting to empathize with—I mean I was hoping he wouldn't tickle me—you're right, a kind of holding-real-still situation . . . But, whereas the Merry Pranksters could get away with a lot because the police knew they were just traveling through, don't you think it's different from actually living in an Oakland ghetto?
A: Different, but probably not much more fraught. To any people, any-where, who have the audacity to be alive to each other, there is always the threat of Maloch swooping down with nightstick and search warrant. Being black isn't what makes living in Oakland, or anywhere else, dangerous; it's being colored. The prison that the audacious are threatened with is built of nothing but categories. Cops know that there is really no way to bust the rainbow.

Q: Unless it crosses state lines . . . What did you mean when you said that I cramped a certain consciousness by talking to those people from Sam's Café on the radio?

A: I mean that the vacuum of centuries is roaring questions in your ear and you take time to play riddles with the cub scouts. Who are you to fritter your valuable energies away in these times of ecological poverty?

Q: I don't know, I guess I must be a cub scout fetishist . . . and you must be a vacuum cleaner salesman . . . Do you approve of the eco-guerillas going out with double crosscut saws and then selecting appropriately obnoxious billboards?

A: Yes, this is a creative and nonviolent act with the effects and immediate rewards. I hope the trend spreads.

Q: Oh, hey, Buster Keaton's on TV now.

A: Far fucking out. Let's watch him.

[Time out. Can't get Keaton. We watch one-third of *Games* instead.]

Q: John Wayne says that if you're going to look into the eye of the camera, you'd better be prepared to deliver the Sermon on the Mount. Would you care to look into the eye of the camera? I guess what I'm really asking is, what are the rules of your game?

A: God's will be done. And if, to be able to tune in on that will, I have to get a little high or come on a little strange in order to free myself of the interference jamming my pipeline, then I may presume to ask God, since it's all in the line of duty, to please don't make my highs too bumpy or my strangeness too ungentle.

We'll always fumble and fuck up, and all our rules will eventually come down with a dose of amendments. It says in *The Urantia Book* that at the Last Supper, Christ promised his disciples that he would return to them as the Spirit of Truth. This is what we want, a compass needle that constantly tries to point out Whatever's Right. Rules we must eventually forsake as we turn more and more to the Spirit of Truth. It is for this spirit of moment-by-moment responsibility, this continual seeking after the unique and correct action for each unique and demanding moment, this Way that is unpointed . . . for this final holy *heart* of us that we must eventually forsake all rules.

Is kind of the kind of game I play.

Q: I can understand the use of prayer as a means of maintaining contact with the universe, but don't you think it's lacking in cosmic humility when you pray for any kind of personal goal?

A: Not at all! If one's heart is like mine, pure and dedicated, he is exempt from humility. Where do you get off with these dopey questions? Don't you know I'm a busy man with lots of important irons in the fire?

Q: Oh, yeah—well, what was the great Spirit of Truth behind your sneaking out of that party with the little tank of nitrous oxide—huh, huh, huh?

A: The Spirit of Stash happens to be one of the amendments to the Spirit of Truth

Q: What do you think your father meant, saying to you and Chuck once, over a gas flash: "You fellows better be right or it's the end of the universe . . ."

A: He sensed that what we were about was threatening the whole human hierarchy, our whole system of Who Really Makes Things Work, and that there had better be Something Better available when the kings and generals fell.

Q: What do you think our kids are going to do that will shock and dismay us as much as the things we've been doing have shocked and dismayed our parents?

A: Nothing. Ever. If our efforts have been sincere. Are Grape Nuts as hard to chew as they were when you were a kid?

Q: Oh, is THAT what you were supposed to do with them? . . . But how come you wouldn't let your kids read *Zap Comics*?

A: Once, on our way to film *Atlantis Rising*, we were encamped at Ed McClanahan's amid a mighty passle of kids: my kids, Babbs's kids, Ed's kids, Chuck's kids . . . and as they played in the backyard us grown folks rested ourselves on the back porch and smoked, drank, shot the shit, and read of the new crop of *Zap* and *Zap*-style comics that Ed had brought from his office. Fierce stuff, gory and righteously disturbing stuff, the only stuff I'd seen with any of the real raw excitement that you feel from when art is in there dealing with the issues, since I'd first come across Ron Boise's work of statues screwing. Fascinating stuff . . .

And after a bit one of the books worked its way into the kid action going on; we noticed a change of energy activity that had been all-encompassing began to fragment. When a kid read a certain of the comics he would turn darkly into himself until, gradually, the communication that is the basis of play fell apart. I asked Babbs: "Do you think that these comics are going to make our kids better fucks in the future, or worse?"

"Worse, I think," he answered.

"Me too," I said.

We set about gathering the books from sight.

Because, in some of the comics of that period particularly, along with the art, there was often something else in the works of even geniuses like Crumb and Wilson and Shelton, speed-trip- like digressions where you could see the artists working to exorcise their own personal demons by, however unintentionally, casting them into whatever swine happened to be susceptible, which wasn't us grown folks because we were either full up with our own demons or had the defense built up by our own exorcising, so we were safe. I wasn't so sure about the kids.

It's like this: I've got nothing against my kids watching a couple make love but having them watch a flagellant is something different. But that doesn't explain it either. I've got it: it's the *consciousness the artist is communicating* that I'm concerned with; not the activity the art is depicting. I've always brought city stuff back from the city for my kids, *Zap* included (so I actually *do* let them read *Zap*; as a matter of fact, I can't recall any of the *Zaps* that I ever withheld; it was mostly the *Zap* spinoffs), some stuff even to read aloud to them because it was so fine you know that the consciousness producing it must have been unimpeachable, *whatever* the subject matter or how luridly it was dealt with, stuff like Lenore Goldberg, and Captain Pissgums, and Fritz the Cat and Mr. Natural and Wonder Warthog and, Lord, *most* of the ones that everybody reads—but I now read them through first to try to plumb the *consciousness* serving as the impetus, and, some I withhold.

I mean, W. C. Fields was a great artist but would we ask him to babysit when he was working off a bad hangover?

Q: What's the last thing that made you lose your temper?
A: I have to admit, it was my kids.

Q: What's the last thing that made you laugh hysterically?
A: My mind is a bramble of shredded wheat. Who can unravel the memories from the riboflavin, I ask you? But I guess it was a week or so ago at an acid-laced poker game when things digressed to the point of a hand of nine card stud with Doses, Jukers, and One-eyed Pukers wild.

Q: Is there any connection between those two things?
A: Yes! Of course there is a connection! What two things?

Q: I forget. Memory and riboflavin, I guess.
A: Ah, of course. In that case, no, there is no question. Next connection, please.

Q: Do you think eternal consciousness would be Heaven or Hell?
A: I don't know about that but I know that forty hours of STP with a big hand on the nape of the neck saying "You wanted to see the books? So then *look* at the books!" can be fairly Hellish. There's a beautiful chapter in *Wind in the Willows* where Rat and Mole find the little lost muskrat child, resting there, safe between the hooves of (the *hooves* of!?) who had been taking care of the helpless animal, and Mole and Rat see, in the *hooves* of, great sights, great tragedies, great delights . . . too much, finally, too much.

And the final gift of (the *hooves*?) then, is the merciful gift of (what hooves? I can't remember . . .) Forgetfulness.

Q: What about that weird ice cream flavor you once invented as an early indication of your abnormality?
A: As ice cream maker in my father's creamery I one time achieved a culinary coup by combining all the leftover flavors, added a large amount of red food coloring, and calling it "Blood Royal," reasoning that the name would tempt new and adventurous customers to our brand. I planned to follow this triumph with two other delights—"Scum Ripple" and "Crud Crunch"— but was torpedoed by the first narrow-minded grocer that discovered a quart of Blood Royal in his freezer. In what seemed to me a very uncalled for phone call to the creamery, he cancelled his account and advised my father to tell the nincompoop that made this batch to look for work in a butcher shop instead of a dairy. Maybe I should have taken this advice; it's difficult for abnormality to flower properly in the antiseptic confines of a creamery.

Q: There was a film critic who said that the Marx Brothers "often used a Sufi parable to launch into their excursions into madness."
A: Far out! But I can believe it. There was a pervading smell of sanity in the fuss the Brothers raised that seemed to come from some place other than the local yeshiva. Sufi Marx? Who'da thought it . . .

Q: So how come you can't call Hugh Romney by his rightful name?

A: Because I simply cannot imagine myself stumping through the mosquito-ridden bush to finally find our missing colleague standing gaunt and bowed with decades of humanitarianism performed in the most desolate reaches of the globe, and say to him: "Wavy Gravy, I presume?"

Q: You've used the expression, "being tight with one's own image"—what does that mean to you?
A: I don't remember ever saying such. But you, Paul, are a truthful lad, so I must have said it. What must I have meant? Hmmm . . . Well, I *do* think about my fucking image, I confess. I don't intend to but often I find it there in the hallway, prancing and whimpering like a dog begging to be taken for a walk in the park, and I am compelled, out of kindness if nothing else, to deal with it:

"Hello, Image, how the hell are ya?"

"Take me out, take me out! I'm fading, I'm warped, I need some *light!*"

"Yeah, I've seen the light you attract, champ. Now stop this nonsense and get back in the basement; I'll let you know when it's time for your walk . . . "

So what I must have meant is trying to keep straight with all the lies I promised yesterday and still not have to pay for a rabies shot.

Q: Once there was the Great Acid Test Graduation. Now, what's your current post-graduate fantasy?
A: Well, to tell the truth, I've been taking a few refresher courses. I may re-enroll and go on for my doctorate.

Q: What've you learned lately?
A: I've learned to keep a little niacin and ginseng handy, and to have a mantra on tap in the backup system.

Q: Do you think it's possible that you're overly dependent on the *I Ching*?
A: The *Ching* is an oracle and willing to work for but not to indulge you. It's very specific about this; whenever you overuse it, it invariably scolds you and draws your attention to this infringement, as with, for example, the hexagram Meng/Youthful Folly which says this in The Judgment:

> *Youthful Folly has success.*
> *It is not I who seek the young fool;*
> *The young fool seeks me.*
> *At the first oracle I inform him.*

If he asks two or three times,
      It is importunity.
If he importunes,
      I give him no information.
Perseverance furthers.

Q: You could always resort to a movie script instead for the same stage directions—Consternation changing to Horror—but if, no matter what you throw, the *Ching* will still apply to your situation, then obviously it serves as a Rorschach test, and it would seem to me that the closer in touch you are with your unconscious, the less you'd have to consult the *I Ching.*
A: No. Getting closer to your unconscious is where you are on a psychological field. The *Ching* exists in another field. There is no development implied in one's ability to throw the *Ching*; you never throw the *Ching* any better or worse than you did the first time.

Q: There was a student rebel poster during the 1968 uprising in France that said: "Psychology aims at the systematic subordination of individual behavior to false social norms"—do you see any change in terms of encounter groups and psychodrama?
A: Once, at Esalen, I happened in on the end of a week's dance therapy. There were the graduates, all aglow with a week's total encounter and breakthrough, recapping their recent victories. Fritz Perls was there too. "Vait!" he said.

[The radio suddenly announces that the charges against Bobby Seale have been dismissed. "Holy cow!" Kesey shouts. Then the president says from Birmingham that America is "not divided at all." Responding to both Krassner and Nixon, Kesey continues:]

"Vait!" Fritz protested. "Vhere are you the *rest* of the veeks?"
"Vwat—I mean *what* do you mean?" asked the dance therapist, cautiously.
"He means," I interjected helpfully, "what does Superman do between phone booths?"
"I mean," Fritz answered for himself, "you are dividing your lives between *this veek . . .* and *all the other veeks!*"
Which means to me that the idea of "sessions" may ensure failure of psychology aims, that to avoid a schizophrenic dichotomy we must either (1) let psychodrama push back the rest of our lives, or (2) let the rest of our lives

push back the psychodrama, or (3) live the drama without benefit of Alfred Hitchcock.

I mean, I heard the fatality report for the weekend in Lane County: A girl was killed when her horse fell on her. A guy crashed in his single engine plane. A guy drowned waterskiing. A mountain climber killed falling down a mountain. It's when you take a break that you stumble, and psychodrama is a vacation, a luxury. Look at the cars driven by the participants, at the houses they live in. Could Bobby Seale afford psychodrama? Does he need it? Does he even have *room* for it?

Q: Now that we won't have Bill Graham to kick around anymore, how do you envision the future of rock concerts and festivals?
A: I'm afraid Bill Graham's pandering has muddied these waters for good. Maybe this is why I feel my personal energies swinging back to writing.

Q: It doesn't seem fair to make Graham the scapegoat for an entire industry, including the groups that demand so much bread in front.
A: You're right; it isn't fair. People get what's due them without any help from other people. But Bill Graham's a very powerful guy and has survived much worse thoughts than I ever had about him, and I use the word "pander" because it implies that particular kind of middle-man, that buffer between the whore and the horny, and this was a place that Bill won, defended, and finally wisely forsook—all with great class and with never any apparent loss of personal integrity. Maybe the waters needed muddying. If the vision is ill it was probably doomed from the start and Bill Graham merely part of Fate's motorcycle. And if I object to a panderer I mean it in no way as a moral or a personal objection; it just seems to me like a sort of fatuous featherbedding. Do we need them? Did you ever see "Mother Nature Presents!" tattooed across an upreared pudendum?

Let me make myself more clear on this, as our great president might say. Bill Graham, as it happened with a lot of us, found himself heir to a large hunk of the Revolution, and I think that he, as did a lot of us, mismanaged his allotment. I also think it's up to them as considers themselves capable to finger the mistakes, and if we keep our finger in the mistake too long, or make a mistake in our fingering, then it's up to those as think *they* are able to, to finger *our* mistake. But we must learn to leave each man's righteousness to him and stick to the work we're involved in. I can't presume to say Bill Graham is a bad man or an un-righteous middle-man—in fact I *admire* his apparent righteousness—but I can accuse him of being a bad pimp.

Then, on the other hand, maybe I'm just getting back at him for calling me a "hip Liberace."

But, I'll tell you, Paul, these are hard questions. I don't like the sound of me answering too-hard questions. I sound oracular, like I know more than I do. My words have a disproportionate weight. Like, I got a long letter from a PhD in Biology about the article in the *Last Supplement* on Cancer, and another about the article on Immunization, asking essentially: Are we certain we have looked into such things as cancer and smallpox vaccination enough to allow statements about things as important as some old lady who might go for the laetrile cure instead of going to a doctor, or some kid's future with smallpox? No! We are not qualified! This isn't to say that we couldn't be if we put our full energies into these areas and stopped trying to live like rock stars, but right now, no, I'm not qualified. No more than I'm qualified to make judgments regarding other people's karmic state or depth of their revolutionary commitment. But I'm easy; some kid with big eyes and a notepad could come up and ask me how the universe was created and if he looks like he thinks I know, pretty soon *I* think I know and I'm running it down to him like the gospel. I'm easy but in *no fucking way qualified*!

So, Mr. Krassner, I not only cease, I *vow* to cease answering these and other such questions and to shut my mouth and the door to my writing room and finish the new totally fictional version of *Cut the Motherfuckers Loose* and answer out of my range no more.

Passing off what-might-be-true as fiction seems a better vocation to me than passing off what-is-quite-possibly-fiction as truth.

Q: Didn't you once believe that writing is an old-fashioned and artificial occupation?
A: I was counting on the millennium. Now I guess I'm tired of waiting.

Q: Would you recount the incident of that old man with the bicycle we saw on the road near La Honda?
A: Ah, gee, Paul, I don't know . . . let me see . . . we're driving down out of the La Honda hills and turning left at the ocean, along the roller coaster of the California shoreline in Faye's 1964 black Mercury convertible with the top open to the great blue sky . . . and we see this apparition up the hill ahead, advancing down the highway toward us in dreadful silhouette of hunk and paraphernalia and even *two other bicycles* tied atop the one battered World he was easing down the grade in grim combat with gravity . . . there on the shoulder as we pass, his face worked like suede by the half century of his tanning, his faded grape-picker clothes loose on his knotted frame, his big

dedicate boots that probably had walked their way through at least two previous masters before aligning themselves with this man's inviolable cause, digging heels into the gravel as he eased his bike down the hill . . .

And we drive on down the coast and go to a cave I know, a tunnel built during the second world war by the Coast Guard so two men could walk two hundred yards through the chiseled earth to sit all day where the tunnel opens out through a cliff overlooking the Jap-infested Pacific, to sit there all day every day through the years of our battle with the Japanese and watch with binoculars over the barrel of a big gun for periscopes that never came . . . then leaving the cave and driving back north hours later through the sunset we spy this old guy, some miles further along and on the other side of the road this time and now pushing his apocalyptic vehicle *up* a hill! Touched with awe and sympathy, we swing in behind him. His head turns and he frowns back at us like an angry and enlightened Sisyphus.

"Do you need any help?" we shout heartily.

"No!" he roars back with such ferocity that our good-hearted grins turn to gapes. After glaring at us a moment to make sure we all fully understand his meaning, he turns and resumes his stoic journey up the hill.

That "no" was not a no roared merely to 1964 black Mercuries, but to airplanes, trains, motorcycles, and LEMs. It was the no of a man who had kicked the petroleum habit and wasn't about to joypop any little five mile lift in even a convertible. Our heartiness subdued, we drove around and left him to his way.

Someday, if we last, there'll be millions of that old man, opting in favor of an austere freedom instead of making monthly payments on a plush prison. Cars will still speed through their rivers of stench, airplanes will still carry the Important on their hectic flights to Folly and Fortune, but on the back-roads and ox-bows of the land this old man will still be pushing his vehicle with absolute disdain along with the millions of others who come to share his vision.

Q: Okay, one final question: Mr. Kesey, would you let your daughter marry the Lennon Sisters high on SST in her underwear at a Black Panther Party even though erogizone research has shown that such a union label would cause the patchouli oil gland to dry up beyond all interstellar recognition?
A: Could you rephrase that question, please?

Q: Let me put it this way: How was the universe created?
A: Thanks, Paul. It's sure been great. Now, in closing, I'd like to say this.

Ken Kesey Summing Up the '60s, Sizing Up the '70s

Linda Gaboriau / 1972

From *Crawdaddy*, December 1972. © 1972 by Linda Gaboriau. Reprinted by permission.

It was a long, winding path that led me Springfield, Oregon, and an "interview" with Ken Kesey. Kesey and I have a few mutual acquaintances. We were both first turned on by the government, he in the west coast scene at Stanford, and me on the east coast at Harvard. The people from those two groups couldn't help but know each other. And then there was Paul Krassner, who, with Kesey, had coedited *The Last Supplement of the Whole Earth Catalogue*. When I spoke to Krassner, he warned me that Kesey was turned off to the media and not doing any interviews—hadn't in three years—but he suggested that I call Kesey and speak to him personally. I did

On a hunch, Kesey told me to come and "see what happens." When I got there, he told me had been intrigued by my voice on the phone—he thought I was in my forties and couldn't figure out what a middle-aged Canadian Broadcasting Corp. chick wanted with him.

So late last summer I found myself down on the farm with Kesey, Faye, and the three kids. Other Pranksters—Hagen, Babbs and Gretchen, Hassler—live in and around the village with their kids and their animals. They visit each other, country neighbor style, and Babbs and Kesey are setting up a newsletter.

Kesey and his family live in a big, semi-converted barn. Under the eaves, looking over the barnyard and the chicken coop where the peacocks live, Kesey has his "study" and spends a few hours there every day. At the time he was hanging out there with Buber and the Bible.

The day I arrived, the Frisco Angels were there. It was the first time they had come to visit Kesey in a few years, and they had been there for a couple of days. Like the usual Angel outing, the visit had degenerated and Kesey had sent Faye and the kids to his parents' house in the village and was waiting it out. The Angels finally took off that evening, and Kesey disappeared into the hills to drop some mescaline and cool out. To put it all back into place.

When he came back to the farm a day later, we began eyeing each other, sharing a pot of tea or a joint. I watched and waited to see whether Kesey felt like talking.

As it turned out, Kesey wanted to talk. Not necessarily to me, just to talk. It had been a hard winter and spring—Faye had been ill and Kesey had chosen to turn all his energies toward his family. There were other friends spending the summer on the farm—Bobby Miller (Arthur's son) and Erica, Tangerine, her kid, and Bobby Steinbrecher, who was working on editing the Prankster film; Ray Brock (as in Alice's restaurant) and his new young old lady; and Shirley Abicair, an English folksinger Kesey had met during his trip to England.

Afternoons we all gravitated to the porch of Shirley's little cabin near the duck pond and drank mint juleps. (Kesey makes the best mint juleps in the State of Oregon, where the mint grows wild.) Everybody said they were surprised to see Kesey so talkative because he had been keeping pretty much to himself for months. I guess the timing was right. Things had started to fall into place and Kesey was ready to talk about it. I got a glimplse of the man Tom Wolfe wrote about, the guy who talks in easy downhome parables.

I had been there about a week when, one evening, Kesey and I and Shirley and crazy Brigitta, who had just flown in from Sweden, decided to go into Springfield and have supper at the Ali Baba Café. After all the Arab food, we went to visit Luther in his suburban-style ranch house. (Luther is an ex-pilot who has a printing shop in Springfield and for the past couple of years has been printing Prankster posters, pamphlets, and community newspapers for next to nothing.) We smoked some of Luther's hash and talked about talking. Kesey suggested we play one of the old Prankster nonverbal games—"the half-hour glower." All the names were thrown in a hat and drawn out in pairs. The pairs were to sit down facing each other with only knees touching and look into each other's eyes. (Since all of us but Kesey were novices we made it a "quarter-hour glower.") My name came out of the hat with Kesey's and after that, Kesey and I knew much more about each other.

I was supposed to return to Montreal that weekend, so Kesey suggested we tackle our taping session the night before my six a.m. flight. About midnight we settled in his study with a bottle of Tangueray and a couple of joints. Kesey had set up the trusty old Ampex which had traveled with them all on the bus. We were talking about another common acquaintance we had discovered that afternoon: René Daumal and his book *Mount Analogue*. About ten years ago, somebody at Berkeley discovered the book and translated it as a guide to disciplined consciousness expansion. (Jodorowski is now working on a film version.)

Kesey began by explaining why the book had struck him as part of the subversive side of the '60s. Only after listening to the tapes a couple of times, did I realize the trip Kesey had taken me on that night. It seems like a summing up of the '60s. Following the road that had led him back to Springfield, Oregon, where he was born. [Kesey was actually born in La Junta, Colorado.—ed.] Stopovers in Stanford, Frisco, La Honda, on the road to Mexico. Hanging out on Desolation Row. Moving out to Edge City. Paying dues in jail. A pilgrimage to England. And finally Back Home . . .

Kesey: *Mount Analogue* is an interesting springboard in what happened to me. A kind of spiritual Janis Joplin Trip—the idea that what you're doing indicates that it's going to stop in mid-phrase, unless something new comes in. At the beginning of the book, this is what is implied. It came to me by way of Karl Lehmann-Haupt, Sandy Lehmann-Haupt's brother. Karl's now heavy into Gurdjieff. And when he brought the book, I not only thought it was bad literature, I thought it was morally subversive. I felt about it (and then changed my mind about it) the way I felt about two other things: one was John Coltrane and the other was Bob Dylan . . .

When I first heard them, they upset me so that I wanted to do something about stopping them. Like Coltrane, what he was saying, although it was valid, was going to drag the consciousness, which I felt was expanding in a new direction, back into a primitive state. I'm talking about just seeing him one night at the Jazz Workshop. It must have been in '61, about the time he was playing "My Favorite Things." He had on a plaid red shirt I remember . . .

There's something about a person in a red plaid shirt fooling with the barriers, with the frontiers, that upsets stay-at-homes. When Coltrane played, he was speaking about darkness that was beyond my wanting to think about it. An existential pit.

Speaking of existentialists, let me tell you a story about Jean Genet. I was in Palo Alto with Ed McClanahan, and Ed McClanahan says let's go over to this professor's house 'cause Jean Genet is going to be there speaking. It's kind of a reception for him. So me and Ed and his wife, Kit, and Paul Robertson, and Gordon Fraser, and his wife, Judy, all headed over there. It turned out to be a high rent Menlo Park scene, with a lot of myrtle hanging around the fence, and grad students hanging around the swimming pool with salads being served on a patio table by these Bay Area women who are totally tanned, thirty-seven years old and their breasts haven't fallen a bit. Served to about eight black guys in double-breasted black suits, black ties, and black shoes, and white shirts. And Jean Genet sitting in this little lawn chair, with a big-eyed-and-breasted Jewish interpreter at his feet, looking at him with all the adoration in the world.

It was a very tense situation. I wasn't aware of what was going on. I didn't know anything about the thing Genet had going with Cleaver to come over here and try to free Bobby Seale. I didn't know that these were the Panthers and that this was a thing they had put together in France . . . to get him to come over here and use his energy and his intellectual power to try and free Bobby Seale. All I saw was this little guy who is so bleached by so long in the shadows that he'll never be tanned. A completely soft, white, strange-looking little guy, surrounded by the stark blare of these black guys standing around him and these people coming up and asking him these existential questions.

I went up and introduced myself to him. I had on a pair of purple shoes. So I stood up and pointed to my shoes and said, "L.A." Genet stood up, pointed at his shoes and said, "Toronto." I felt like we had made some kind of connection and I just wanted to talk with him. I didn't want to get into anything heavy with him, 'cause you really can't with somebody interpreting.

Finally they called us all inside where Genet had this interpreter stand up and read this statement he had written, about Bobby Seale and the Panthers and what they were doing. The point was that there had to be some kind of justice squeezed from the American people for these—and I remember the phrase—these virile and beautiful young black men. And as it went on, this long letter, I began to think, "Wait a minute, Genet, what are you pulling?" He was just sitting there, completely white and malevolent, like a toadstool, buttering them up, these six or eight very fierce-looking black guys, one of whom I found out later was David Hilliard, who had gone to France to get Genet in order to use him to try to advance a certain thing they were doing here.

But as I was watching and listening I thought: there's nobody who uses Jean Genet. He's too slick. He has opted from consciousness as we know it, becoming—I've seen Sandy Lehmann-Haupt become this way—a totally amoral person. So that he's karmically frictionless. His life begins at birth and ends at death, and as he sweeps around and looks things over with his eyes he sees things in terms of how they work within this framework. The total dead-end existentialist, just sitting there, looking for action.

Then the Stanford faculty started asking him what they could do about what was happening. And he began to come on at them, standing up and coming on in fierce French being translated into eloquent English. As I say, he's slick. He's got the kind of mind you can only have if you withdraw a long ways and put it together in sort of a confined secrecy.

Cassady, just to interject, couldn't live with his wife or his kids. To do what he did, he had to leave them. Even though when he went there you could tell he liked being there. But when he was there, Cassady did a thing he would never do around us. It was the way he deferred to his wife. The way he couldn't help himself but communicate with her and his kids on a level he felt beneath his best. And when he was doing that he couldn't muscle us the way he was muscling us most of the time. You know, when he was lying soft there with his head in his wife's lap, he was a different Cassady than when he was really coming on hard with us. So he had to cut himself off to do his number. Genet is the same way . . . a person on a peak. On a mountain top. The way he watches, the way he deals with people, is from this lofty peak.

As he was talking with these Stanford professors, the vibes became more and more perverse. Strangely perverse. He was lacerating these guys through this big-eyed girl who would listen to him and then deliver. Listen to the professors, then deliver back. When you hear that, you know there's no true dialogue. Communication is not what's happening. It's finally just a way to lay the whip on. It can't be a dialogue. You slap a phrase down. You wait for the reaction, then slap down another phrase. And the slapped person can't retaliate 'cause it has to travel through this interpreter who's obviously in love with the guy who's swinging the whip.

I was getting more and more tense. I was loaded when we got there, and I was having to hold myself in. I don't like to see people demean themselves the way the Stanford faculty was doing before the Panthers and Genet. And more than that, I don't like to see people enjoy seeing other people demean themselves. So every time one of the Stanford faculty would get up to argue with Genet about what he was saying—and what he was saying essentially was: guns, knives, and bombs—one of the Panthers would jump up and take him on. It went on like this until I could no longer keep my yap shut . . .

I told them a story. About this time in Springfield, Oregon, we were having our first Springfield Creamery Jugs basketball playoff. On our team there was this black guy named Jay Bird and another black guy named Nick

Jones, who was a big U. of Oregon star and is now playing for the Warriors. He got it together there for the Jugs. He could communicate with them and of course basketball is essentially communication. When you see a good basketball game, the ball's moving from guy to guy and the goal's really secondary. And this Nick Jones was like the Jug's switchboard.

Well, I saw a strange thing happen during this basketball season. Nick and Jay Bird played all the time with another half dozen black teammates on the team on the court with them now and then. The referee this season was an off-duty state policeman. He must have had haircuts twice a week. When he called signals on these black guys, he did a thing which he might have got away with in a regular high school game. But there were a lot of other blacks and long hairs who had come to see us play. And by this audience, the ref was busted. When he called a foul on a black, he blew the whistle and held his finger just a little too long, revealing to all something he didn't even know he had—a heavy streak of racism. And I saw the black guys on the team begin to draw their energy from this and begin to get off behind it.

Meanwhile back at Menlo Park, David Hilliard was coming on strong at one Stanford professor when I walked in and started telling him about our basketball team. It was pertinent to what was going on right then. But everybody stopped and turned around and looked at me like I had walked in there and farted and belched and tried to tell ethnic jokes. David Hilliard told me to shut up or they'd take Genet out of there. He said, "We don't hafta listen to this crazy man!" I asked him to wait and listen, 'cause it was part of what was happening. But all of a sudden all the Panthers jumped up, picked up Jean Genet and practically carried him out of the house along with three-quarters of the other people who were there. Out of the house and onto the lawn. So I was left in there with nothing to do but finish this story about the basketball team.

The story was how I had seen these guys on the basketball team begin to draw their energy from the ref's prejudice and start to do amazing things behind it. Amazing passes and checks and scores. But I saw also that when we would pull into the lead this energy would fade, because it draws you from having somebody discriminate against you. You get it on because somebody is putting you down or doing something unjust. You go against that injustice with righteous fury, but as soon as you pull into the lead you fold. I saw this time and again with these black guys.

Then one night I came to the game and brought Rumiako. (*Kesey's pet macaw.*) There was another game going on before ours, so I walked into the stands. And this state cop ref freaked (you could see these last weeks had been murder for him, out there in front of everyone making calls that he knew deep inside were wrong). Freaked and blew his whistle, stopped the game in progress and said, "Get that bird out of here." I was amazed. I hadn't realized how freaked he was. I told him to cool off and ref the game, 'cause Rumiako was just sitting on my shoulder in the stands and had nothing to do with what was going on on the court.

But when it was time for our game, all the guys went out on the court and the referee told them that if I didn't get the bird out of the stands, he wouldn't let our team play. These black guys couldn't believe it. Like me, they were amazed that he had taken his insanity to this point. So finally I said I'd take the bird out and as I walked out I saw our black teammates flash on something—that this referee wasn't just against them and their color. He was against all of us and all color.

That's what I wanted to say to the Panthers, not to let Genet suck them into playing a black-white game . . . especially when he'd be back home in a couple of weeks and they'd be left with a few new burns and nothing else to show for it. And as Genet stalked off with the Menlo Park sunshine on his bald head I experienced the same sense of moral outrage I first felt upon reading *Mount Analogue*. A book I later reversed positions on, so I may do the same with Genet.

Now Coltrane and Dylan . . .

Why I was threatened by Dylan is the best example. I saw very early that he was doing something with our consciousness, the extent of which will only be known hundreds of years from now. Dylan's not only a poet, he's as well a prophet, a prophet like happens once every five hundred years or so. When you heard Dylan in those first songs, he was really talking to you in some way that was not customary linear communication. There'd be a phrase that would strike like a Rorschach, setting off a personal image that would start a whole crystallization of thinking and leave your head in a place it had never been before. It's as if, inside of us, there's always been the proper solution, and Dylan tossed in the proper crystals. But the crystals weren't connected. One thought running and connecting with the next, and that one connecting with the next to present an inductive argument. This was imagery leading out and connecting lyrically to form brand new thought crystals in people's heads. And that's as subversive an act as you can possibly imagine.

This all reminds me of a dream I had a while ago. This was a dream that happened after waking up, not getting up and going back to sleep. Faye had enrolled us in a new class. She had sent away and gotten in the mail a class with the name of a hall that we were to go to, with the number of the room—it was 125A. So we took this bus, driven by a Mexican bus driver, to this old European-looking college. We got there and went along the corridor to 124, 125—and 125A turned out to be in the ceiling. The key unlocked this door in the ceiling. It opened, and out of it fell sand, all over us. Then a ladder came down and we climbed up the ladder and went inside. It was a long room, as long as this barn, dimly lit with benches along both sides. There was no teacher that you could see and there was about forty or fifty people in there. People of various ages, doing a lot of strange things that had no meaning that we could interpret. When we went in, there was no traditional opening made for us, like a professor might have made by saying, "Attention, class, these are the new students," etc. This opening wasn't made, so we just had to go sit on the bench. People were reciting strange things, and as they would stop, somebody would start tapping on the wall with pieces of bamboo. Other people were just moving and making noises. We began to feel very uptight sitting there, the way you might feel if you went into the marketplace in a strange town, all dressed up like American tourists. All the people are doing the marketplace thing, talking in a language you can't understand dealing with each other, and *you're not part of it*. That's a Dylan feeling. That's the feeling he talked about in "Something's Happening and You Don't Know What It Is, Do You, Mr. Jones?" (It finally even came around and got Bobby himself.)

Anyway, in this dream, Faye had to get up and go to the bathroom or someplace; and I was sitting there by myself. I was watching and seeing— finally I see, "there's something important going on here, something really important. They can't stop and bring us in in the traditional way, because then there's no way of doing what they're doing. To forge this new communication that's going on, they have to continue what they're doing, even when it seems rude and heartless. It's up to us to discover our own expression, our own way to enter into it!" There's a lot of the dream that I've forgotten, but I can remember waking up and feeling inspired the rest of the day by that kind of communication that I think now is the answer to all our global problems. A total communication of dance, song, of word-salad Dylanesque expression, where conversation doesn't restrict itself to the way we're used to conversing, but goes to the true core of humanity.

It's like what you see when you've watched the Family Dog trying to put together a communal scene in San Francisco. And they have to argue for three hours about whether they're going to use colored toilet paper or white toilet paper. And you see old Chet Helms get older and strunger-out with it. And you know that nothing's going to help, all these meetings will go on to no avail, until they're able to communicate in this visionary way. None of us know really what it is yet. We just have these dreams about it, and sometimes see people who are able to do it.

How do we forge this? How do we put it together? That thing we played at Luther's, "the half-hour glower," works to a small extent. But how do I do that here in this community where my mom and my grandmother live. It would spook them. I want to be able to communicate off the wall and *not* alienate the people that I care for.

(*As we changed tapes, the conversation went from forging new ways of communicating to pursuing enlightenment. Kesey picked up with the example of Martin Buber.*)

Buber speaks of a thing—it's no longer just a question of a man finding enlightenment, which men have tried to do since they started building campfires, but it's a question of a whole people finding enlightenment, a great group finding this new consciousness.

It's like the time I saw the Beatles at the Cow Palace. One of the great, fantastic experiences of my life. We'd taken a lot of acid and Babbs was driving the bus and "Help" was playing on the loudspeakers. The freeway was just jammed with cars, and spotlights were playing on the Cow Palace. By the time we got there, our level of magic knew no stopping. We drove right in, they parked us right at the front gate, we walked right in, had these perfect balcony seats, were just in time to hear the Sound Incorporated, the ones who used to play before the Beatles . . . we were ready.

We were so loaded that the Cow Palace looked like an enormous organism; the people were all cells of the organism. When the Beatles came out, and all those teenybopper Instamantic flashbulbs started to go off all over the place, flash, flash, flash . . . a thing happened in my head like it was not only the Cow Palace but the inside of my head too. And when John, Paul, George, and Ringo got up there and started singing and coming on, I saw them create a very strange thing—a pyramid of attention which is the cancer of rock music. This is the pyramid that our western consciousness is still built on. I've felt it a lot, when I get up and talk to a college and look out and see these blank faces looking up at me. All I have to do is get myself going a certain way and pretty soon I can say anything I want to and it's believed because the American audience is trained to relinquish its consciousness to this pyramid (see back of dollar bill). When you stand up there, you feel this great flood of power. But, if you talk long enough, you realize that this intersection of attention up there is where you always find Hemingway and Janis

Joplin and Malcolm X and Kennedy and Manson. At this apex is where you find the super-hero of the day, the one who seems to hold the answer for the hungry hordes, the human pinnacle who will lead us up from the love-less mire into the light. But the hero can't do it because he is just another human, just a plain man or woman coming on real good, yet the crowds are loading on hopes that *no* human can fulfill. And when they begin to see that the hero can't handle it, they overload him with a blast of spiteful adoration and burn him out like a fuse.

I've long felt that as soon as you are up there and see this is happening, the only thing to do is step down *into* the pyramid. So that you step down amongst the people and fuck up the concentration.

When I saw the Beatles up there, I saw this concentration of power like never before or since. And it was getting freakier and freakier 'cause what these guys were singing about was Love. I remember feeling at that time that they represented, each one of them, one of the letters of L-O-V-E. When they sang to a fourteen-year-old girl sitting out front, "I want to hold your hand," she felt something from them she wasn't getting from her folks or her boyfriend.

So if you get something up there singing about love, and attracting peo-ple, what you have is a cancer. It's aware of what it's doing, but it can't pro-duce and neither can it stop doing it. The Beatles found themselves in a dangerous situation. There weren't enough cops to hold this mindless cel-lular pushing forward. It was literally getting more and more uptight. They would sing, "She's got a ticket to ride," and the people would scream again and push forward. The people up close were being crushed but there was no way then for the four guys who had put this thing together in a studio, and practiced it, to suddenly sing the crowd *back*.

These guys could have got up there and started coming on together, the four of them, off the wall, impromptu, with that kind of power they could have said, "Ok, you people, you know that all however many thousand there are of you can't have all of us, or probably *any* of us, and you probably don't want any of us anyway. What you truly want is the guy or the girl standing next to you. So stop turning it toward us and begin turning it toward each other." If they could have done that, they could have taken this room full of kids, snapped them awake, and sent forth a crowd of calm, sane, and per-haps even enlightened youngsters. But they couldn't do it, they could only do that which they had practiced.

And even though they'd never admit it, not even to each other, I think they knew during those days that they had the power to bring this off—this new consciousness. But they couldn't do it because they couldn't get it together, the four of them, to the extent of coming on, singing and communicating together, outfront naked and unrehearsed!

It's like when Janis Joplin was singing—what she was saying was "Look at me, folks, up here, but I'm involved with you people out there. And unless something happens, and it has to happen right here in this audience and on this stage, with you guys letting me off the hook and me letting you off the hook . . . unless it happens here soon you know the end I am bound for." That for me was the plea that was always pounding underneath her voice, a plea for equality, for everybody cutting loose the star and the audience alike and standing naked together. But nobody has the hair yet to be that naked, to finally confront everybody on all levels with their responsibility.

Then there was Jim Morrison. I used to think, what a burn. I went to see the Doors, after I got out of jail. It was the first big rock concert I'd been to see since I'd been in jail. And I'd heard a lot about the Doors, knew their songs and that they were supposed to be far out. It was still about the time when a lot of us thought the millennium was just about to happen. So we took some acid and went to see the Doors at Winterland. God, it was awful, super-awful. All these kids walking around looking at each other out of the sides of their eyes, scared but faking it cool. When the Doors got up and sang "Break on through to the other side," they just couldn't. Though the Doors was their name, they never had "broke on through," they never really had expected to, they just knew that it was fashionable to say so. So there was a built-in paranoia, a paranoia that we're still spinning down from. And it will take a long time. Like there at Winterland there were five thousand people, all of them kidding each other into believing that "I've brought it on through to the other side . . . what about you?" A totally paranoid state, because no one dared admit that *nobody* had "broke on through!" The only people who ever *do* dare are the people who are freaking out on acid at those scenes. They get up and scream and take off all their clothes and run around talking about the way things really are, yelling, "It's all a *lie*, a *lie!*" Then everybody cools them, "hush, hush, hush; we don't wanta hear that . . ."

When we went outside Winterland after the concert, Terry the Tramp was standing out there and he was one very high angel. I said, "How you doing, Tramp." He said: "Doors are getting smaller all the time, smaller all the time." Because people were pressing out to get out the door. There was this pressure of hysteria that people get when they know the doors are too small and they're trying to get away.

Did you ever see Buñuel's *The Exterminating Angel?* The movie takes place after a very fancy Spanish chamber music concert, these almost Fellini-like people are entertaining each other at a villa after the concert. It's a delightful party and lasts late. About four in the morning, this woman had just finished playing the harpsichord and somebody says, "It's late, don't you think we ought to go home?" And somebody else says, "It's been such a nice party, let's stay a little longer." By morning they're still there and the hostess is trying to get off with her lover, but nobody will leave. Finally by the next evening, they finally get around to admitting it. They *can't* leave. And the door's open, but they can't leave. They're stuck in there together, fifteen or twenty people, really freaking by this time. Pretty soon they're hungry. One guy dies of a heart attack, they seal him up in a closet because he's stinking. They can't get away from each other. It becomes very much like an STP high where you feel like you're stuck in the horrible situation forever, with everybody going crazy because existence alone is too much for us to handle without a little oil of divinity.

Not that a healthy eastern sense of Existentialism isn't necessary for the functioning Western mystic. Even my guru Jew, Martin Buber, made use of the Oriental philosophies; at the university, he studied ancient Chinese philosophy, especially the teaching of Lao Tsu, and Chang Tsu. In Germany and later on in Jerusalem, he went out of his way to meet scholars from China and India and to question them about the political and spiritual paths their countries were taking. Toward the end of his life, his granddaughter, the wife of a specialist in Chinese studies, was in Hong Kong and sending him extracts from the Chinese newspapers about the Communist struggle.

In 1909, at the age of thirty-one, he had translated some of the talks and parables of Chang Tsu into German. Although later in life he said he could no longer feel that it expressed his beliefs, he still asked his students to bear in mind that this essay belonged to a stage that he had to pass through before he could enter into an independent relationship with Being.

When I read Camus, *The Stranger*, and when I read *Mount Analogue*, these were like tiny windows that flash by on two passing trains. Standing there, looking out of this one window just for an instant, I see into this other area, and there I am a young boy, sending off for some decals which I pasted on my skin and on glass—decals of Batman comic book heroes. And when my package of decals arrives there is as a bonus, this small book of magic. I got interested in magic, then sent away for a catalogue of stage illusions. I got into a lot of theatrical magic and did shows all through high school and in college. I went from this into ventriloquism into hypnotism. And from hypnotism into dope. But it's always been the same trip, the same kind of search. You get so that you recognize people on the same kind of search. Most of the people I know are the kids in high school who ordered magic tricks.

And that feeling, that existentialist flash, was the same as the Zen feeling which came about this time. I'm at Stanford, drinking my first wine with a bunch of beatnik types, talking about life with a capital L, and painting Zen on the wall with black paint. This was right down the road from North Beach, where everybody went because of Cassady. Cassady led us there by way of Kerouac. An amazing thing—people read *On the Road* and headed out on a trip that took us first to North Beach, then to Bohemianism, thence to Existentialism, Zen, Dope, Rock, and the rest of the psychedelic '60s and finally on into this new decade, graduates of a school without precedent.

Anyway, to go on about Buber, when he was younger he saw the unification of Self with the All Self, attainable by man in intervals of his earthly life. The Chinese of antiquity had seemed to offer him a guide to this mystic and ecstatic experience in which a person lost his personality through absorption into the universe.

The French mystic sees the reverse of that same coin. It's not a spot you can really pin down, but that you recognize by the sort of carnival barker excitement that your head enjoys when it gets near that spot. A turf very far out but still definitely your own personal turf. For instance, I'm a hard shell Baptist, born and raised, and though I thought I had left it I found it in myself at every turn, this basic, orthodox Christianity. Well, there was stronger in me than I knew all along the Baptist, orthodox conservative (I'm farther right than William Buckley)—and this puritan ethic part of me recognized those subversive things in Dylan and Coltrane—recognized these more for the anarchists that they really are.

The first time I took STP was in Larkspur, at this place where Rohan used to live. We'd all just come back from Mexico, and I'd gone through a bunch of strange scenes in San Francisco. We were still very much together as a group on the bus. Owsley came over and said he had this new drug he wanted us to try. I don't know how it happens that a bunch of people decide to get high—but we just decided. We bought some sponge, because we were trying to build for Rohan a soft sauna bath where you could lie around. (It never did work.) So all this sponge was lying around.

Owsley came to me—he was taking the stuff out with a spoon and letting people snort it or lick it off. He asked me how much of the stuff I could take, and I told him I could take whatever he could dish out. Which is the sort of dumb thing I do once in a while. So we really got loaded and held it together that night long just because we held it together. We kept with each other and we were able to remember the strands of emotion and feeling that ran between us as it got more and more spacey.

On acid, it gets very high, but at least you're down within a day. But STP goes on twenty hours, then thirty hours, then forty hours, until it's hard to remember anymore what it was all about. What put the grease between the balls of your life that made it easy and fun? Or at least possible?

I can remember looking at my hand and seeing it as just part of this large billiard ball game going on in space, with atoms bouncing off each other this way and that way. And Ramrod was standing up and walking around saying every once in a while, "No matter which way you turn, there you are." We held it together that night, then the next day Ramrod came up with a ball of opium to sort of ease us down.

I've been into a lot of heavy drugs and been to a lot of far out spaces, but I felt a thing happen that night which was as far out spacewise as anything I've been into. I felt like a flying saucer had lit on our house. An interaction of energy that all of us could feel when we shut our eyes—something read-justing us. Like there were these women and men in the future all dressed up in plastic mini-skirts and plastic outfits, moving up and down, adjusting and getting it all shaped up. But BLEAK. Very bleak shit. Nobody could pos-sibly want to screw. You're way past that. Putting your hands on somebody's leg is no different from putting your hand on a rock.

Like I say, we survived, but I knew I had a time coming with STP. It hap-pened a couple of years ago, during a dreadful occult period. That time we didn't hold it together. And I forgot something during that period. I lost a thing we take for granted, something that's been forged over I don't know how many thousands of years of human effort, and it's now in us. But when you're very high for a long time, you forget this thing. All I knew when this high was over was that I'd forgotten it, and it was the most important thing I'd ever known and I'd known it since I was a kid.

It's about this time I decided to go to England, to take Faye and the kids to England, 'cause it was just heavier than I could handle. I decided to take some more acid for the first time in a long time. I thought maybe I could refind this lost thing, but I couldn't 'cause it's not in the drug. It's in the way we're brought up. In the way our folks deal with each other. The way our uncles and our dads shot the shit behind the pump house. A way of relating that when it's gone, leaves you mighty bleak.

I was trying to get the car packed the day before I left for England and here came this guy. There I was high on acid, just trying to get the feeling of the farm before I left, and here came this guy walking through the snow. A short-haired guy, about twenty-two or three. Spaced and high. I couldn't tell what he was spaced on, and I can usually tell. Really strange and yet powerful in his eyes. He came up to me and said:

"Kesey . . ."

"Yeah. . . ."

"Did you feel that?"

I did. It went through me like a wave. Then he said he wanted to talk to me. I told him, "Listen, man, I know what you're doing is valid, I did feel it, but I can't handle it right now. I've got all I can take right now. Just leave me alone, let me go off to England and rest a bit."

So he left. And the next day, I was talking to my probation officer, sitting on the car. And here came this guy walking through the snow in his stocking feet. My probation officer was very impressed with the looks of him, told me I'd better talk to him before things got drastic. I walked over to meet him.

"Kesey . . ."

"Yeah, who are you?"

"You know who I am . . ."

"Well, give me a hint . . . Where are you from?"

"You know where I'm from. Listen, we've got to talk. Right now the world is hanging between the Valhallists and the Scientologists."

And the way he said it, maybe because it was a lot of stuff I had been thinking about at the time—he had me. So we went in the house and left my probation officer standing out there. By this time, I had decided he wasn't high on anything because nobody could keep that intensity, that peak, going that long on drugs. You've got to have it going some the other way.

So we went in the house, and he did that thing again where he passed that bolt of energy toward me. And I felt it again. So I asked him what he thought the solution was between the Valhallists and the Scientologists, because I didn't want to be either one. He said:

"You and I know what the solution is. It's just an illusion. It's all just an illusion."

And I knew that what he was talking about was right. Like one time I was driving back from L.A. with Babbs, and this voice came to me which said, "Stop the car!" So Babbs stopped the car. There was a big full moon shining. And this voice says, "Go out into the field." (That's the only time I've ever really heard a voice, and I wasn't even very high.) So I went out into the field. And this voice said, "Get a pair of Polaroid glasses, take one of the lenses, turn it half way around, put it back in the frame, and wear them."

Now if you've ever taken the lenses of two Polaroid lenses like these, and put them over each other and turn them like that, it goes dark. So what's happening is a grid. When you do it like this with one like this on one eye, and one turned half way on the other eye, the grid happens in your mind. And what you're looking at out there begins to fragment. So when this guy said it was all an illusion, I knew what he was talking about. But I said, "No, man, it's not *just* an illusion." It's not a thing you can speak of as *just* . . . Until you have appreciation for the beauty of it, you can't speak about it like that. Then I told him I couldn't deal with him anymore, that I was going to England, and I kicked him out again.

So I went to England. I spent a lot of time visiting this church over there. Not into this church, but into the graveyard. The graves were like four hundred years old some of them. There I began to get a sense of what I was doing in England, what I had gone there for, and what I had lost with that STP. I call it the tiller.

When we took acid ten years ago, we cut off our periphery time sense. All the stuff that had come before us, and all the stuff that was to come— we said, forget that, let's deal from here on with the present. Just forget what we're going to do and what we've done. It's all contained right in this instant." At this time I was seeing a lot of Fritz Perls, who was into this thing of having to get into the present to realize our senses. He used to say he wanted to bring us to our senses of knowing what's going on right now.

We really got into it. We got so we could do it and be right there, in the present like that, you're like Muhammad Ali when he beat Liston. You move into a state of magic. Powers are available to you that you couldn't find in the past or in the future. But after a while, being in the present is like being at sea, in a boat, and you've been there a long time, drifting and existing. Then you look over yonder and you see a light. You decide it's a drag just sitting there in the ocean, in that boat, and you want to try to head toward that light. So you put up your sails and start to try to head out toward the light, but you find that you've lost something else. The thing that enabled you to steer the ship. The thing that was behind you. So you're sitting in this boat in the present, looking toward the light in the future. When I reached for the tiller behind me, after the STP, I found that it wasn't there anymore. I no longer knew what man was doing cruising along through the world.

When I went to England and hung around these churches and these graveyards, and watched the people over there, I thought of America as being a part of this consciousness that had come to England. There's a promise implied to England by America. A promise that we're going to finish something that they were working on and couldn't quite complete.

In that church graveyard I began to feel from these guys whom I didn't really know, who were buried there, that the shit that a man does decays. The shit that man *is* decays. But you can see up over the edge of that graveyard, over the curb, down across the cobblestone, to where the kids are playing on tricycles, that Man's spirit goes on and continues to do what it was that the best of him wanted to do. That continues to work. That spirit is the thing that has stirred man and kept him from cracking up on his foolishness.

The thing that got us here and moved us across the country—that spirit is a thing that we flipped off, thinking it wasn't important.

But without it, we can't maneuver the vessel we're in. When Coltrane and Dylan got right into the present, where you're in a discovery position, not trying to make any statement that's ever been made, they did it by cutting off that tiller. They were speaking right from there. Which is the way Cassady was trying to speak, so the words were coming out before you even got a chance to maneuver them around. The threat of this, and the extent of it, has left like the bulk, the energy bulk of our nation, like this fleet of rudderless ships. Full of intention and energy and direction, but they're reluctant to reach back and grab hold of that rudder. They mistrust it. They've been burned too often by Maggie's farm and the Industrial Revolution.

Buber was doing this the same way Dylan's music is now. I mean, he relinquished his mojo for the sake of this rudder. The stuff he writes now is nowhere near the poetry it used to be. He has had to turn his head way, way down to speak now in terms of very simple images and drama. And emotion. Straight, Western, funky emotion.

Eventually, I think we'll get to where we have that rudder in our hand firmly once more, and that light ahead of us again and still be in the present. Once we've got it strong again, then we can turn loose our heads and really sail. Like we've always sort of been promised that we could. I don't know if it's going to happen to our generation, but the promise is there, enticing and explicit. But it was ushered in with that *Mount Analogue* feeling. It didn't just come from that book. It came also from Burroughs and *Naked Lunch*. Now I read Burroughs, and he's great, fantastic. But he doesn't make you feel good, or give you any sense of this oil of divinity that will keep you greased and going from day to day.

The Indians believe that before you can really expect to find any enlightenment, you have to raise a kid to maturity. And take out once again on your own path. Maybe the kid we have to raise to maturity is ourselves.

Ken Kesey: The Prince of Pransksters

Rick Saunders, Bob Nesbitt, and Vaughn Binzer / 1976

From *Marijuana Monthly*, Vol. 2 No. 3. © 1976 by *Marijuana Monthly*.

Anyone with the guts and civic responsibility to turn on the Hells Angels can't be all bad.

—CRAZY BOB

The Intrepid Traveler

For those of your *Marijuana Monthly* readers who don't recognize the vehicle in this [picture], its name is Furthur and it belongs to Ken Kesey. For those of you who don't know who Ken Kesey is, he's the guy who wrote *One Flew Over the Cuckoo's Nest* (and *Kesey's Garage Sale* and *Sometimes a Great Notion*), and he's also widely known through Tom Wolfe's *Electric Kool-Aid Acid Test* as owner and pilot of the Magic Bus whose only destination is Furthur. Ken was the Intrepid Traveler whose band of Merry Pranksters toured the country in the Bus in the '6os consuming inordinate quantities of Acid and blowing everybody's heads, including their own—*and* the Hells Angels as well.

Kesey and the Bus are for the present back on the farm. Kesey ploughing and digging and the Bus basking (and rusting) while cows munch grass indifferent to the glorious past of the DayGlo apparition now comfortably settling into the green Oregon turf.

Stewart Brand had a notion (and not a great one) to "snatch the Bus away" from Kesey and stick it in the Smithsonian Institute with other relics. Brand must have been a history major. He writes in the *CoEvolution Quarterly* that he was around for some of the '6os and came to realize that "the Bus is a true and unusual artifact of a true and unusual time in American grassroots history." So Brand wrote to the Smithsonian and told them about Furthur. They responded that they had never heard of the Bus, but agreed that "this is a dimension of cultural history with which this museum must come to grips . . ." And sure enough, just as Brand dreamed, the Smithsonian got around to asking Ken for the bus. But Ken's not ready to give it up, as *Marijuana Monthly* learned in our phone interview with him recently.

Rick: Hey, someone better lock that front door!
Phone: Click.
Bob: Hi—Ken?
Ken: Yeh—

Bob: Ken, this is Bob Nesbitt from *Marijuana Monthly.* Our Creative Director, Vaughn Binzer, and the Publisher, Rick Sanders, are on another line.
Ken: Great.

Rick: We'd just like to ask a couple of questions to bring people up to date on where you're at. What about the court case?
Ken: I can't talk about that. You see, there's no way I can talk about it while it's pending. The lawsuit won't come off for a while.

Rick: I heard or read somewhere that people were being asked to send you money to fight the thing. Do you want us to put some kind of blurb for money? Shall we ask our readers to send Ken a few bucks?
Ken: No. I'm going to try to do it on my own. We're going to get together and talk about it—what to do. That thing of sending money in is good, but if we can break through that to where just by force of consciousness we can bring in the money from where it's supposed to come from. That's my gripe—it's not that I don't have the money so much as it is: I don't want money from other people—I want money from *these* people!

Rick: Well, if you ever need help, you know where to come.
Ken: I've just spent two days in the deposition, man, and it was the most hideous event of my life. Man, there's nothing like coming home from a noisy deposition to a "nice quiet joint."

Rick: Can we talk to you 'bout that?
Ken: No, I don't want to talk about it.

Vaughn: When did you go to University of Oregon?
Ken: As a student? Between '57 and '60.

Vaughn: Did you ever wrestle anyone from the University of Arizona?
Ken: Could be.

Vaughn: I think we wrestled.
Ken: What weight were you?

Vaughn: I was 191 then.
Ken: I wrestled a guy from Arizona in a freestyle tournament. How old are you?

Vaughn: I'm forty-one.
Ken: You don't sound hardly forty. I'll be forty-one soon too.

Vaughn: Happy birthday. Are you a Leo?
Ken: No, I'm a Virgo. We make tremendous wrestlers—great tenacity.

Rick: I want to ask one more question about the film. How would you have done it if you were allowed to—if you were the director?
Ken: You should read my script. It's good as hell. How's that!

Rick: I thought the answer would be "The right way."
Ken: I can't really say that. Personally I feel that you have to make people a little bit mad to have them understand what the story is about, so you have to twist them a little. I have a lot of ideas about how to do it, starting with the theater lights completely up at the beginning and having sounds of wind blowing through pines and then voices of old women talking to young Indian kids—then working from that to having the theater get darker as finally you see stuff on the screen that looks like pines which become tombstones and finally as you close in on them they're beds and you're on the ward. Things like that. That's how I'd do it.

Bob: What about psychedelics?
Ken: Do you mean would I pass out something to the audience?

Bob: That's not a bad idea, but no, I mean lighting and effects, the sort of effects you can get with film.

Ken: The only thing I know that comes remotely close to what I would like to have people see at the beginning of that movie is *The Cabinet of Dr. Caligari.* The way that stuff is twisted and the way everything moves and keeps writhing during the whole movie. Hey, guys, I have to get off this phone. I just got home from depositions and I feel a need to plough!

Rick: One quick question. What's happening with the bus? We heard a rumor that it's going to the Smithsonian, that they want it.
Ken: They do. But I'm not giving it up. I'm going to let it rot right out there in the pasture. I'm going to make a planter out of it.

Rick: Far out. Anything you want to say in closing?
Ken: Yeah. Stick something in there about *Spit in the Ocean*, our magazine. Tell them to send ten bucks for four copies.

Rick: We have the first issue here.
Ken: Great. The first is edited by me as you see. The second issue is just being printed and the third issue is in the works. That's Leary's issue. It's pretty esoteric. I have a hard time following it—it's just straight Leary spacey stuff. It's about getting off the earth you know—going to outer space and that kind of stuff. He edited and did most of it in jail.

Rick: What's the address for the magazine subscription?
Ken: Ken Kesey, Pleasant Hill, Oregon 97401. The third, as I said, is by Leary and is mostly about communicating with higher intelligence.

Bob: O.K.
Ken: The fourth issue is all edited by women from San Francisco, and mainly by a woman called Lee Morris. She's a San Francisco underground comic artist—and good! It's an all woman bit. Even the joker is wearing tits. So we have four issues cooking, and that's ten bucks for four of them. Also the last one has the "Episodic Adventures of Grandma Whittier," which you want to pay special attention to: an emerging talent.

Rick: I know you don't do drugs anymore, "ha ha," but next time you're in L.A. cruise by and we'll have a glass of milk or something else just as cosmic.
Ken: I was down there for that Buddhist Festival.

Rick: You should have come by and got high.
Ken: Rick, the next time for sure.

Rick: See you, Ken.
Ken: Fine. Bye.

Phone: Click.
Rick: He's going to let that bus rot? What a bummer!
Bob: It's a futureplanter!!

Editors Note (*Marijuana Monthly*): Ken Kesey has filed an $869,000 damage suit against the makers of the movie *One Flew Over the Cuckoo's Nest.* Kesey claims he was verbally promised 2.5% of the movie's gross, but has never been paid. He is now asking $869,000 in damages plus 5% of the gross. This would amount to about $1.5 million.

Kesey, who has never seen the movie version of his book, says that reading the final screenplay convinced him that the film is dishonest. He complains that the movie emphasized the struggle between the lead character, McMurphy, and the nurse without stressing the elements in American society which drove the characters insane.

Getting Better

John Nance, Paul Pintarich, and Sharon Wood / 1986

Recorded on KBOO December 16, 1986. © 1986 by KBOO. Reprinted by permission of Sharon Wood-Wortman and KBOO Community Radio.

Sharon Wood: Where did the title *Demon Box* come from?

Ken Kesey: Oh that's been the name of this whole collection of work for a long, long time, even before I wrote the story that has that name. It is based on a notion a guy named Clark Maxwell had a hundred years ago about . . . oh it's too hard to explain real quick here, but it has to do with our minds, and in our minds we have this little box, and on one side of the box is the good and on the other side is the bad, and the effort to sort the good from the bad is costing us more than we're getting. And I use this metaphor loosely through the book to try to shed some light on the psychedelic movement of the '60s.

Paul Pintarich: Now this is your first piece of fiction—it is fiction, isn't it? Fictional essays, or how would you describe it? Your publisher described it as fictional essays to me, but . . .

KK: It's one of those things that as you read it you can tell that a lot of it is real stuff that I've kept notes on, but I have bent it to fit into the themes of the book. So it's fiction.

PP: What period does this represent? I mean, how long a period of writing?

KK: This is the '70s and into the '80s. It's a fifteen-year period of writing.

John Nance: But I understand you say you're really focusing on that '60s psychedelic period. Is this the journal—or is there something more you want to say about that?

KK: This is when I talk about the "come down" years. This isn't about the '60s. This is after the '60s. The stories all start in 1969, which I really feel

101

like was the time when things began to fall apart. You remember *Alice's Restaurant* when he's singing, "I don't want a pickle / I just wanna ride on my motorcycle"? Remember he's riding along on his motorcycle and goes over a cliff, and he's going over the cliff he sings, "And I don't wanna die / I just wanna ride on my motorcy . . . cle"? And he says, "I knew it wasn't the best thing I ever wrote, but it was the best I could do coming down." And that's the way I feel about it. It's not the best thing I ever wrote, but . . . all my Kentucky writer friends told me, "Son, you've been in the field for twenty years. We need you to report. Never mind literature."

PP: I was getting to that. There's a lot of people that have asked me, and I'm sure they've asked you: maybe when you wrote *Sometimes a Great Notion*, which a lot of us consider a minor masterpiece, that might have been writing out everything. It's a hell of a thing to compete with. Do you feel that way at times?

KK: Well, how many no-hitters can you pitch in the Major Leagues?

PP: Is that what you consider it, a no-hitter?

KK: I doubt that I'll ever equal *Great Notion*. I don't think I have the capacity. I don't think I have the energy or the concentration to do it. I don't feel bad about that, except that when I talk to American writers—and one of the great things about being famous is you get to talk to other famous people, so I've had Norman Mailer here and I've had Arthur Miller here and I've had a chance to talk to Richard Hugo and people like that, and one of the things we always talk about is what happens to American writers. Why don't we get any better?

JN: But that idea you had, particularly following *Cuckoo's Nest*. I mean you're talking about a *boom! boom!* kind of effect there. Very powerful. And I've often wondered myself what that meant to you to go two resounding successes one after the other.

KK: I've never had any doubt as to who I was. That's never bothered me.

JN: How would you describe yourself then?

KK: Well, I'm not Shakespitter, but I'm better than Barry Manlabel. I know where I exist. But that isn't it. It's what you ought to be.

JN: Who's ought?

KK: My ought. And then not only my ought, but there's bigger oughts than mine. And I feel about this book—I'll tell you, I'll get right down to it so we don't have to fool around. I feel that what's important about this book to me is I found a place to put my gonzo: Devlin Deboree, that persona that I speak through in almost all these stories in *Demon Box*, this isn't me anymore than [interview cuts out here] is Mailer. And yet the American writer has moved under the stage so much that he's almost forced his characters off the stage.

JN: He goes there willing, though, too, doesn't he?
KK: It's not just willingly. Look at you guys and the microphone here. There is a force moving the American writer into a corner. And that has to do with media, it has to do with reviewers, it has to do with critics, it has to do with something that Shakespeare never had to deal with. Now when you read *Lear* or *Richard III* you have no sense of Shakespeare on the stage. Those characters walk that stage free and unencumbered. You can't say that about a Hemingway character. You can feel Hemingway behind the scene pulling the strings, right. And you can feel when you read an Updike character. Or just when you read almost any of the modern American characters. This is who we have become. We have become players on our own stage. And so this box that I have tried to create is where I'm trying to put my gonzo before he eats me alive.

PP: But don't you think, though, that since John Gardner's influence on moral fiction and so forth that a lot of this is coming back? Now, look at Larry McMurtry's *Lonesome Dove*.
KK: Great book! Best book in the last *thirty* years!

PP: And that's back to traditional way. Good characterization and so forth. Now do you anticipate going back to this yourself?
KK: I would love to. I envy the hell out of Larry.

PP: But you've got an Alaska book somewhere that you're trying to finish.
KK: Oh yeah, I've got three hundred pages of this written. . . . I started working on a book, but here's what happens, see: I was working hard on this. I was deep into it. But I found that the gonzo, the Kesey persona, had so much interrupted that book that I couldn't do what Larry is doing in *Lonesome Dove*. And I know writing well enough to know that—you know, you can tell that when Larry takes out on that book that's as much an adventure for him as a writer as it is for you as a reader. It's a beautiful damn book. And all I want in my twilight time is to be able to write and love it. I don't want to have it whip me around a post.

JN: What will that take, I mean to get that persona? You think you buried it with this *Demon Box*?
KK: I haven't buried it, but I've got a box where I can put all the stuff like it.

PP: Is this an exorcism?
KK: Oh no, I've got three times this much stuff about the Deboree characters and about all of those characters that come out of the Tom Wolfe time.

PP: How does this character and this reflection on this period date you? I mean it seems sort of anachronistic to me.
KK: Oh, it is. It is.

PP: It's almost stale.
KK: I wish it'd been out ten years ago. And have you read the Hemingway book? [*The Garden of Eden*] Sad book. It's a good book if it'd had come out in the '30s. But coming out now it's wrong.

JN: What is the wrongness of that, and how would you describe it?
KK: You're talking about women with short hair and in slacks. That had a certain hit then. And if it'd been published then it would've had that hit. But now it doesn't have that hit. It's a different hit.

JN: But it has a hit as far as reflecting on his personality. It says a lot about him that he could never say.
KK: But that's not what a writer wants to do, really. I mean, Shakespeare doesn't say anything about Shakespeare. I'm tired of saying stuff about Kesey. That becomes, finally, almost an industry.

JN: But if Shakespeare were to write today, could he step back from being Shakespeare? With the kind of exposure, the kind of stuff—he would have had to go out and sell his books. Could he have pulled back and been allowed to be old Bill Shakespeare cranking out something back there and maybe it's gonna make it—
KK: It would have been harder for him because there'd been Baba Wawa wanting him on television.

JN: Did he have to go, though?
KK: Well, you don't like to be impolite. When people ask you a question, you assume that they ask you because you know. You know, if somebody

asks me the weight of Mars, they assume I know, and I try to make something up. And this is what a fiction writer does. And pretty soon you're
caught. That was not something that Shakespeare had to deal with.

SW: You talk about your twilight years. How old are you?
KK: Seventy-nine, eighty, am I?

JN: At least eighty-two.
SW: Does that mean you're not going to answer my question?
KK: No, it means I'm talking about working talent. I'm talking Muhammad
Ali. I'm talking about when you can deliver a punch. And move correctly.

PP: You sound like Mailer doing this stuff.
KK: Mailer's no dummy. . . . He's a smart damn man and he knows what he's
talking about and he knows the stuff we're up against.

JN: There's a certain pacing about that, I mean, you can come out and
maybe save yourself for the ninth round to the twelfth. In between you've
really got to know what's in there—
KK: I don't feel like this—I hope this isn't *my book*. I got books in me yet.

PP: Long ones?
KK: I don't know if I've got long ones. I don't know if I've got another *Great
Notion* in me. . . . I saw a kid win the World Juggling contest on television
last week. He juggled twelve Indian clubs. Now, I know the Flying Karamazov Brothers. There's none of them can do that. This kid is probably fourteen, sixteen. Maybe you can only do that a certain time. When I was doing
Great Notion, I had more balls in the air than I can keep in the air right now.

JN: I wonder how much of that is really conscious, or does it just kind of
flow through you? Could you have calculated that, or was it just happening?
KK: I'm a professional. Yeah, I know what I'm doing. And I'm doing it as
full-out as I can, all the time. I got the metal to the floor all the time.

JN: You refer also to some kind of power other than your own. Whether that
comes through in the writing. Are you conscious of that when you're writing, or are some of the words just coming out?
KK: Well, we're now talking muse, the muses. As Wendell Berry says,
it comes from musing on something, from reflecting and thinking on

something. And we went through a period of time in which we were being taken by the muse without having to reflect. It was moving us.

JN: There was a lot of schlock that came out of that too.

KK: That's okay. I don't mind a lot of schlock. I'll sit through four hours of bad Grateful Dead to hear one hot piece of stuff.

But to get back to this thing about American writers, and what it is about American writers: You know when I talk with Mailer and Miller and Vonnegut and Wendell Berry and Larry McMurtry and everybody about who got better in writing, you know who is the only person they can agree on that got better? Now, think about the last hundred years or so: Who got better? Yeats. Yeats got better, and he was writing good stuff at eighty.

PP: How about Joyce?

KK: Well, I don't know that he got better. I think he got more willful.

PP: How about Henry Miller? Do you like Henry Miller?

KK: I love Henry Miller, but I don't think he got better. I don't think Faulkner got better. I don't think Hemingway got better. I don't think Steinbeck got better. Styron, none of those people. They hit their stride at a certain time and from there on glided to the grave.

PP: Do you write poetry?

KK: Lots. I like the Robert Graves thing, that poetry is the language we speak through the ages. I have a real sense of my talent and I know where I stand amongst people, and I know how good I am and how good I ought to be, and I'm not near as good as most great writers. And I ought to be better. And that rubs you somewhat, but when you're courting the muses and you really want to be touched by the moving spirits, you find that you can't do it in New York, you can't do it in Hollywood. I find that even if I'm not writing, I'm closer to it out in that field than I am when I'm back in New York. Now, with this book coming out, I tell you the thing that really made the difference to me was I have taken these stories and these pieces of stuff back to New York a number of times. These pieces have been available to Viking for ten years. Why haven't they published 'em? Why haven't they seen 'em as a work? It's because they are trying to go with the gusto. There's a certain amount of media movement—marketing. And if I'm trying to sell those cows, I don't take those cows and drive them to New York. I bring the people from New York out to look at the cows. So I got an editor, finally, and I haven't had an editor in ten years. I mean, Viking has changed hands three times; I've had five editors. I've had all of these people who I've finally convinced that I'm trying to do something, and then they change houses, or the house changes hands. They move, and so, finally, I've got this guy, Chuck Verrill, who really came to me by way of Gurney Norman, who came to me by way of Ed McClanahan, all my old buddies from that great writing class in Stanford.

JN: McMurtry—was he in that class?
KK: McMurtry was in that class. Wendell Berry was in that class, Ernie Gaines, Peter Beagle—

SW: What class was that?
KK: This is the famous . . . Malcolm Cowley taught it.[1] This is the famous Stegner writing class at Stanford. All of the people that came out of it have done well, and I've tried to understand why a number of times, and I think it goes back to Malcolm Cowley. Malcolm Cowley taught us something about writing which has to do with more than writing. It has to do with respect for writing, and respect for people who have written. And whenever I do a writing seminar, the first thing I tell them is that it's just as hard to write a bad novel as it is a good novel, and that you don't ever want to hurt anybody, and that when somebody publishes something good, every writer triumphs, and so it's not a competition.

PP: That's what Cheever said, "It's not a competitive sport."
KK: Yeah, John Cheever came and guest lectured at us and he said this very thing. He made this point that so often in writing classes writers get positioned against each other. Like people are always asking me, "What do you think of John Irving?"

PP: Poets are worse.
KK: Poets are worse!

JN: But five minutes ago we were talking about the quality writing and you're making those kinds of judgments along the way about who the top

---

1   Ed McClanahan points out in *Spit in the Ocean #7* that "Here Kesey, who attended writing classes at Stanford off and on over a three-year period, is conflating the class of '58–'59 and the class of '60–'61. The former was taught by Wallace Stagner and Richard Scowcroft, the latter by Cowley and Frank O'Connor."

writers are and greatness kinds of labels we put on people and where you measure up. It does in its nature sound competitive. "I'm great, but I'm not that great." It starts to be a ranking system.

KK: It's like throwing the javelin, though. You're not throwing the javelin against Petronov. You're throwing the javelin against distance and weight.

JN: But when it becomes a media event, it starts to be measured, making it your insides against their outsides. What you know inside against how they appear—and it really is not the same kind of battle.

KK: I'm moving off the page, back in front of people, back around the campfire. And when I talk to writers or when I talk to musicians, when I talk to filmmakers, I have to overcome the fact that they're writers or musicians or filmmakers. I'm not interested in all of that stuff. I'm interested in only one thing and that's the magic of it. You use whatever you can to make it go.

PP: Are we talking about storytelling?

KK: Storytelling and opera and rock 'n' roll and . . .

JN: But this again puts the writer out, as opposed to Shakespeare, out on the stage. I can recall even at Oregon the things that at those spring competitions you were out there singing and writing things and so on, and that's one of the things I remembered about that time. You were out there as a writer, but also as director/performer, and there was something about your personality seemed to be drawn to that. And you did extremely well.

KK: Yeah, well, I think that's what the writer was before Gutenberg.

PP: He was maybe back in the caves spinning yarns, putting people . . .

JN: It's like the old Norse storytellers . . .

KK: The show that went from castle to castle trying to keep civilization together by telling how beautiful the women were in the other cave. And how the strong man killed the dragon. That to me is what you're judged by. You walk out into an area and it's relatively easy to draw the spotlight. That's the thing that a lot of people don't understand. My dad used to say about me, "You could draw a crowd in a desert." But what do you do with the crowd once you've drawn 'em? Can you tell 'em the truth? That's the thing. Can you stand shoulder to shoulder with people you respect through the ages? You know, the Baal Shem Tov of Hassidic literature. Or can you stand up there with Rimbaud? Can you stand up there with Faulkner? These are really allies in an ongoing revolution fighting against a deadly thing in our nation today.

PP: Which is . . .
KK: growing fascism.

JN: I was going to ask you about evil. Talking about demons, right away you come up with a concept that somehow that question came to me.
KK: Melville, man, Melville. *Moby-Dick* is the book.

JN: What is the evil today?
KK: It has to do with there is something there that we have to combat all the time and it isn't necessarily a human being. It takes the form of a human being now and then, but it also may be a whale, it may be something inside of you, but it is ever-present and it's off of evil—this is the thing about *Cuckoo's Nest*: people think that Big Nurse is the villain; she is not the villain; she is a minion of the villain. But she is not the villain; the villain is something else. If you reduce it to her being the villain, it loses its importance. So it's finding what the villain is. Okay, let's get back to *Demon Box*. The villain I was going after in this book, successfully or not, was What was it that brought us down?

JN: From where?
KK: From where we were when we were in the '60s. From this feeling of caring for each other. What was it that brought us down? What separates us? What makes us vulnerable?

The Fresh Air Interview: Ken Kesey

Terry Gross / 1989

From *Fresh Air*, 1989. © 1989 by NPR. Reprinted by fair use.

Terry Gross asked Kesey what he thought about Wolfe's book and how accurate it was.

Mr. KEN KESEY: Oh yeah. It's a good book. Yeah, he's a—Wolfe's a genius. He did a lot of that stuff, he was only around three weeks. He picked up that amount of dialogue and verisimilitude without tape recorder, without taking notes to any extent. He just watches very carefully and remembers. But, you know, he's got his own editorial filter there. And so what he's coming up with is part of me, but it's not all of me, any more than Hunter S. Thompson is loaded all the time and shooting machine guns at John Denver. That's the sort of thing—interesting in the media but he's got a lot more life to him than that.

GROSS: What effect did the *The Electric Kool-Aid Acid Test* have on you? For instance, did it make the police feel more determined to try to bust you again?
Mr. KESEY: Yeah. But I haven't been worried about the cops that much. The effect of *Kool-Aid Acid Test* is they'll say that you're Richard Gere and you've got a great big wart on the side of your nose. And they begin to play it up in the cameras and then pretty soon it becomes the thing that a lot of teenage girls are in love with, and pretty soon you're looking at it too, until you're cross-eyed looking at your own wart.

GROSS: Why do you use the wart as an analogy?
Mr. KESEY: Well, because I was a lot more than the Tom Wolfe depiction. And I think this is a problem for a lot of American writers and has been for

a long time. You know, Hemingway, he really doesn't get into trouble until he becomes dazzled by his own image. He sees the rest of the United States looking at him and he moves over and sits there, and he looks at himself too. And then when he tries to go back and get inside of his own skin he can't quite fit into it as well as he used to; he's gained weight.

(Soundbite of laughter)

Mr. KESEY: He can't put his own skin back on. And when you're writing, it's not a good idea to be observed too much. Unless you want to live in New York and wear white clothes.

(Soundbite of laughter)

Mr. KESEY: If you really are interested in being a real straight old-fashion writer, it's better to live down in Mississippi like Faulkner and work out in the woodshed and not be seen but once every ten years. I think that being the observed always turns your eye back on yourself and you become kind of blinded by your own radiance.

GROSS: You started doing LSD through a government experiment. An experimental program in, I think, it was in 1959. You were one of the volunteers who, you know, volunteered to take this experimental drug and have it tested on yourself. How did you become a volunteer for these experiments?
Mr. KESEY: One of the guys that was our neighbors, was a—he was a psychologist and he was supposed to show up one day and just really he didn't have the common hair to do it and says does anybody else like to take my place? And I, at the time, was training for the Olympics. I made it to be an alternate in the 1960 Olympics team and was . . .

GROSS: As a wrestler?
Mr. KESEY: Yeah, as a wrestler. I'd never been drunk on beer, you know, let alone done any drugs. But this is the American government. They said, "Come in here. We've just discovered this new spot of space and we want somebody to go up there and look it over and we don't want to do it. We want to hire you students." And I was one of 140 or so that eventually turned out. It was CIA sponsored. I didn't believe it for a long time. Well, Allen Ginsberg said, "You know who was paying for that was the CIA." I said, "No, Allen, you're just paranoid." But he finally got all the darn records and

it did turn out the CIA was doing this. And it wasn't being done to try to cure insane people, which is what we thought. It was being done to try to make people insane—to weaken people and to be able to put them under the control of interrogators. We didn't find this out for twenty years. And by that time the government had said, okay, stop that experiment. "All these guinea pigs that we sent up there in outer space bring them back down and don't ever let them go back in there again because we don't like the look in their eyes."

GROSS: Do you remember what your very first trip was like when you were a volunteer in this government program? And what kind of preparation were you given for it? Were you given any?

Mr. KESEY: None at all. Except I read a little piece in *Life* magazine about how they'd given it to cats and cats were afraid of mice once they had LSD. But I think that we'd been preparing for a long time. You know, I knew the Bible. I knew the Bhagavad Gita. I knew the Daodejing. I had read Hermann Hesse's *Journey to the East*, which gave us an underpinning, spiritually, so that these phenomena that were happening to us had something that they could relate to. We just happened to come at a time when it was not only a lot of stuff happening, chemically, there was a lot of new changes in music and in film. Burroughs was just beginning to do his work in literature and there was a movement afoot that this was just a part of. And it was exciting. It was wonderful.

GROSS: What was the very first trip like, though, under the experimental conditions?

Mr. KESEY: Groovy, man.

(Soundbite of laughter)

Mr. KESEY: It was groovy. We suddenly realized that there's a lot more to this world than we previously thought. I think, you know, because I'm asked this question a lot. It's been twenty years or so and people are always coming back saying well, what you think? And I'm—the one of the things that I think came out it is this, that there's room. We don't all have to be the same. We don't have to have Baptists, coast to coast. We can throw in some Buddhists and some Christians and people who are just thinking these strange thoughts about the Irish leprechauns, that there is room, spiritually, for everybody in this universe.

GROSS: You were among the first people to take LSD out of the clinical setting and use it in a social setting. How did you first get it out?
Mr. KESEY: Of the hospital?

GROSS: Yeah.

(Soundbite of laughter)

Mr. KESEY: Well, after I had gone through these drug experiments and
was in this little room in the hospital, looking out through the little window
at the people out there who were the regular nuts. They weren't students
going to experiments. I'm looking at them through my crazed eyes, I saw
that these people have something going and there's a truth to it that people
are missing. And that's how I came to write *Cuckoo's Nest*. I got a job at the
nut house and worked from midnight to eight writing that book and taking
care of these patients on this one ward and made a lot of good friends—
some that I still have. And I found that my key opened a lot of the doors to
the doctor's offices where these drugs were being kept.

(Soundbite of laughter)

Mr. KESEY: That's how.

GROSS: Huh. And then you have friends who were able to make it in their
own laboratories.
Mr. KESEY: Yeah. But it was never anywhere as good as that good gover-
nance stuff. That's the government, the CIA always has the best stuff.

GROSS: Now you brought up *Cuckoo's Nest*. And I was wondering when
you were working in the psychiatric ward, which is what *Cuckoo's Nest* is
based on, and I think you sometimes went in there high on hallucinogenics.
Do you think you ended up writing *Cuckoo's Nest* in a way projecting your
experiences as a quote "sane person high on drugs," projecting those experiences on to people who maybe had like serious problems?
Mr. KESEY: Well, these people had had serious problems. I mean I saw
people hallucinating and people in bad shape. Make no mistake about it,
being crazy is painful. And being crazy is hell—whether you get it from
taking a drug or whether it happens because you're just trying to lead the
American way of life and it keeps kicking your legs out from under you. One

way or another, it's hell on you. And it's nothing that's fun about it and I am certainly not recommending it. It is a lens through which I did stuff, but it's hard on the eyes. But I think I had a very valid viewpoint and much closer than a lot of the doctors were having.

At that time, you know, everything was Freudian. If you were messed up, it was because of something that had happened to you when you were in the bathroom as a kid. And with these experiences—and I don't just mean drug experiences—there were a lot of other things that were going on that were emphasizing this. John Coltrane's music was saying the same thing. It was saying something is wrong and is making us a little crazy and that is making us crazy enough to hallucinate, whether we were promoting it ourselves or it was being imposed on us. I don't want to argue that now. But when I would—I felt so good after being on there all night to know that I was wearing a green uniform and—I mean a white uniform instead of a green uniform so I could leave in the morning and go home, otherwise there wasn't that much difference between me and those people they were locking up. It gave me an empathy that I could never have come up with. A better example is those first few pages of *Cuckoo's Nest* were written on peyote. And I don't know any Indians. I don't know where the Indian came from. I've always felt humbled by that character. Without the character of that Indian, the book is a melodrama. You know, it's a straight battle between McMurphy and the Big Nurse. With that Indian's consciousness to filter that through, that makes it exceptional.

GROSS: Have you given up drugs? Or, I don't know, maybe I shouldn't be asking this, but do you . . .
Mr. KESEY: We're into it now, go ahead.

(Soundbite of laughter)

GROSS: Do you still do them at all or . . . ?
Mr. KESEY: On religious occasions, yeah. I like to walk up on a mountain on Easter and get a sense of rebirth. Some people jog. Some people meditate. You know, there's certain people who whip themselves on the back, there's—everybody has their own way of trying to see past the veil and this is just the one that I happened to come up with. My metaphor is this, is that you don't need a huge tuning fork. We used to think we needed a tuning fork eight feet long and weighing 2,000 pounds just to find middle C, but

now all you need is a little bitty tuning fork once a year maybe. But no, I don't know anybody who really goes out and gets ripped anymore.

GROSS: At what point did you decide to give up the kind of Pranksters life. The story that I've heard is that other Pranksters went to Woodstock. You didn't want to go. And when they came back, they came back to a sign hung in your driveway that just said: "No."

Mr. KESEY: Well, there were sixty-one people when they headed out to Woodstock. And after they were gone, I went upstairs—and we live in a barn. We still live in the same barn. We fixed it up and it's a pretty nice place. But at that time there was still hay in the loft of the barn. And I found out one of these little hippie warrens where they dug in with their little ratty old sleeping bags and their copy of *Zap* magazine. In stock right down in a hay bale was a candle which had burned right down to the hay before it had gone off. And I thought, hey, enlightenment is one thing but being this loose is . . . I mean my grandpa wouldn't have allowed them up there and my great grandpa wouldn't have, and there's certain things that take precedence over enlightenment.

Collaboration in the Writing Classroom: An Interview with Ken Kesey

Carolyn Knox-Quinn / 1990

From *College Composition and Communication*, October 1990. © 1990 by Carolyn Knox. Reprinted by permission.

Last year, Ken Kesey and a group of University of Oregon graduate students collaborated on a novel during a year-long writing class. Their novel, *Caverns* (Viking Press, 1990), was published under the group name of U.O. Levon.

The following is an edited version of our conversation in the Keseys' red-barn home in the Willamette Valley countryside near Eugene, Oregon. Here he addresses a number of current topics of interest to composition teachers: collaborative writing, peer editing, publishing in the classroom, learning to write by writing, designing a novel, and the teacher as class-participant. Kesey also talks about the creation of a cohesive class mind and the importance of performance for an artist/writer. And, at the end of the conversation, Kesey and two students, Chuck Varani and Bennett Huffman, talk about how word processing with a big-screen monitor let Kesey communicate the process of the artist at work to his apprentices.

Knox-Quinn: Will you begin by describing your class in a general way?
Kesey: It started out that there were two rules in the class. One was that you couldn't tell anybody what the plot of the novel was until it was done. The other one was that I made up half the class. If it came to an argument about something, I was fifty percent of the class. I knew that we wouldn't have to go into a lot of democratic discussion. Nothing hampers creativity like too many cooks.

As time went by we came up with the third rule and most important rule. The rule was that we didn't do any composition outside of class. I found that people were beginning to go their own directions and prose style. Doing it there in class really made a difference. Suddenly we started hearing a lot more and a lot better prose. We needed to move like a team with a quarterback. The more we did it, the more it was like a team.

This third rule was enacted when we were about a fourth of the way through the book. As you go through the book, the early part is by far the weakest part. When we began to do the composition in class, we began to hit our stride.

I think this is the way to teach writing. You teach wrestling by having guys get out and wrestle. You teach basketball by having them play basketball, and you teach writing by having them sit and write. Writing and rewriting are different things. A lot of college people learn how to rewrite well, but not how to write well. I've had an interesting thought lately. You don't become Isaac Stern to make a recording. You become Isaac Stern to play the violin. You don't learn to write just to publish. You learn to write so that you can write; you can feel it flowing through you.

When we would sit down around the table, after we had drawn lots, and start writing our little section, this was only a half-hour period—boy you could hear the brain cells popping. They knew they had to write and had to fit it in with the other stuff. You couldn't be too much yourself. You had to try to fit it into the tone of the novel, and then you had to read it aloud in front of this jury of your peers.

Knox-Quinn: What were you drawing lots about?
Kesey: We divided the chapter into increments one to fourteen. We designed the chapter on one of those white boards with wipe-off ink [picking up a felt tip pen as if he were showing a new gadget]. We designed it up there: "Gabby gets up, walks outside, has a cigarette, thinks about her past." That's number one. Number two is: "She meets somebody, talks to them and they go to breakfast." That's number two. Then we'd put those numbers on lots in a hat. We'd draw lots and write.

They would write, and when it came reading time they would read that section. Then the next section would be read. We'd read it into a tape recorder that we passed around the table. It gave people a chance to hear what the person had written before them, to make a few alterations in what they were writing. Then we handed the tape over to a secretary who transcribed it on the computer.

We would do this on Monday and by the next class meeting, which would be on a Friday, we'd usually have forty to fifty pages of prose written and ready to read on the computer.

Knox-Quinn: Did you read it as a class?

Kesey: Sometimes we did, but by the time the class was really going well, people were coming in all the time and reading whenever they could come in and see the stuff.

Knox-Quinn: Could they change it? Could anybody change anything?

Kesey: Yeah, it was open for work. We would go through it and make large editings on it, but the next phase was that each member of the class had a chapter that they had to work on, do the rewrite on, to make all those seams fit together, to take out discrepancies. Adjustment I call it. Here's a good example: we knew that we were going to need an archaeologist because of the theme of what we were doing. I had just assumed the archaeologist was going to be a man, but when the class went to design the characters they brought back the archaeologist as a fifty-year-old woman who's been study-ing the Anasazis. It was not something I would have thought of. Having her be a woman changed all sorts of relationships that would happen naturally amongst these characters. It changed the tensions.

I thought of it like adjusting the struts in an airplane, an old biplane. You had to adjust this and that made the wing go up a little, and you had to bring that wing down. That kind of adjustment was going on constantly.

By the time the second term was over, we had a draft. We knew where we ended up. We started and we ended up. During the third term, we did the extensive rewrites. This was the job of each member of the class. They'd take a pile of manuscript home and make that adjustment. Fix the seams, bring it back, read it aloud, and start on the rewrite.

If I were to do it again, I would have maybe one class meeting in which we explained what was happening, and then we would go to work on it right away.

Knox-Quinn: What would you explain during that first class meeting?

Kesey: When I first went into the class, I explained to them that I had no idea what the plot was, who the characters were, where it was going to be located, what time frame it was going to be in, or anything at all. We were starting from the beginning.

Then we went a number of months doing what they call in jail "scop-ing each other's credentials." We talked literary blather [laughter] to just get comfortable with each other. That's fun. Writers love to talk writing, but talking writing is a lot different than writing. It's like talking basketball. You can talk basketball forever. It's different to pick up a ball. I think I'd pick up the ball right away and we would go right into the plotting and making decisions.

Knox-Quinn: How did you plot the novel?
Kesey: The way we plotted it was this: I said, "Start from character," and "Let's not do it about this time in history." The other thing I said was, "Move out of Oregon. Let's go somewhere else, and let's write about something we really don't know anything about."

Knox-Quinn: Why?
Kesey: Because so many people that write about something they know something about are all bound up emotionally with it. It becomes psychotherapy instead of writing. I just finished reading about Robert Burns's "Tam-O-Shanter." It's about ghosts and boogie-ies and all sorts of stuff that he knows nothing about. He never saw any of that stuff. He had to go and research that stuff [laughs]. It frees you from yourself. You don't end up being Diane di Prima talking about shaving her armpits. That may be interesting to her, but not to many others.

So we launched out into an area that I think is relative to the present but it doesn't take place in the present. I read this piece to Rebecca Preston from NPR. As soon as it was over she said, "Oh, I see this is about the new age." I said, "That's right. It's about the new age only we've moved it. Instead of writing about now, we're writing about back then when it was at its heyday in the '20s and '30s." But she picked up on it right away. She understood why it would have been a mistake to write about it now. It's too cumbersome a mechanism to try to really dig into a current topic. To write a thing about El Salvador, for instance, it would be better to write a thing about Montezuma and have that reflect on El Salvador.

Knox-Quinn: How did you decide who the characters were?
Kesey: [To Bennett and Chuck] How did we do that?
Varani: Well, you told us to come in with a character.
Huffman: On a card.
Varani: On a card, describing some character's need.
Kesey: Make up a character.
Varani: Yeah, make up a character. So we all came in, and we all read them.
Kesey: I studied Stanislavski, *My Life in Art*. He says that when you're studying acting what you do is try to find out what the character's need is. What's Richard the Third really trying to get? What's he really want, and what's he

going to do? Everything springs from that spine, he calls it. I think that is the same way writers write. They dig into the character. They ask the character, what does the character really want and need? So the card thing gave us a really simple mechanism.

Starting with these characters first, you try to figure out what is a plot that will bring them all together. It had to be a quest, something like *Canterbury Tales*. In fact, it was called for a while *Indiana Loach and the Temple of Canterbury Gloom*. So the characters all get to go somewhere and be together.

The necessity of bringing the characters together dictated the plot, which is really the way it is in life. People are people, and they get together, and they have to do something. What comes of it will surprise you. Whereas, if you make up the plot, and then make up the characters to go into it, you've got puppets. These characters did stuff none of us ever expected, said things that we couldn't have made up. They had life.

Then by the third term we did another thing that I think was really important. We reserved Gerlinger Hall for the reading. This was to be the class recital. It's different than sending a novel off to an editor; different than ending a class. It means that you're going to have to make a presentation up in front of people. You could just feel the nervousness increase in the class as that date got closer. We decided to wear 1930s garb. I don't remember who it was that came up with that idea. It was a great idea.

If you're going to practice the violin steadily day by day for years and years you might as well get it in your head that one of these days you're gonna have to take that on the stage, have people out there listening to you play. Goethe said it: "Don't act. Compete." This doesn't mean to be competitive. It means that you're going to be out there in a win/lose situation. As soon as you put yourself in that situation, as soon as you walk up on stage or send a piece of stuff in to be published, you're in a win/lose situation. That means you've risked something. You've put something on the line. You can be hurt. And the people who don't ever put anything out there and that don't get hurt, then they are never fully alive. People that play it safe end up, you know, driving Volvos [laughter].

I'll do this again someday and I think that I'll do a play instead of a novel. I'll do it the same way only at the end of the year, instead of a reading we'll put on a play. It's made for presentation. Publication really means just that: you do it to the public. Getting it printed is one form of it, but presenting it to the public is so important.

The book took place in 1934. We just kind of arbitrarily picked that. Sometime almost nothing is written about. We thought, "Where can we take the people in the novel that isn't already beaten down by other novelists?" So we made it up through Idaho and Utah and Wyoming in the desert area. My brother took us all over to Bend so we could go down in a cave. Get down in there, and turn all the lights out. Get a feeling what it's like.

Knox-Quinn: You were researching what you were writing about at the same time?

Kesey: Yeah, and the books just showed up in the library, and the pictures. We found out we had to learn about bats. So we were all current with each other. We needed to have some things in common.

For the first assignment of the class I said, "Bring in a character sketch about yourself in the third person." As we read these things we found that everybody has a certain thing in common. A lot of writers really are questers. They are not just trying to write. They are trying to quest. They're looking for truth.

This is a really good idea for a teacher, having the kids come in and write a third-person character sketch of themselves. It gives you a picture. You get to know the person right away. As you read through this stuff you see there's no need to teach any of them to write. They can all write.

We got into Joseph Campbell like you couldn't believe. There was that whole series that was broadcast last year, which had to do with primal images found in caves. The Joseph Campbell shows were broadcast exactly when we needed them. We didn't pick it up from him. This was all happening currently in the class. It was wonderful.

Knox-Quinn: Does the age of the students make a lot of difference? What about teachers of high-school or junior high-school students?

Kesey: I think if I had a high school, I would set the class right down there and say: "OK, right now, take your pencil and put it to this piece of paper. I want you to fill that piece of paper with penciled words. Fill it with words. Now, you've got fifteen minutes. Do it. Don't think about it. Do it." And when it's over: "Now, stand up and read it out loud." Do that again the next day and the next day. By the end of a certain number of months those people are going to be able to write.

Knox-Quinn: You were writing with the people in this class. You were writing the novel too. That doesn't happen in a class very often. Teachers assign students to write, they don't write.

Kesey: Oh, gosh, yes. When I sent this book off to Viking, my heart was in my throat like nothing else I'd ever done. When we did this reading over there for Gerlinger Hall—I perform a lot, but this was a risk. We didn't know. So I felt more under the hammer than I have remembered feeling in years and years.

I will get an assignment or I'll get an idea, and I'll send it off. If somebody doesn't like it, somebody else will like it. They'll give me a suggestion, and I'll work on it. But this, we didn't know at all. So when we got the word that Viking had taken it—that by God, they're gonna take it—it was a great victory. And when I was out there writing, it was very exciting.

This whole thing, especially with college students that are coming in with their own work and you have to read them—that is not teaching people to write. That's teaching them to rewrite, and it's just too hard a task for me. I have a hard enough time brushing my own teeth, let alone other people's [laughter].

When it was over, we were moving fast; we knew we had to finish it. When I'd finish a class, man, I'd walk upstairs and just collapse. I felt like each of those classes were like wrestling tournaments.

Knox-Quinn: The classes were about three hours long?
Kesey: About that, yeah. Everybody had their own habits, their own style, and people were completely different from each other. We were all completely alike in that we had habits and we had a style. Working on a computer helped.

I thought that I could come off the back of that computer and go to monitors around the table, lots of them. Three people can work on a monitor, maybe four. They'd be all working on the same stuff. We finally tried, but it was a nuisance.

I focused the video camera on the screen and ran a line from the camera to my big TV so you could see the stuff this big. Ideally, you'd have a large screen there and people sitting in close enough contact so that everybody could watch it. We found in the rewrite that three people, maybe four, was about the most you could work with per computer.

This is how, as a professional, I can teach stuff. I couldn't teach writing without doing it. I have to be writing this stuff. People have to be looking over your shoulder [at the monitor] as you do this, as you see that this phrase here is redundant and this is bad. Outside of the context of the thing, general abstractions don't work, unless you've got something specific for it to go on.

The other thing about this group style is that some days you just don't have any new sparkling stuff. But when you got thirteen people, somebody always has something neat and it's as though somebody on your team is on and you're off. This woman from NPR, Rebecca Preston, she asked why a lot of people seemed to be doing group things like Dolly Parton and Emmylou Harris. Because it's fun. You get tired of doing things by yourself, and it's a lot of fun to have a group that you're working with. That old team effort. We keep hearing so much about the pride is back, stuff that's all muddied up by Budweiser beer, but it still works when you have a good team working with you.

Knox-Quinn: Earlier, you were talking about the students coming in with their own work and there being some competition. Is there a contradiction or problem between competition and creativity?

Kesey: Well, people compete with each other instead of competing with gravity and inertia. Real things that you compete with are stagnation. When Larry Bird is really shooting well, he's not competing with another guy that's shooting well. He's competing with distance and it has to do with Zen. When Goethe says, "Don't act. Compete," he doesn't mean with another playwright to see who's the most popular, which has become the American way of competing. It's a weird thing. Instead of competing with the real foe. And the real foe in teaching right now is not other kids. It's Coke commercials, it's the lethargy.

Also we're competing with the past. My old teacher is back in town, my old University of Oregon teacher. His name is James Baker Hall. He's finally come back to Oregon because he's finished teaching and he's going to do more writing. He writes these short, minimalist perfection works. He's really a great writer, but he'll never be recognized as a great writer because he's like a little jewel that's hidden away within himself. He taught me the greatest thing I ever learned about writing. I was reading a story called "Soldiers" by Hemingway, and he pointed out a phrase in there where Krebs is sitting there and watching the bacon fat grow cold on his plate. And he says: "There it is. That's the story. It's there, the bacon fat growing cold. It has to do with a guy who's been to war, and he's come home, and something has gone cold and hard in him." And I got it! And that kind of turn-on, that kind of thrill, that's what teaching is all about. When you give something and the person knows that he got it. That'll recharge you on both ends.

To do it with high-school kids you have to overcome a tremendous amount of stuff that's thrown up in the way, of flack and crap. Because this [approach] is an end run around the conventional kind of teaching framework, I'll bet if you could take any bunch of kids in the school, by the end of the year, you would have a work. And they would all have contributed, and they would all be proud of it. The very fact that you don't let them tell others what it's about draws people together into a little cult. It's far out enough that they can see themselves a little bit rebellious. Just step over the current trends. Step over!

That's why the punks are trying to do that. It's a valid thing, that whole new wave, cyberpunk. Have you been reading cyberpunk? It's good as hell. It's describing everything in minute detail. "As he watched her he could feel the adrenaline flowing through the capillaries and into the tips of his phalanges and they were moving an increment." And everything is described in minute detail like Data on *Star Trek* would describe it. It's kind of exciting.

Knox-Quinn: Are you going to show me what you would do with the computer in this class?

Kesey: I'll tell you what let's do, let's fire up that thing, and we'll correct some of these pages that are really muddy. [Kesey starts to run a word processor on his big, old IBM computer.]

This is some stuff my editor said was too long. [He's looking at a hardcopy of his novel, which he keeps next to the keyboard. It is drawn with lines and penciled-in editing notes. His students and I look over his shoulder at the monitor as he talks to us about the editing changes he is making on the computer.]

Knox-Quinn: If you had had a bunch of computers would it have changed the class?

Kesey: If we would have had a bunch of monitors, yes it would have made it much easier. We still would have had only two or three people working on it at a time and people sitting at monitors, but they wouldn't have access to the keyboard. I think you could have two keyboards perhaps, but you couldn't work with many more than that because people would just be fussing with each other. [While Kesey is busy starting up the computer, Chuck talks.]

Varani: Working with Kesey, while he was on the computer, was one of the really high points, I think, with all of us sitting there together. That's something you never really do. Like he said, he had a lot on the line, more than we did. We were just students. That was the most valuable thing I got out of it. While doing the rewriting. Looking over his shoulder. Doing the actual composing of it right there. Having him read his stuff along with us.

It was like, you know, Leonardo and Michelangelo. You know, those guys, they all studied under people. They were apprentices for whoever. And they got to learn watching these masters, and they went out and had their own school, and people learned from them. And this reminded me of that. We got a chance to see someone who has been doing this for twenty years and to just learn by just doing it.

Kesey: [Checking his copy for changes he wants to make] You know, it became tremendously complicated working on this story. And it became necessary to have people over the shoulders of people reminding each other of what was going on. Saying, "We can't do that, remember, he lost that thing in the last chapter. We can't use it." Usually when you're writing you've got all that in your mind. But this, we had to have it all in all our minds. Someday, somebody will do a thesis on this style. That's why I've kind of kept all this stuff, so that somebody can go through and look at it, not in terms of whether the book is a great book, but just as a way of teaching, an important way of teaching.

Knox-Quinn: Because of the creation of the class mind?
Kesey: It's more like what Chuck said. You're in where the statue is being chipped. And you're watching the hammer move and the chips fly and you get a chance to every so often chip some of the statue yourself. The only way you're going to teach somebody sculpting is to have a hammer in your hand. You can't just look at their stuff and criticize it. You have to be working on your own stuff and have them see you do it. We're too used to the other form.

[Kesey, engrossed in the task of editing, talks softly about why he is deleting text or making other changes.] Now this sort of whole shot, I'm taking it out. This became a wonderful, fun, thing to do. The first draft was 450 pages and we dropped it down to 360. [Kesey talks to himself about the keyboard commands and makes appropriate noises as he punches the keys.] We're taking that out [deletes a section with a keystroke]: Pop!

Editing requires concentration. When finally Kesey emerged from narrating for us his own editing process, it was dusk. The cows needed to be fed. Chuck, Bennett, and I made ourselves useful throwing bales of hay off a flat wagon bed as Ken tractored through the fields, past herds of cows and one faded, but once brightly painted old bus, sinking into the Oregon mud.

Comes Spake the Cuckoo

Todd Brendan Fahey / 1992

It was just another Saturday on Ken Kesey's farm, but it felt like Shangri-La. Some shaven-headed freak stood staring down from the rough-hewn stage, glassy-eyed and grinning through a musky amalgam of marijuana and pine, slapping a pair of spoons against his chest and thigh—a demented rhythm section in an unknown band, one of the dozens to play in the moss-draped south-40 of a man uniformly known as America's First Hippie. While every cop in Eugene stood poised on the roadside overlooking a commercial replacement for the Grateful Dead's aborted late-August doubleheader, the Cuckoo strode around his own eight acres, miles away, in a striped referee's shirt, signing autographs and posing reticently for the cameras—an icon who, in the words of Hunter Thompson, "has found out a way to live out there where the *real* winds blow."

As the proud owner of a plane ticket to Portland, before Jerry Garcia's brief collapse in August of 1992 to thirty years of excess, I felt I had but one honorable decision: "Buy the Ticket, Take the Ride." And so by 9:00 Friday evening, I had flown to Eugene and befriended a local bluegrass band with whom I hitched a ride the next morning to a rustic encampment in nearby Pleasant Hill. By noon, I had videotaped the infamous Bus from every conceivable angle, as it rested in all its brokedown splendor between a pair of Douglas firs. By 4:00, I was bearing witness to tree-people emerging from the hollow—a gentle, pachouli-scented race, bound by dreadlocks and sweet sativa. By 10:45, Ken Kesey took the stage, towering over the crowd like a redwood in a bayou of scrag-oak, to read from one of his children's books against an eerie Northwest sunset—an actor who somehow never made it in Hollywood, and a living testament that "the '60s aren't over; they won't be over until the Fat Lady gets high."

Fahey: I interviewed Timothy Leary a couple weeks ago over dinner, and he had some very kind and heartfelt words to say about you; and he was also talking about what he saw as the future of information. He felt that the novel is a somewhat archaic art form, in that the brain can absorb so much information so rapidly. I was wondering what you might think about the future of the novel.

Kesey: I agree. I have been sayin' for the few years that I've been working on this novel [*Sailor Song*]: it's a flash in the pan, as far as history goes. Because the storyteller was there to begin with. He used the fire and he used his voice; he used shadows and monsters and he used poetry and music. And all those things worked on the audience. When you just get into print, you reduce the input quite a bit. But it makes for a nice thing to package and distribute—like a box of tampons. But I think that for us to really deal with a young audience, we're going to have to pick up the pace.

Ol' Leary's been saying this forever, and I've always agreed with him. It's kind of like a compulsory in the Olympics: every so often you've got to write a novel to make people pay attention to the other stuff you're doin'.

I just came back from a book tour, in which I had Viking not just line me up with bookstores where I was just reading and signing my book but also line me up with theaters where I could perform my children's stuff. It made a lot more sense; also, it was a lot more colorful. When you're up there with robes and masks and monsters and dance and drums, the story gets up off the page and moves around.

Fahey: [Grunts in agreement.]

Kesey: When Shakespeare was writing he wasn't writing for stuff to lie on the page; it was supposed to get up and move around. And I think that writers are going to have to face this; they were performers originally. That's what storytellers did—they told a story. And the better they were at telling it, the more famous it became.

The Chopes were writers that moved from castle to castle. The word *Chope*, C-H-O-P-E, means "see, to see, and be seen." So you went from castle to castle and you told about the castle you just came from, and how beautiful the maidens were and how powerful and manly the knights were. You helped prop up a young civilization: They couldn't have done it without them.

Now, we've got electronic means to do that, so you wouldn't have to actually travel to castles. Come out of that box, there, and address the audience. The whole MTV audience, that *is* the new audience. And the people who are being purists and ignoring that, are those who are going to be left behind. As Dylan says, it's a new road; if you don't like it, get out of the way.

Fahey: Timothy felt that, in history, you'd be as famous for your computer book, the *Caverns* piece, as anything you've ever done.
Kesey: That's the only time it's ever been done like that. And it's a pretty good little potboiler novel. Tim was trying to have a thing where a person with a computer could plug into that [*Caverns*] and also add stuff, write stuff in. You've kind of got to have a love affair with computers that I've never had. He's always been plain infatuated with that techno stuff; where I'm more interested in gnomes and elves. [laughs]

Fahey: Why did you decide to make a shift from the more obvious form of short stories to children's stories in the mid-'80s?
Kesey: The audience was a whole lot better. You can put the same message in that kids' story and deliver it to quite a large audience, because it's the big folks who buy the books, and they always read the books before they pass them onto the kids. And so you're not only reaching a new, young audience, you're reaching your same old audience. And the messages in my kids' stories are the same message in my novels.

Fahey: Sure.
Kesey: Totalitarianism, and how you can overcome it. Which takes you back to a lot of old trickster stories and spider stories from Africa.

Fahey: *Animal Farm.*
Kesey: And monkey stories from the Orient. But the new novel, the real new novel, hasn't been written yet. It will be written with a new type of pen. If Shakespeare were alive today, he wouldn't be using the quill pen; he would at least be using the Pentel® Rolling Writer®, or something. You use whatever is available during your time. And the most powerful tool of composition we've got now is that camcorder. There'll be kids who write a novel using the camcorder as a pen; and the novel will sell as though it's a novel, but you'll play it through your video.

Fahey: That's another thing Leary said; he said he thinks that anyone writing a novel these days should have it half videoed.
Kesey: Yeah. In fact, I'm taking *Cuckoo's Nest* and reading it into a video camera, just sitting there—

Fahey: Fantastic.

Kesey: Viking wanted me to do a recording for an audio book. But when you're actually raising your face up and looking into the camera, as opposed to just having a microphone, you have a lot more presence. This is the new edition, this ability to have your face pop out of the screen. 'Cause a good storyteller uses his face a lot, uses his eyes.

Fahey: Let's go back to the very early '60s, to Perry Lane.

Kesey: OK, let's *do*. [laughs]

Fahey: I've always been curious whether you had a sense of being the role model, the leader . . . history has kind of pronounced you the Father of the Counterculture. I was wondering if *you* thought of yourself as that back then, or if that's been something generously awarded to you.

Kesey: Oh, no. I don't even think of myself as that *now*.

Fahey: But back then. Back in those heady times of the Bus trip and Neal Cassady . . . did you have a sense?

Kesey: I really *did* have a sense that what we were doing was important, historically important, in a way that still hasn't been understood or recognized. The '60s aren't over; they won't be over until the Fat Lady gets *high*.

You think of the stuff that came out of the '60s: the environmental movement, the feminist movement, the power of the civil rights movement; but most of all, it's the psychedelic movement that attempted to actually go in and change the consciousness of the people, either back to something more pure and honest, or forward to something never before realized, knowing that the places we were in, the status quo, was a dead-end—a dead-end spiritually and, as we are finding out, a dead-end economically.

That stuff that happened in the '60s, all of us who were part of it . . . you can tell when you break new ground. If you're a farmer you can tell that this sod has never been broken before, the plow is laying open great, purple earth and something comes out of it and you can *smell* it. When you're a writer, when I was working on *Sometimes a Great Notion*, I could tell I was breaking new ground; there's an energy that comes out, that's probably not unlike the energy that comes out of nuclear fission—it wasn't just me. It was not *anybody*. It wasn't rock and roll; it wasn't art; it wasn't cinema or dance. *Something was happening* at that time, and it was a wave that some of us were able to surf on. And none of us started the wave; I don't think there's any way you could start the wave. The wave is still going.

After this recent tour across the country I've run into people who I haven't seen the likes of for twenty years: really interested in something new, not just interested in sound-bites. There's a new seriousness, especially amongst college kids; they know that all of these simple old homilies really are not important.

I've been telling everyone that I'm mainly interested in warriors. Tim is a warrior. Most of the people I run into are interested in *being* warriors. When they read Tim Leary, or when they go to see a movie by, let's say, Gus Van Sant, or when they go to a Dead concert, they're doing it not just to be entertained; they're doing it because they want to become better warriors. And we've had a real crackerjack bunch of warriors. I mean, Allen Ginsberg is a tremendous warrior as time goes by. He's a warrior first and a poet second. There was a time when he forsook being a great poet, the future of poetry, and became a warrior. He uses his poetry to be a warrior. And that's the same way I feel about my writing: I'm much more interested in helping warriors know more about their task than I am in just trying to titillate them with stories.

Fahey: Did you ever meet Robert Hunter when you were in the Veterans Hospital experiments?
Kesey: You mean the Dead's—

Fahey: The Dead's lyricist. Was he in there at the same time you were?
Kesey: I don't remember meeting him [fades] . . . he and Garcia didn't live far from us. There was a place called the Chateau; Hunter, I think, at that time roomed with Phil Lesh. And Garcia was at the same place. Oh, yeah. I've known Hunter for a long time.

Fahey: He's written some tremendous poetry.
Kesey: Yeah, he has. He was up here for our Field Trip last fall. You know, everybody thinks Garcia wrote those songs; it was Hunter. Hunter doesn't perform or sing much, but he got out here and sang, and he couldn't remember the words to "Ripple," so all the audience had to help him out. [laughs] All those great dance songs; he's written so many. He's not as good as Dylan, but he's right up there.

I saw Garcia night before last down at Oakland. I emceed that show. [audible smile] It's like every ten years, all these people have to get together to check each other out and see what we're doing. 'Cause we don't see enough of each other; we're spread too thin. It's really good to get back together with Hunter; especially when you get [the Dead's second lyricist, John] Barlow. You get to talk about stuff that you've *forgotten*. That's why it's good to see Leary.

Leary can get a part of my mind that's kind of rusted shut grinding again, just by being around him and talking, 'cause that's where he works. He knows that area of the mind and the brain, and he knows the difference between the two areas. He's a real master at getting your old wheel squeaking again.

Fahey: I'm reading a quote by you—it was a little insert in *USA Weekend* back in July. Betsy Clayton has you quoted as saying, "The Haight is just a place; the '60s was a spirit." I've only been up to your place once, but to me it seemed like what the '60s were all about. Do you try to keep that atmosphere alive, or is your place a pretty normal place most of the time and you just let loose once in a while?

Kesey: No, it's pretty much the same all of the time. [soft chuckle] It's nothing that you have to try to keep alive; it'll live on its own. I think you have to kill it. That kind of spirit doesn't die naturally; you have to lock it up in shackles and feed it lots of red meat and browbeat it into death. It doesn't die of its own accord.

Children keep it alive. The way the birds have been drunk today. All the grapes hanging out there fermenting. All the birds—a beautiful, sunny day—the birds have been eating those grapes and they're drunk and teetering around and the robins are falling off the branches and reeling around on the lawn, and the children are parading around with their fall garb, and it's always *there*. It's always *anywhere*. All you have to do is let it live. There's no effort that needs to be made to let it live; there's effort that needs to be made to keep it from dying.

Fahey: What are your creative plans after *Sailor Song*, besides the videotaping of *Cuckoo's Nest*? Can you let us in on some secrets?

Kesey: Last night we got out there and we set off our big bonfire, and I had all my sea monsters dance and cavort around the fire. This is part of the movie that Gus Van Sant shot, *The Sea Lion*. Gus is, right now, involved in doing *Even Cowgirls Get the Blues*.

Fahey: Oh yeah, Tom Robbins.

Kesey: Uh-huh. And as soon as he's done with that, we'll get into editing the footage that he shot of *The Sea Lion*. And then I'll try to bring the Dead in to do the soundtrack for this, like they promised ten years ago. This is the thing I'm most interested in—to move a kind of Wagnerian drama into these rock and roll venues, so that it's not just playing "Uncle John's Band" [laughs] over and over again.

And whenever I get together and talk with the guys about it, oh, they're just so eager. But they go vehement that they have to move to do it. It's so cumbersome; it's hard for them to do it. They're almost run by their machinery.

But that's the thing I'm most interested in: performing a big rock and roll opera, where we move those ol' scrabbly-lookin' musicians down there in the pit where they belong, and put dancers and singers and magicians on the stage, and have that broadcast to *large* numbers of people, ten, twenty, thirty thousand people. And do it with video enhancements, so that you are able to see faces up there.

The people who have this equipment, they keep making the mistake of thinking that you can endlessly watch Garcia's hand run up and down that keyboard [sic], but that isn't any more interesting than watching Rachmaninoff's hand run up and down the keyboard. People want to see drama; they want to have a story told to them. They want to be part of some kind of beginning, middle, and end that they can relate to, the same way as the tribe can relate the story about going out and killing the deer, and evoking the deer spirit, and raising the spirits of the tribe with the blood of the deer. That stuff still has great potency.

And when you're around the whole Dead scene, like I was on Halloween, and you see out there in the parking lot as many people as are inside, they're there as a tribal thing; they're there as part of a rendezvous and a powwow. And all it lacks is that story. The only thing that has happened like it, that I've ever seen, is *Tommy*. I guess *The Wall* was something on the order of this, but I didn't see *The Wall*. And I know the Dead are capable of it, and I know the audience is ready for it. And it's what I'm most interested in.

Fahey: One last question: I saw the interview with you and Bob Costas, and he was asking why you did certain things that you've done throughout your life, and you said because you're an American; and that as Americans, we're searchers and pioneers. And I was wondering what frontiers are there left for Ken Kesey to explore?

Kesey: The frontiers that we broke into in the '60s are still largely unexplored. When I was doing those experiments at the Vet's Hospital, they gave us an enormous array of drugs, and they gave us an enormous array of tests.

They tested our motor skills, our memories, our ability to create, to imagine, they tested our urine and our blood—all the results of those tests still exist somewhere. For those to be valid experiments, we need to follow up on that—to see if our brains have deteriorated, to see if there's been any damage like they claimed.

When we first broke into that forbidden box in the other dimension, we knew that we had discovered something as surprising and powerful as the New World when Columbus came stumbling onto it. It is still largely unexplored and uncharted. People like Leary have done the best they can to chart it sort of underground, but the government and the powers do not want this world charted, because it threatens established powers. It always has.

People don't want other people to get high, because if you get high, you might see the falsity of the fabric of the society we live in. We thought that by this time that there would be LSD given in classes in college. And you would study for it and prepare for it, you would have somebody there who help you through it; you would know what to sing, where to be, how to stand out among the trees. We were *naive*. We thought that we had come to a new place, a new, exciting, free place; and that it was going to be available to all America. And they *shut it down*.

People ask, "What happened to you guys?" And I always tell them, "We got *arrested*." Just everybody I know got arrested and had to serve time.

Fahey: But you got arrested for pot though; it wasn't LSD.
Kesey: Yeah, but it doesn't make any *difference* once you're arrested. The fact that they're beating on Rodney King—it didn't matter what they were beating on him for; they were beating on him.

And it meant that a lot of this stuff had to go way underground. And other drugs sprung up. I've never seen crack or a lot of these new drugs. Don't know anything about them. I don't know what they do for you, or whether they do anything good for you or not. But I do still have a lot of faith in the spiritual purity of LSD and pot. And I think that if grass were legalized, it would help our drug problem enormously. As John Madden said, "There've been a lot more people hurt on AstroTurf than grass."

[Laughter on both sides]

Fahey: Do you think that as long as LSD is illegal, the youth today will experience any of the same modicum of freedom that you had in the early '60s?
Kesey: No, I don't. For one thing, all these people that were taking these

drugs back then were college age; and we had all read a certain amount of Oriental literature, and we had read Hesse, and we had a spiritual underpinning of knowing the Bible and knowing the Bhagavad Gita, knowing the Judeo traditions. And that gives you stars to sail by. And without those stars, just thrown into chaos, a lot of people are lost.

Luckily, we've still got some *old* mariners around, like Tim Leary, who keep doling out enough clues that these *young* mariners keep afloat.

Ken Kesey: Writing Is an Act of Performance

Dan McCue / 1993

Even counterculture superstars have to sometimes go to the supermarket.

And so it was that Ken Kesey, author of *One Flew Over the Cuckoo's Nest* and *Sometimes a Great Notion*—not to mention the central character in Tom Wolfe's *The Electric Kool-Aid Acid Test*—was in the position to literally drop everything for someone he didn't know.

Kesey had spent the better part of the past three decades engaged in "living" his books rather than actually committing them to paper, but when he did release a bit of writing here and there from his farm in the wet hills of Oregon's Willamette Valley, the work often surprised his fans.

For instance, during a five-year stretch beginning in 1986 there was *Caverns*, a mystery written in collaboration with the graduate class he taught at the University of Oregon; *Demon Box*, basically a grab bag of miscellany; and *The Further Inquiry*, a rejected screenplay turned into a book in which he put his erstwhile band of fellow travelers, the Merry Pranksters, on trial.

And right before I set the telephone ringing inside his Pleasant Hill home there were *Little Tricker the Squirrel Meets Big Double the Bear* and *The Sea Lion*, two children's books that began their existence as performance pieces.

As Kesey picked up the receiver to say hello, one could still hear the rustle of paper grocery bags as he and Faye settled into the kitchen to unpack them.

Having someone call completely out of the blue seemed the most natural thing in the world to Kesey, who listened, offering an agreeable "Mm hmm," as the caller spun a hurried tale that amounted to an introduction by a mutual acquaintance.

"Well," he said cheerily when the caller paused, "how can I help you?"

Talk to Ken Kesey for a while about writing, and you almost forget that he's been a literary outsider for more than a quarter century. His life seems perfectly centered, and his sentences all seem to end in a smile, rather than a period, as he says them.

But it's also clear that he's paid a price in certain circles for the life that he's led and the career that he's fashioned. When he recently once again tackled the novel [with *Sailor Song*, a skewering of religious cults, organized lodges, and land developers], critics reviewed his persona as much as they did his work. Many of them, still smarting from his rejection of the New York–based publishing world, were less than kind.

"You know, I wouldn't have let Tom Wolfe do [*Acid Test*] if I had known what I know now," he says of the long shadow the book and, more to the point, the image it created, cast over his subsequent projects.

"In that book it's like he's looking at me from an East Coast crow's nest," Kesey continued. "But what he's really looking at is this huge wart beside my nose, and he writes about this wart so eloquently that other people are looking at it all the time and staring at it, and then you find one eye begins to cross down and then you're looking at it. You become cross-eyed at your own wart."

With that, Kesey hesitated, as if to take the measure of what he would say next. After a moment's deliberation, he said, "You have to take that into account when you're writing with this kind of light on you.

"It's different than if you're writing as a stranger. When I was doing *Sometimes a Great Notion*, my personality was in it, but my personality was not something that anybody knew," he said.

Still, Kesey said he saw no alternative to pressing on with his writing in his own way, likening the process, as William Faulkner did, to the "dog having to go against the bear, just to keep calling itself a dog."

It is Indian Summer in Oregon as Kesey and I have this conversation, and *Sailor Song*, the author's first full-blown novel in twenty-eight years has just been released by Viking. In writing it, Kesey chose to include his *Sea Lion* tale for children, making it an important part of the book's storyline. This afforded us the chance to discuss his feeling about children's stories, beginning with why he got involved with the form in the first place.

"I'm real certain of my kids' books," Kesey said. "I've read them and performed them enough to know that this is a working piece of stuff. You're not telling stories that are meant to explore the psychological depths of a character—you're just trying to tell a story, like Poe or Zane Grey. And that's just so much more interesting to me."

By comparison, Kesey said, "It's hard to be certain of a novel. They're just so vast," he said. "But with a kids' story, the kids you're reading to, they don't know you from Ralph Waldo Emerson. [laughs] They've never heard of Tom Wolfe. They've barely heard of the Grateful Dead, so if the story can't stand up on its own, no amount of posturing or critical praise is going to change it in a kid's mind. It's got to make it according to that kid's set of rules, and I think those rules keep you pretty honest."

Surprisingly, given that it would naturally be assumed Kesey would be talking up his latest novel, he said he actually prefers *Ticker the Squirrel*, the story of a wily rodent who outwits the bears of a mythical forest called Topple's Bottom.

"It's a better story," he explained. "It's basically a story that my grand-mother told me and that I haven't changed very much except—as my grandma told me when she heard me read it one time—'I gussied it up quite a bit.' But the story itself has all the classical storytelling tricks in it: Repeating things three times, using a lot of alliteration, using a lot of changes in tempo, casting large things against small things. Every time I read it, I'll be surprised by another nuance I'll discover."

"Did you ever see [Disney's] *Beauty and the Beast*?" Kesey asked abruptly. "A super movie. People will be watching that movie in a hundred years; they won't be watching *Silence of the Lambs*, and the reason why is the story. It's so good, in terms of pure storytelling, that you can just barely do anything to hurt it."

If there's an element of Kesey's personality that's obscured his percep-tiveness over the years, it's the fact that his persona is a pure distillation of the child within the man—and again, this is never more evident that when he's performing his stories for children.

Last October, for instance, he ventured to West Harlem, New York, to read *The Sea Lion* to an audience bused in by local church groups and homeless shelter. Decked out like a kind of hippie shaman, Kesey used magic tricks, slides, and audience participation to flesh out the story. This theatricality, he said afterward, is the shape of all literature to come.

"Writing really doesn't happen until it connects with the mind of the reader, or . . . I think we're getting to a time in which we can call the reader the viewer. If we don't confront the reader as viewer, we've going to lose a lot of them."

A week prior to this conversation, the director Gus Van Sant had brought a film crew up to Kesey's place to film him performing *The Sea Lion*.

"To me, that is the real publication of it, more than the book," Kesey said. "The book will be there and one thing doesn't preclude the other, but a performance is much better and so much more fun for the artist as well as the viewer.

"You begin a novel, and you can just cross yourself off for about two years of being worth living with," he added with another hearty laugh. "It's corrosive work—and not just for you, but for everyone around you. You find yourself in the morning kicking the dog, throwing things at the cat, and screaming at the parrot."

Sailor Song, in fact, was written over the course of several years, and its writing was accompanied by a nagging fear that the thread of the story would run dry during the long process of committing it to paper.

"I think every writer is fearful of that," Kesey said. "See, you don't ever really know for sure where the inspiration for a piece of writing comes from. If you did, you'd just reach in there and grab the handle and turn it on.

"But with *Sailor Song* I had a strong enough sense that this, what I was doing, was really close to the bone of my sermon, and if I just kept myself interested, that the story would just come. . . . I guess a more simplified way of saying it is, you have to trick your muse over the course of writing a novel.

"She'll sit around and watch daytime television if you let her, and you have to do something to poke her out of her stupor," he laughed. "And I have learned a number of ways over the years to trick my muse."

While Kesey's larger than life persona is difficult to keep entirely out of his work, he said he tried harder to keep it at bay in *Sailor Song* than in some of his other recent work, like *Demon Box*.

"I really felt like *Demon Box* was my gonzo," he said. "I felt like my personality was pretty much contained in that, in a way. I wanted *Sailor Song* to be different.

"But you know, the thing about being a writer that's getting older is that you find yourself being more and more like a grumpy old man, by which I mean it's harder to repress your personality," Kesey continued. "Now, I don't think that's good for you, but you find yourself doing it.

"Also, the gonzo that I'm using in *Sailor Song* is somewhat different from the one I used in *Demon Box*," he said. "The central character is not quite me. This is kind of me in the future. I've put a pin on this personality that's not quite like the ones that I used to do."

"If I were Dostoyevsky, I could pretty much keep myself out, but once you start tricking your muse, you find you trick yourself as well. You've got to get her up from watching daytime television, but you're also a little jacked up too, so it's hard to keep personality entirely under wraps. But most of the time, when I do let it in, I'm aware of what I'm doing and I'm doing it for effect."

Still, recriminations peak through. Circling back to his comments about the impact acid tests had on his subsequent life and work, Kesey allowed that the notoriety Wolfe's book gave him may have been an advantage in some respects and not in others.

"In a way, I guess, I really wish I didn't have to take that public perception of me into account as I work," he said.

When Kesey is in the throes of a novel, manuscript pages pile up quickly. "For this one, I've got big boxes of manuscript pages that are maybe ten to twelve inches deep and two that big across, and if you were to go through them, what you see is the process behind the finished work," he said.

"When I'm writing, I experiment with the prose to get the right tone and to get the right character," Kesey explained. "To get the tone in this book, I experimented a lot because I wanted to arrive at something between cyberpunk and traditional, turn of the twentieth-century, Emily Brontë prose. I wanted to bring the old and traditional and set it against the new and uncertain."

As he writes, Kesey said, he's constantly revising his pages. "When I read over what I've written, if something isn't right, it really stands out and jars me, and when that happens, I often have to work a long time to get it ring true," he said.

"Another thing that sometimes happens is that my characters get away from the plot. They'll head on out and do what they want to do, and sometimes they just don't follow what I'm trying to do in the novel," he said. "When that happens, and when something obviously becomes superfluous, I have to go back and take lot of that out."

Kesey said, when it comes to central characters, he tries to leave them "open" inside, allowing room for readers to project their own thoughts and perceptions into them. To explain what he meant, he pointed to Hollywood.

"Part of the genius of Robert Redford as an actor is his ability to be a character and yet leave enough room for the audience to inhabit the character as well. You really don't know that much about the character, but over the course of the performance, you're kind of taken inside the role and by the end you're almost playing it inside your own mind as well.

"The western *Shane* is another good example of that, and the title character is a great American character," Kesey said. "He's a little bit mysterious, a little tragic, alone, and you can sit there and watch the movie and all of a sudden, you become Shane. It's a little harder for you to do that with, say, Ishmael, which is a more fully developed character on the page."

Real writing, according to Kesey, is writing that understands who it is being written to. "It goes right around and stands in front of that consciousness and confronts it, speaks eye to eye with it," he said.

"This business of standing off to the literary side and shuffling work into somebody's ear and hoping it goes Boom! in their brain . . . well, I think we can just about count that over. We may have really big literary heroes for a little longer, but I don't think that's going to last."

Instead, Kesey saw musical artists usurping that position—but only if they have the wherewithal to reimagine their own relationship to their audience and to their work.

"Let's imagine this," he said. "Take Michael Jackson, because he's got the talent to carry this off; if he were to look at what he is doing and decide, instead of just tiddling the kids, I'm going to create a work comparable to Pink Floyd's *The Wall*, something with some depth to it, he'd be considered one of the great artist of our time.

"When I talk to the Grateful Dead, I keep telling them, 'You guys have got to get off that stage and get down in the orchestra where you belong, and allow stuff on the stage to happen that conveys drama and plot and character,' he said. "That's what the Greeks did, what the Indians did, what the Africans did. They used drums and flutes and dance and fire to convey a story. That's exciting to me."

Given how keenly Kesey seemed to feel the need for the artist to change, it seemed naturally to talk about how the audience for literature has changed in the decades that have passed since Kesey first began writing in the late 1950s.

"Um, well, television has changed everything so enormously that it will never be the same, and for us in the writing world to bemoan that fact . . . that's like complaining about hurricanes hitting Florida. There's nothing you can do about it but try and live after it," Kesey said.

As a writer "you have to compete with Big Bird, and the latest big situation comedy, and you have to compete with all of the car chases and shootings and low cleavages that are there constantly in front of the viewers' minds—and if you try to respond by doing all the old stuff that used to catch attention, you'll just find yourself left out in the cold," he said.

If Shakespeare were working writing today, the bard of Stratford-upon-Avon would be trying to work, "in what is the most popular and exciting and juicy form," Kesey said. "Today that might be MTV and tomorrow some other forum, but it all comes down to this: Being where the audience is, because that's where the action is. Now, implied along with that, whether you're a writer or a dancer or a filmmaker, is the realization that the greatest sin that you can commit is boredom," he said. "My Dad told me a thing once that I've always remembered: good writing ain't necessarily good reading. He always emphasized to be sure that what you've written is something that people will enjoy reading.

"Now, it's difficult to do this, especially when you're distracted by potential reviewers," Kesey said, subtly shifting gears as he continued. "Right now, everybody's talking about this [unfavorable] review [of *Sailor Song*] in the *New York Times*—they've talked about it enough that I've been able to forestall myself and not read it," he said, laughing. "In fact, I've quit reading all that stuff.

"I decided that good reviews, they don't really help you, they just pump you up; and bad reviews, well, all they do is hurt you. After that review came out, my editor called and said, 'Well, you know it's a good book. You don't have to be affected by a bad review.' And I said, 'That's like saying Rodney King knew he was innocent.' It doesn't make a difference; when they're hitting you with a stick, it still hurts."

Kesey said rather than get caught up in all that, he'd just as soon stay busy in Pleasant Hill. Soon, he said, he was going to begin work on the further adventures of Tricker the Squirrel, to be followed by a children's book in which a female character named Shula descends into the spirit world.

"I'd like to see what happens when Shula meets Buddha," he said.

Comparing the demands of writing for children with the demands inherent in writing for adults, Kesey said that with *Sailor Song*, "the audience I'm dealing with is not only older, they're also kind of specific. At one point I was trying to figure out, 'Who am I writing this for?' And I knew I wasn't writing it for the East Coast critics because if I did, I was going to get my 'heart broken and my nuts crushed,' as Hunter S. Thompson says," Kesey said.

"In a sense, I feel like the audience I'm writing for today is kind of the MTV, skateboarding circuit, that segment of the population that perhaps doesn't know it likes to read yet, but that is nonetheless interested in the future of our country and the environment, and in what's happening in TV and drama and in other mediums.

"You know that magazine *Mondo 2000*?" Kesey said, referring to the glossy cyberculture magazine published in the 1980s and 1990s that covered everything from virtual reality to the emergence of computer culture to speculations on the benefits of "Smart" drugs. "I want to speak to that consciousness," Kesey said. "A consciousness that's just a little bit above science fiction, but a little below Saul Bellow."

As Kesey's laughter subsides, he had just one more question to tackle, although by now the answer seemed fairly obvious. Did he ever nurse regrets about being a maverick within his own profession?

"No. Not at all," he said. "I've watched a lot of writer friends do this and that, and one of the things you learn is that sometimes you have to make a choice. I mean, it's very difficult to write and maintain a marriage and a family because [being a writer and] playing the game seems to demand that you go back and live on the East Coast, do lunch, and have certain acquaintances—and I never cared about those things.

"I don't feel like I've missed anything by living out here, and what I've gained is immeasurable."

An Interview with Ken Kesey

Matthew Rick and Mary Jane Fenex / 1993

From Blotterati.com. © 1993 Matthew Rick and Mary Jane Fenex. Reprinted with permission.

Ken Kesey's sitting at a table with a stack of books beside him, and a bag of markers, pens, and rubber stamps to assist him in the project of autographing copies of *Sailor Song* and *The Sea Lion*, his two most recent works. To his side is a blonde-haired boy named Lutien, who is helping Kesey on the project. The stamp in his hand is done in the style of Northwest Indian art.

"It's like this frog is appearing out of the fog," Kesey is telling the child. "This is a fog frog." Introductions are made and then he resumes decorating copies of his books. "Go ahead. I'm ready."

Matthew Rick: Of the pieces you've done, do you have a particular favorite?
Ken Kesey: "Tricker the Squirrel" [*Little Tricker the Squirrel Meets Big Double the Bear*] I think is the best piece I ever wrote. It's intricate and well wrought. The best long piece is *Sometimes a Great Notion*. I'll never come up with a better book.

Mary Jane Fenex: Why?
KK: I don't know, but Alberto Salazaar ain't gonna win the New York Marathon. There's a thing you have when you're young. Me and, oh, Norman Mailer have talked about this. About how hard it is in America to get better. Especially at writing.

MJF: Do you think it's the influence of American culture that we can only go so far?
KK: I saw Jerzy Kosinski just before he died—before he committed suicide—and talked to him about this. He said in Europe you make one good book, one good movie, and you're set. In America you're expected to best yourself every year and that in itself is crippling.

143

With *Sometimes a Great Notion* I was able to work twenty or thirty hours at a whack and I had all this stuff in my mind. I've been to too many Dead concerts. There've been smokin' holes where my memory used to be.

MR: The things you did with style, with narrative, with splicing stuff . . .
KK: It was exciting. Gurney Norman, a good writer friend of mine (*Divine Right's Trip*), said he really envied me that book because there's something about taking a plow and breaking new ground. It gives you energy. And when I was really sailing along on that, I knew that I was doing stuff that had never been done, and nothing I've done since has been anything like that.

"My best work is this kind of stuff," Kesey says, pulling coins out of his pocket and doing a quick slight of hand trick. "That has to do with art at its best. It leaves you with that little crack in your mind. The bus trip . . . 60,000 books every season and there's only one of those. And that communicates something that can't be bottled and sold, so people don't think of it as valuable."

He taps a marker with the palm of his hand. Two coins fall out. Lutien is staring in awe. Lutien: "How'd you put that in?"

KK: I was doing magic acts around Oregon, my brother and I, when I was in high school. And my brother and I would travel around with my dad—he was manager of a creamery, and we'd do these shows for these kids—farm kids—before television, hardly any radio. We'd do these shows and the look that would come on these people's faces—it was wonderful. And I remember one time driving the bus through Boise. We were playing ball on top. The cops'd told us to get out of town and we were just about out of town and there were these two kids and we were playing ball on the top of the bus, making all of this noise. We saw these kids, and we threw a ball at them. One kid caught one. The other kid caught one and the bus went on. And I always thought about what do they tell their folks? "Where did you get the ball?" And that to me is art at its peak. There's a feeling for it in this country again. Of magic. You can feel it.

MJF: How do you define magic?
KK: Magic is seeing something that extends beyond the visible.
I'm just hoping to do a thing that I've been talking about a long time, which is what we were doing with the Dead twenty-five years ago. Bill Graham kind of took it over and we haven't gotten back to it. I call it ritual reality.

MR: Could you tell me more about ritual reality?

KK: Matthew, the virtual reality—it's that word *virtual* that goes back to the word virtue. Goodness. Goodness is something that is about to happen. It hasn't really happened. It is by virtue of its nature it will happen. But it won't happen without some kind of observance of it. Ritual is necessary for us to know anything. You've got to get out and pray to the sky to appreciate the sunshine; otherwise you're just a lizard standing there with the sun shining on you. We need the rituals or else we have to contrive our own because all of our rituals have been coopted and corrupted and taken from us and used by Coca-Cola and Nike.

A ritual has to be a little dangerous. It doesn't come cheap or free. The rituals we are trying to put together, we don't know what they are, but we feel the hunger for them. Everywhere I go, I feel the hunger for people wanting to be a part of a ritual. Not to be there and have somebody present something to them. It's almost being taken away from us by disco, by MTV, by bottled performances. That's why I like to see this whole punk group. The statement that they're making with their stuff. . . . This is ritual.

MR: What do you see as the role of the twenty-first-century shaman/mystic?

KK: Everything's still basically the same as it used to be. Fire hurts you when it burns you. If you fall in water, you drown, rocks bruise you, wolves bite you, you go through a certain bunch of things that are the same. The job of the shaman/mystic I think is to pull things away from the Freudian mind. Let's quit examining ourselves and trying to make ourselves psychologically perfect. We aren't and never will be.

I have a friend who teaches psychotherapy and they go through death experience and I said, "Hey you can roll around on the ground and agonize as much as you want, but it's not like it really is when you really have some-body you care for die." That confronting reality, we've been turned away from it. We don't want to think of the bad stuff that's going to happen to us, but it's life and we need to be able to reach our arms around it and say, "Hey, it's awful, and it's beautiful and I love it." People like Ginsberg, he teaches you to do that. That's why Kerouac was such a great writer. He tries to say, "Hey look at these people—these pops, these jazz players." Y'know you can't think of anybody in Kerouac's books that he puts down—except for Lou Little, the football coach at Columbia and he is hard on his case. . . .

I was driving around one time after Jed died. He'd been dead about two weeks and I was driving to a wrestling match and I was weeping and talking to him and I said, "Oh Jed, we really loved you," and I thought, "That doesn't sound right. Loved." You can't use it in the past tense. We still love him. Death does not stop that love at all.

When we were at the hospital these couples began to come around who'd lost kids, so for years after that, I still do, I write to people who lost kids. Because you don't think you need that. It's important shit.

When Pirsig's kid died, he wrote *Zen and the Art of Motorcycle Mainte-nance.* He wrote me a letter and we knew that this had happened to us, but it was larger than that. It had poetry to it and if you don't have that . . . if you don't have that dab of poetry and beauty and stuff, it's just too hard. You can't stand it. If love isn't stronger than death, then fuck it. I can't bear it. So I wrote the Kennedys after the one kid od'd, and I got a great letter back from Teddy Kennedy. That changes how you feel about somebody like that. When I was back in D.C., he came over and shook my hand and thanked me for the letter. That wavelength is above and beyond all this other political stuff.

Ken Kesey: The Art of Fiction No. 136

Robert Faggen / 1993

From *The Paris Review*, Issue 130, Spring 1994. Copyright © 1994 by The Paris Review. Used by permission of The Wylie Agency LLC.

At the center of Kesey's work are what he calls "little warriors" battling large forces. Over the years, some critics have praised his work for its maverick power and themes of defiance; others have questioned his wild and paranoid vision. He has been dubbed a renegade prophet, a subversive technophile, a spiritual junkie—characterizations that Kesey does little to discourage.

He lives in a spacious barn that was built in the '30s from a Sears Roebuck catalog. It is decorated in bright DayGlo colors. The stairs ascending to his loft-study are covered in streaks of neon green and pink, recalling the psychedelic designs made famous by Kesey's bus, Furthur. Inspired by these visual remnants of the '60s, Kesey works late into the night, observed, as he points out, by a parliament of owls.

This interview was conducted during several visits with Kesey at his Oregon farm in 1992 and 1993.

INTERVIEWER: Your only formal studies in fiction were as a fellow in Wallace Stegner's writing program at Stanford. What did you learn from Stegner and also from Malcolm Cowley?

KEN KESEY: The greatest thing Cowley taught me was to respect other writers' feelings. If writing is going to have any effect on people morally, it ought to affect the writer morally. It is important to support everyone who tries to write because their victories are your victories. So I have never really felt that bitter cattiness writers feel toward their peers.

INTERVIEWER: Yet you had a difficult relationship with Stegner. What were the differences between you?

KESEY: Shortly after *Cuckoo's Nest* came out, I did an interview with Gordon Lish for a magazine called *Genesis West.* I don't remember exactly what I said about Stegner, but it made him angry. When I heard he was angry I tried to see him, but his secretary wouldn't let me in. We never spoke again after that. Wally never did like me. At one point, I read that he had said he found me to be ineducable. I had to stew for a long time over what Stegner didn't like about me and my friends. We were part of an exceptional group, there's no doubt about it. There was Bob Stone, Gurney Norman, Wendell Berry, Ken Babbs, and Larry McMurtry. All of us who were part of that group are still very much in contact; we all support each other's work. Stegner was the great force that brought us all together. He put together a program that ruled literature in California and, in some ways, the rest of the nation for a long time. Stegner had traveled across the Great Plains and reached the Pacific but, as far as he was concerned, that was far enough. Some of us didn't believe that it was far enough and when we went farther than that, he took issue with it, especially when it was not happening in the usual literary bailiwicks that he was accustomed to. I took LSD and he stayed with Jack Daniel's; the line between us was drawn. That was, as far as he was concerned, the edge of the continent, and he thought you were supposed to stop there. I was younger than he was and I didn't see any reason to stop, so I kept moving forward, as did many of my friends. Ever since then, I have felt impelled into the future by Wally, by his dislike of what I was doing, of what we were doing. That was the kiss of approval in some way. I liked him and I actually think that he liked me. It was just that we were on different sides of the fence. When the Pranksters got together and headed off on a bus to deal with the future of our synapses, we knew that Wally didn't like what we were doing and that was good enough for us. A few years ago, I taught a course at the University of Oregon. I began to appreciate Wally much more after I had been a teacher. Every writer I know teaches— at some point, even if you don't need the money, you have to teach what you were taught, especially if you were taught by a great coach.

INTERVIEWER: Did your experience at Stanford drive you to an anti-intellectual stance?

KESEY: The reason you read great authors—Thomas Paine, Jefferson, Thoreau, Emerson—is not because you really want to teach them, though that's one of the things you find yourself doing because you know it's important that they be taught. You study literature because you're a scholar of what's fair. It's just a way of learning how to be what we want to be. We go to concerts to hear a piece by Bach not because we want to be intellectuals or scholars or students of Bach, but because the music is going to help us keep our moral compass needle clean.

INTERVIEWER: What connection is there between Ken Kesey the magician-prankster and Ken Kesey the writer?

KESEY: The common denominator is the joker. It's the symbol of the prankster. Tarot scholars say that if it weren't for the fool, the rest of the cards would not exist. The rest of the cards exist for the benefit of the fool. The fool in tarot is this naive innocent spirit with a rucksack over his shoulder like Kerouac, his eyes up into the sky like Yeats, and his dog biting his rump as he steps over the cliff. We found one once at a big military march in Santa Cruz. Thousands of soldiers marching by. All it took was one fool on the street corner pointing and laughing, and the soldiers began to be uncomfortable, self-conscious. That fool of Shakespeare's, the actor Robert Armin, became so popular that finally Shakespeare wrote him out of *Henry IV*. In a book called *A Nest of Ninnies*, Armin wrote about the difference between a fool artificial and a fool natural. And the way Armin defines the two is important; the character Jack Oates is a true fool natural. He never stops being a fool to save himself; he never tries to do anything but anger his master, Sir William. A fool artificial is always trying to please; he's a lackey. Ronald McDonald is a fool artificial. Hunter Thompson is a fool natural. So was the Little Tramp. Neal Cassady was a fool natural, the best one we knew.

INTERVIEWER: Neal Cassady was a muse to the Beats and became one to you as you started writing. When did you first encounter him?

KESEY: It was 1960. He had just finished the two years he served in the pen. He showed up at my place on Perry Lane when I was at Stanford. He arrived in a Jeep with a blown transmission, and before I was able to get outside and see what was going on, Cassady had already stripped the transmission down into big pieces. He was talking a mile a minute and there was a crowd of people around him. He never explained why he was there, then or later. He always thought of these events as though he was being dealt cards on a table by hands greater than ours. But that was one of my earliest impressions of him as I watched him running around, this frenetic, crazed character speaking in a monologue that sounded like *Finnegans Wake* played fast forward. He had just started to get involved in the drug experiments at the hospital in Menlo Park, as I had. I thought, Oh, my God, it could lead to this. I realized then that there was a choice. Cassady had gone down one road. I thought to myself, Are you going to go down that road with Burroughs, Ginsberg, and Kerouac—at that time still unproven crazies—or are you going to take the safer road that leads to John Updike. Cassady was a hero to all of us who followed the wild road, the hero who moved us all.

INTERVIEWER: Were there literary influences as well?

KESEY: Many of us had read Ginsberg's "Howl," Kerouac's *On the Road*, Kenneth Rexroth's work, Ferlinghetti's. I knew their work when I was a student at the University of Oregon. I had a tape of Ferlinghetti saying, "I'm sitting now outside of my pool hall watching the hipsters come by in their curious shoes." I wanted to go down to the North Beach area and see Mike's Pool Hall. That's where I met Ken Babbs and Bob Kaufman, a great poet and a casualty of exploration of the synapses.

INTERVIEWER: Do you think the drug experimentation produced mostly casualties? Do you think Cassady was one?

KESEY: I think most artists who, as the saying goes now, "push the envelope" wind up as casualties. If you think about the history of writers and artists, the best often don't end up with pleasant, comfortable lives; sometimes they go over the edge and lose it. I've been close to enough casualties to learn how to avoid that pitfall. Some critics like to argue that some of the Beats had a death wish. Cassady certainly didn't have a death wish. He had a more-than-life wish, an eternity wish. He was trying to recapture, as Burroughs says, the realities he had lost. He was storming the reality studio and trying to take the projector from the controllers who had been running it. When that happens you are bound to have some casualties.

INTERVIEWER: How did Cassady become the driver of your bus, Furthur?

KESEY: Cassady was around us often. There was one incident in particular when he truly impressed me not only as a madman, genius, and poet but also as an avatar—someone in contact with other powers. He took me to a racetrack near San Francisco. He was driving and talking very fast, checking his watch frantically, hoping we would get to the track on time. If we got to the track just before the last three races, we'd get in free. We made it just in time and we bet on the last two races. Cassady had a theory about betting he'd learned in jail from someone named Knee-Walking Jackson. His theory was that the third favorite at post time is often the horse most likely to upset the winner and make big money. Cassady's strategy was to step up to the tellers at the ticket booths just at post time. He'd glance up to see who was third favorite and put money on that horse. He didn't look at the horses, the jockeys, or the racing sheets. He said to me, This is going to be the one, I can feel it. He asked me for ten bucks and I gave it to him. He put three dollars down with my ten. Given the odds we would have made some good money. We went right down to the line to watch, and it was a close race, neck and neck. I'm no horse fan, but I was getting into it because it looked like the third favorite could win. There was a photo finish and Cassady suddenly tore up his tickets and left. I followed him back to the car and could hear the announcement: We have a photo finish and the winner is . . . It turned out to be the favorite. Neal was so confident of his vision that if he lost, he never waited around or looked back.

Cassady was a hustler, a wheeler-dealer, a conniver. He was a scuffler. He never had new clothes but was always clean, and so were his clothes. He always had a toothbrush and was always trying to sell us little things and trying to find a place where he could wash up. Cassady was an elder to me and the other Pranksters, and we knew it. He was literally and figuratively behind the wheel of our bus, driving it the way Charlie Parker worked the saxophone. When he was driving, he was improvising an endless monologue about what he was seeing and thinking, what we were seeing and thinking, and what we had seen, thought, and remembered. Proust was his literary hero and he would quote long passages from Proust and Melville from memory, lacing his revelations with passages from the Bible. He was a great teacher and we all knew it and were affected by him.

INTERVIEWER: What did you learn from Cassady?

KESEY: I've listened to the tapes from the bus trip and reread his letters and autobiography—*The First Third*—for years. I've tried to distill his teachings as best I can. The most important lesson is also the most ironic: most of what is important cannot be taught except by experience. His most powerful lesson behind the rap was not to dwell on mistakes. He used the metaphor of driving. He believed that you got into trouble by overcorrecting. A certain sloth, he thought, lets you veer into a ditch on the right side of the road. Then you overcorrect and hit a car to your left. Cassady believed you had to be correcting every instant. The longer you let things go, the longer you stayed comfortable, the more likely the case that you would have to overcorrect. Then you would have created a big error. The virtue of continual, engaged experience—an endless and relentless argument with the self—that was his lesson.

INTERVIEWER: What do you think of Wolfe's account of you and the Pranksters in *The Electric Kool-Aid Acid Test*?

KESEY: When the galleys came out, we all read through them in one session. I had no major problems with the book then, though I haven't looked at it since. When he was around us, he took no notes. I suppose he prides himself on his good memory. His memory may be good, but it's his memory and not mine.

INTERVIEWER: You met Jack Kerouac and Allen Ginsberg at a party in Manhattan during the bus trip. What happened at that encounter?

KESEY: That was the first time I had met Kerouac. It was an important moment for me. I'd known Ginsberg and Dick Alpert—before he became Ram Dass—back at Perry Lane. Ginsberg was good friends with Vik Lovell, the guy who got me involved in the Menlo Park hospital and to whom I dedicated *Cuckoo's Nest*. Ginsberg and Alpert were part of IFIF, the International Federation for Internal Freedom. That was the Millbrook psychological experiment group that included Timothy Leary. Our group on the bus was known as ISIS, the Intrepid Search for Inner Space.

I have thought about that meeting hundreds of times since then. We wanted Kerouac to be the same way he was when he wrote *On the Road*. I find the same thing happening to me when people show up and expect me to be the way I was twenty-five years ago. Kerouac seemed offended by our wildness, particularly by the way we were wearing American flags draped around our heads. He thought we were being derisive of the United States. But we weren't. We just liked the look of dressing in the flag. I was disappointed in myself for not going up to him and sincerely expressing how much his work meant to me. But it wasn't the right time and I needed to say it in a letter.

After Kerouac died, his agent gave me a letter from his wife, Stella. She was very bitter that people had passed Jack by and instead were looking at people like me as the new literary lions. I wrote her back and told her that I couldn't hold a candle to him. His life's work will stand for centuries. I can't say that about Mailer or Updike or Kosinski. But I believe that people will be reading *On the Road* centuries from now as the true lens into our time.

In his writing Kerouac was true to his vision to the end. He believed there were drama and glory in the most mundane parts of our lives. And all things—running across a football field, the smell of leaves, the sound of a car—became charged with romance in Kerouac's imagination. Kerouac didn't have to have much money, and he didn't have to be famous. But he was part of the ongoing exploration of the American frontier, looking for new land, trying to escape the dust bowls of existence. He had a deep connection to the American romantic vision. Kerouac was a giant to the end, a sad giant. But then giants are usually sad.

INTERVIEWER: How much of Neal Cassady went into the making of Randle P. McMurphy?
KESEY: He's part of the myth. The Irish names—Kesey, Cassady, McMurphy—were all together in my mind as well as a sense of Irish blarney. That's part of the romantic naïveté of McMurphy. But McMurphy was born a long time before I met Neal Cassady. The character of McMurphy comes from Sunday matinees, from American Westerns. He's Shane that rides into town, shoots the bad guys, and gets killed in the course of the movie. McMurphy is a particular American cowboy hero, almost two-dimensional. He gains dimension from being viewed through the lens of Chief Bromden's Indian consciousness.

INTERVIEWER: You were working at the Veterans Administration Medical Center in Menlo Park participating in experiments with psychedelic drugs. How much did those drugs affect you or help you to write *Cuckoo's Nest*?
KESEY: I was taking mescaline and LSD. It gave me a different perspective on the people in the mental hospital, a sense that maybe they were not so crazy or as bad as the sterile environment they were living in. But psychedelics are only keys to worlds that are already there. The images are not there in the white crystals in the gelatin capsule. Drugs don't create characters or stories any more than pencils do. They are merely instruments that help get them on the page.

INTERVIEWER: Do you use LSD or other drugs when you sit down to write?
KESEY: It's impossible for me to write on LSD—there are more important things to think about. Hunter Thompson can do it, but I can't. It's like diving down to look at coral reefs. You can't write about what you've seen until you're back up in the boat. Almost every writer I know drinks to ease the burden of being out on the cliffs, so to speak. But writing under the influence of drugs is a little like a plumber trying to fix the pipes without being able to work the wrench.

I did write the first several pages of *Cuckoo's Nest* on peyote and I changed very little of it. It had little effect on the plot but the mood and particularly the voice in those first few pages remained throughout the book. There were also some sections of *Sometimes a Great Notion* written when I was taking mushrooms. Again, the effect is more on mood and voice than on vision. But for the most part, I don't write under the influence of LSD or other drugs.

INTERVIEWER: Do you take notes when you use LSD or other hallucinogens?

KESEY: Yes, sometimes I use a little tape recorder for notes. There's often a big difference between what you think you wrote under the influence and what you actually recorded. One time a friend of mine and I were taking LSD and thought we had written "The History and Future of the Universe." What we actually wrote down was something on the order of "if you pick your nose long enough the world will unravel." But often when I am taking LSD, there is an accessing of a universal pool of images, forms that I often find, for example, in Indian art. By the time I started taking peyote and LSD, I had already done a great deal of reading about mysticism—the Bhagavad Gita and Zen and Christian mystical texts. They helped me to interpret what I was seeing, to give it meaning. You don't just take the stuff and expect understanding. It's also important not to be in a hellish place with LSD or it can be a hellish experience. You need to be in a secure setting.

INTERVIEWER: Do any of the visions you have using LSD get translated into your writing?

KESEY: I'm fond of computer analogies. There are visions written on those programs that are hard to access or convert to the writing programs. I like to take it mostly for the spiritual experience.

INTERVIEWER: Do you recommend LSD as a tool for writing?
KESEY: No.

INTERVIEWER: To go back to *Cuckoo's Nest*, it seems that Chief Bromden's perspective is crucial. What was the origin of his character?
KESEY: Some have described Bromden as schizophrenic. But his is a philosophical craziness, not a clinical illness. I knew Indians who would eat mushrooms and sit and stare at the beach until the beach stared back at them. They're not unlike Baudelaire twisting himself so that he could look at flowers in a different way. They're still flowers and he knows they're flowers but he also sees them as eyes looking back at him. That's what Chief's

craziness is all about. The idea is to regain control of reality so it's no longer presented by public relations people or funneled through a Coca-Cola bottle. The reaction against control is often violent and destructive and lashes out in all directions, even against things that are beneficial. If a man doesn't have a little madness, he never breaks the control lock that gets placed on reality. It's facing the vast ocean alone, without the safety of land or boat.

My father used to take me to the Pendleton Roundup in northern Oregon. He would leave me there for a couple of days. I spent time hanging around the Indians living in the area. I used to take the bus back down through the Columbia River Gorge where they were putting in The Dalles Dam to provide electricity to that part of Oregon so the fields could be irrigated. But it was also going to flood the Celilo Falls, an ancient Indian fishing ground along the Columbia. The government was using scaffolding to build the dam. When I first came to Oregon, I'd see Indians out on the scaffolds with long tridents stabbing salmon trying to get up the falls. The government had bought out their village, moved them across the road where they built new shacks for them. One time, as we got closer to this dam project, we were pulled over by the cops. We were in a big line of traffic. The bus driver got out and walked up to see what was happening. He came back and told us, One of them crazy drunk Indians took a knife between his teeth and ran out into the highway and into the grill of an oncoming diesel truck, which was bringing conduit and piping to the dam project. I thought, Boy, that's far out. Finally, he couldn't take it anymore. He just had to grab his knife, go out into a freeway, and run into a truck. It was really the beginning of *Cuckoo's Nest*—the notion of what you have to pay for a lifestyle. It started an appreciation in me for the Indian sense of justice and drama. I mean, it's dumb and nasty, but that's class, and the fact that he had the knife between his teeth, that's style. So this Indian consciousness has been very important in all of the stuff that I write. It's not just in *Cuckoo's Nest*. The character Indian Jenny in *Sometimes a Great Notion* is very close to the character of Alice in *Sailor Song*. It is the dispossessed Indian spirit that's trying to reconnect with the white male spirit.

INTERVIEWER: In describing the Native American who hurled himself at the truck, you said he had both class and style. How do you distinguish between class and style?

KESEY: A woman who was a circus acrobat did one act for thirty years. She climbed atop of a 180-foot aluminum pole and stood on her head as her brother balanced her. One day she fell and died, and I remember reading about it in the paper. She fell, the pole fell, because it got too far over, and her brother couldn't keep up with it; he probably stepped on a peanut. She began to fall but she held her pose the whole way down and didn't scream. And of course she must have thought about it thousands of times: What am I gonna do if it ever gets to the point where I know I can't stop it, it's going to go all the way over, and I'm going to die. Can I hold my pose and not scream? She did, and that's class. Paul Krassner, who was there, told me, Yeah, but the fact that when she hit, she did the splits, that's style. So class is more important than style, but they're connected.

INTERVIEWER: What authors and works do you consider strong embodiments of class and style?

KESEY: Hemingway, because he built his work very rigidly and structured it with a lot of muscle. But Faulkner is so much better. In "The Bear," the prose just tumbles out like water out of a spring, especially in that primeval moment when we see a man posed on the back of the bear with the knife, hugging and hanging on. There is class in the character and class in the style. This takes training and discipline beyond anything Hemingway could imagine. This is Faulkner being true to a very deep source and letting it run, letting it go, not perverting it. Hemingway's prose holds up a mirror. He walks around in front of it and works on style. Faulkner's prose doesn't have time for a mirror. It's tumbling and tumbling, and this takes trusting and courage.

Eudora Welty has tremendous class, not just in her work, but in the way she walks, the look in her eyes, the way she has conducted her life. Kerouac had lots of class—stumbling drunk in the end, but read those last books. He never blames anybody else; he always blames himself. If there is a bad guy, it's poor old drunk Jack, stumbling around. You never hear him railing at the government or railing at this or that. He likes trains, people, bums, cars. He just paints a wonderful picture of Norman Rockwell's world. Of course it's Norman Rockwell on a lot of dope.

Jack London had class. He wasn't a very good writer, but he had tremendous class. And nobody had more class than Melville. To do what he did in *Moby-Dick*, to tell a story and to risk putting so much material into it. If you could weigh a book, I don't know any book that would be more full. It's more full than *War and Peace* or *The Brothers Karamazov*. It has Saint Elmo's fire, and great whales, and grand arguments between heroes, and secret passions. It risks wandering far, far out into the globe. Melville took on the whole world, saw it all in a vision, and risked everything in prose that sings. You have a sense from the very beginning that Melville had a vision in his mind of what this book was going to look like, and he trusted himself to follow it through all the way.

INTERVIEWER: What do you see as evil in the world and how do you depict it?

KESEY: In my novels and stories, evil is always the thing that seems to control. In *Cuckoo's Nest*, it's the combine. In *Sometimes a Great Notion*, it's the symbol of the river, eating away, leveling, trying to make that town the same. In *Demon Box*, the villain is entropy. That natural running-down of energy is the fear that the refrigerator is going to be empty, that we're not going to have enough of something; that fear makes you vulnerable to every kind of scam artist trying to sell a solution. But the real villain is not entropy. It's the notion that entropy is the only choice. And there are a lot of other choices that we can find in religion, philosophy, or art.

INTERVIEWER: In *Cuckoo's Nest*, Big Nurse is often regarded as the embodiment of evil. Do you think that is an accurate representation of her?

KESEY: Recently, I was over in Newport at the opening of the Oregon Coast Aquarium, which has been seven years in the making. I was performing *The Sea Lion* in the Newport Performing Arts Center. Afterwards a white-haired old woman approached me and said, Hey, you remember me? I looked her over, and I knew I remembered her, but had no idea who she was. She said, Lois. It still didn't click. She said, Lois Learned, Big Nurse, and I thought, Oh my God. She was a volunteer at Newport, long since retired from the nursing business. This was the nurse on the ward I worked on at the Menlo Park hospital. I didn't know what to think and she didn't either, but I was glad she came up to me. I felt there was a lesson in it, the same one I had tried to teach Hollywood. She's not the villain. She might be the minion of the villain, but she's really just a big old tough ex-army nurse who is trying to do the best she can according to the rules that she has been given. She worked for the villain and believed in the villain, but she ain't the villain.

INTERVIEWER: Do you believe that individuals have to be held accountable for evil, even if they are not the ultimate source?

KESEY: I may, as they say in jail, hang the jacket on them, but I'm not the judge. I can expose something, but as you get older and hopefully wiser, you find that blame and punishment beget only more blame and punishment.

I'm probably, from another person's point of view, the Big Nurse in somebody else's story. The thing that changes as you get older is your belief that certain people are bad forever or good forever. We're not. It wouldn't make any sense to write if we were. With blame, you either resist it or you pick up rocks and throw them at who's to blame. Wendell Berry talks about that when he says we all have the capacity to do evil but we have to learn to forbear it. What keeps us from being monsters are Emerson and Thoreau and the Beatles and Bob Dylan—great artists who teach us to love and hold off on the hurt. The hurt is inside of us, and of course we can always randomly hurt something, but a great artist will teach you to love a thing and not want to possess it or alter it—just to love it. You finally have to love Big Nurse. It's the symbol behind her, the combine, that makes her do what she does. You've got to fight that, but finally you have to love them all—the poor, broken human beings, even the worst of them.

INTERVIEWER: Your novels have been popular in Eastern Europe and translated in the former Communist-bloc countries. How do you account for that?

KESEY: They were allowed in all the Communist-bloc countries because the authorities considered them anti-American. Totalitarians never see themselves as being totalitarians; they always see that in the other guys. And *Cuckoo's Nest* is, to some extent, anti-American. It's about American terror. Big Nurse works for an American bad guy, the combine, the inhuman part of American industrialism.

INTERVIEWER: Why did you break off from writing the screenplay for *Cuckoo's Nest*?

KESEY: I was contracted to do the screenplay, but they wanted me to do it a certain way, leaving out the narrative thread of Chief's perspective and making Big Nurse the center of evil. And there were other disputes.

INTERVIEWER: What do you think of the movie?

KESEY: I've never seen it. We were arguing with lawyers and the issue was whether I had been paid adequately. I was fussing with them. They said, Why are you coming on like that, you'll be the first in line to see that movie. I said, I swear to God I'll never see that movie. I did it in front of the lawyers and I'd hate to go to heaven and have these two lawyers calling me on it. I mean, to lie to a lawyer, that's low.

INTERVIEWER: Do you see the inhuman evil present in nature?

KESEY: No, evil is part of the human consciousness. A baboon may get a harem and rape and hurt, then some other baboon will tear that baboon up eventually. It's part of baboonery and it's gonna be there. The evil force isn't interested in baboons or daisies. The evil force wants to hang human souls on its walls for some reason, and I don't think of it as satanic. It's lukewarm. As Christ says, hot and cold are cool, but evil is lukewarm, and it's a drag.

When I see bad-looking bikers with black leather studs on their wrists hanging out at the Oregon Country Fair, I take it as a sign of health. No, I don't want them hanging around, but trying to eliminate them all, arrest them all, legislate against them all—that's evil. I have asked feminists, If you could, would you eliminate all male chauvinist pigs? If you could come up with some kind of spray to spray in the air and do away with them, would you? Would you do away with all scorpions and rattlesnakes, mosquitoes? Mosquitoes are part of the ecosystem. So are male chauvinist pigs. You've got to fight them, but you don't try to exterminate them. A purifying group or system that would eliminate them all—that would be an evil force. Anytime you have a force that comes along and says, We will eradicate these people, you have evil. Looking back in history, what has seemed the worst turns out not to be the worst. Imagine how the Catholics must have talked about Galileo, how he must have seemed a great evil to them. But as time went on, it turned out that he was not only a good human being but good for the Catholic Church.

INTERVIEWER: Your heroes are often little warriors against big enemies. If the writer is a "warrior," who is his enemy?

KESEY: When I begin to try to follow the money, as they say in *All the President's Men*, up the evil ladder, past the businessmen, past the Mafia, past the leaders in the state, I ask, Who is doing the stuff, who is pulling the cords? It looks an awful lot like God. It's the big fascist in the sky. But all of this religion, government, and civilization bending toward God is dangerous. There's nothing worse for a forest than to have all the trees be the same. So you think, Well, maybe this isn't God. Maybe this is the famous Antichrist who's been the bad guy all along. The good guys, the real God, are hippies in tie-dyes out at the Oregon Country Fair, who are providing a sprinkle of mischief and chaos to keep things from becoming mud all over. As Burroughs says, the job of the writer is that of an exterminator. You're trying to battle the evil bugs that have crawled into our works and get in the way of exploring the hollow. Zora Neale Hurston and Louise Erdrich are good examples of warriors. So is Tom Robbins. People laugh and point at him, but that's just because he's on the West Coast and he won't dress up in the right clothes. His prose is like that motley that the fool wears, and it's easy to be impatient with him, but he's a warrior the same way that old Hunter Thompson is a warrior.

INTERVIEWER: Are there other contemporary evils for which you believe the writer has to account?

KESEY: In Kurt Vonnegut's book *Cat's Cradle*, the worst thing that ever happens to a marine is mud, and there is a thing called ice-nine that you can add to mud to solidify it. But then all the mud around the world starts to go solid. We have to try to fight anything that is going to create solid mud worldwide.

INTERVIEWER: *Sometimes a Great Notion* begins and ends with the image of Henry Stamper's amputated arm with its middle finger extended. Did you structure the book around this image?

KESEY: The image of the amputated arm came to me before I knew whose arm it was. Writing the book was the way to figure out who belonged to the arm and why. In writing the book I figured out what the symbol meant. First, I thought that Stamper was the hero, fighting the union's attempt to control the family. But in retrospect, the river is the controlling force the family is battling. The Stamper brothers, Hank and Lee, are matching wills and egos over Vivian. When Vivian leaves at the end, she leaves the people she loves for a dark future, but one in which she isn't controlled. Mother Nature throws off the forces that try to control her. Old feminism, women's lib, had something to do with that, but I didn't know it at the time.

INTERVIEWER: *Sometimes a Great Notion* is much more ambitious than *Cuckoo's Nest*. Do you think it is as successful?

KESEY: It's my best work, and I'll never write anything that good again. It's a question of time spent on it. I worked on *Notion* for two years without interruption, exploring symbols and characters and letting the narrative take its own way.

INTERVIEWER: Did you have a model for the narrative experimentation in *Sometimes a Great Notion*?

KESEY: Orson Welles's film *The Magnificent Ambersons* influenced

Sometimes a Great Notion quite a lot in its ability to move narrative along by going from situation to situation with just a few lines of dialogue by one of the characters. Someone would say the next thing we needed to know and there would be a cut to that shot. The first part of *The Magnificent Ambersons* covers quite a long period in a very short time, and you get to see the characters in a structured, stylized way—they step out on stage and deliver lines that help with the exposition. That influenced me in terms of structure.

INTERVIEWER: After *Sometimes a Great Notion*, you set out on the bus Furthur. What did you want to explore?

KESEY: What I explore in all my work—wilderness. I like that saying of Thoreau's that "in wildness is the preservation of the world." Settlers on this continent from the beginning have been seeking that wilderness and its wildness. The explorers and pioneers were out on the edge, seeking that wildness because they could sense that in Europe everything had become locked tight with things. The things were owned by all the same people and all of the roads went in the same direction forever. When we got here there was a sense of possibility and new direction, and it had to do with wildness. Throughout the work of James Fenimore Cooper there is what I call the American terror. It's very important to our literature and it's important to who we are: the terror of the Hurons out there, the terror of the bear, the avalanche, the tornado—whatever may be over the next horizon. It could be the biggest, most awful thing in the world. As we came to the end of the continent, we manufactured our terror. We put together the bomb. Now even that bomb is betraying us. We don't have the bomb hanging over our heads to terrify us and give us reason to dress up in manly deerskin and go forth to battle it. There's something we're afraid of, but it doesn't have the clear delineation of the terror the Hurons gave us or the hydrogen bomb in the cold war. It's fuzzy, and it's fuzzy because the people who are in control don't want you to draw a bead on the real danger, the real terror in this country.

INTERVIEWER: What is the "real terror" in America?

KESEY: When people ask me about LSD, I always make a point of telling them you can have the shit scared out of you with LSD because it exposes something, something hollow. Let's say you have been getting on your knees and bowing and worshiping; suddenly, you take LSD and you look and there's just a hole, there's nothing there. The Catholic Church fills this hole with candles and flowers and litanies and opulence. The Protestant Church fills it with hand-wringing and pumped-up squeezing emotions because they can't afford the flowers and the candles. The Jews fill this hole with weeping and browbeating and beseeching of the sky: How long, how long are you gonna treat us like this? The Muslims fill it with rigidity and guns and a militant ethos. But all of us know that's not what is supposed to be in that hole. After I had been at Stanford two years, I was into LSD. I began to see that the books I thought were the true accounting books—my grades, how I'd done in other schools, how I'd performed at jobs, whether I had paid off my car or not—were not at all the true books. There were other books that were being kept, real books. In those real books is the real accounting of your life. And the mind says, Oh, this is titillating. So you want to take some more LSD and see what else is there. And soon I had the experience that everyone who's ever dabbled in psychedelics has. A big hand grabs you by the back of the neck, and you hear a voice saying, So you want to see the books. OK, here are the books. And it pushes your face right down into all of your cruelties and all of your meanness, all the times that you have been insensitive, intolerant, racist, sexist. It's all there, and you read it. That's what you're really stuck with. You can't take your nose up off the books. You hate them. You hate who you are. You hate the fact that somebody has been keeping track, just as you feared. You hate it, but you can't move your arms for eight hours. Before you take any acid again you start trying to juggle the books. You start trying to be a little better person. Then you get the surprise. The next thing that happens is that you're leaning over looking at the books and you feel the lack of the hand at the back of your neck. The thing that was forcing you to look at the books is no longer there. There's only a big hollow, the great American wild hollow, which is scarier than hell, scarier than purgatory or Satan. It's the fact that there isn't any hell or there isn't any purgatory, there isn't any Satan. And all you've got is Sartre sitting there with his momma—harsh, bleak, worse than guilt. And if you've got courage, you go ahead and examine that hollow. That's the wilderness that I've always wanted to explore, and it's connected to the idea of freedom, but it's a terrifying freedom. I'm working on a book *called The Seven Prayers of Grandma Whittier.* The idea is to take someone who is a very strong, very devout Christian and put her into a situation in which she loses her faith and show how she wrestles and comes back from this hollow. And so my grandma, who's a hundred years old this year, and I are in some way linked in an excursion into her dark hole of Alzheimer's. You know she must be something even though she can't remember the Lord's Prayer or read the

Bible anymore. She's alive, but that's it. You can go into that hollow and still come out of it and have a positive life.

INTERVIEWER: And that hollow is, for you, the new wilderness?
KESEY: That's the new wilderness. It's the same old wilderness, just no longer up on that hill or around that bend or in the gully. It's the fact that there is no more hill or gully, that the hollow is there and you've got to explore the hollow with faith. If you don't have faith that there is something down there, pretty soon when you're in the hollow, you begin to get scared and start shaking. That's when you stop taking acid and start taking coke and drinking booze and start trying to fill the hollow with depressants and Valium. Real warriors like William Burroughs or Leonard Cohen or Wallace Stevens examine the hollow as well as anybody; they get in there, look far into the dark, and yet come out with poetry.

INTERVIEWER: Have you ever felt that you were going too far into void, getting too twisted to come out?
KESEY: Many times I feel I have been way out, but I always come back. I have my family, my wife Faye, the farm, chickens, and cows. The earthly world calls out to you in clear voices that you must come back. Those earthly voices are far better than anything I've heard crying in the night.

INTERVIEWER: After *Sometimes a Great Notion*, you seem to have grown dissatisfied with the novel as a medium. Do you prefer public performance?
KESEY: Yes. The first rule—whether you are a writer or a dancer or a fiddle player or a painter—is "don't bore people." My dad used to say that good writing ain't necessarily good reading. A lot of people think good writing is like the compulsories in figure skating; it goes round in circles and doesn't go anywhere. If I'm going to skate, I'm going to race.

At one point, I was trying to write an illuminated novel with pictures and different kinds of print, experimenting with visual form as well as prose form. It's not right yet. But I haven't felt like I have taken a vacation from my work. I feel that I am continuing to probe into that big hollow, but the traditional form of the novel won't do. My metaphor has been that I've been dating Emily Brontë and the old dame just ain't putting out like she used to. The novel is a noble, classic form but it doesn't have the juice it used to. If Shakespeare were alive today he'd be writing soap opera, daytime TV, or experimenting with video. That's where the audience is. The audience is there even if there's a lot of mediocrity in the writing. I have just completed a play, *Twister*. Writing drama for a live audience is exciting, almost addictive.

INTERVIEWER: What do you think of when you think of an audience?

KESEY: I was in a quandary about my audience when I was working on *Notion* until I realized that I'm not writing for the East Coast literary establishment. I am writing for Mountain Girl and Jerry Garcia's oldest girl, Annabelle—she's a great Stephen King fan. She just reads and reads. She likes something that's got a little zip to it. At one point, I realized that's who I'm writing for. If Annabelle Garcia reads this book, gets excited, and grins about it, then I have hit my audience and all the rest just ricochets.

INTERVIEWER: Some of your most recent works have been children's stories, *Little Tricker the Squirrel Meets Big Double the Bear*, as well as *The Sea Lion*, which also appears as part of your recent novel, *Sailor Song*. What are the attractions and challenges of writing for children?

KESEY: When you go into the arena before a group of kids you don't care what Christopher Lehmann-Haupt said about you in previous reviews in the *New York Times*. Your strokes are broader, because all the little fine brush lines are lost on a kid. But the message beneath them has to be clearer. In a kid's story like "Pinocchio" the message is clearly communicated—if you lie, your nose gets bigger. In a novel you have to conceal it, or you're accused of being too obvious. When you're writing for kids, all you have to have is a good story; it will be accepted. Also, you can tell whether it works when you read it to a kid. It's hard for a writer to tell when a novel works.

INTERVIEWER: When you were five, your maternal grandmother, Grandma Smith, told you the original story of Little Tricker.

KESEY: What I remember most about the way she told the story are the repetitions, the series of threes in the events, the alliteration in the language. She taught me the speech rhythms that are essential to being a good storyteller. There is a drumbeat, in which you have to get your idea across in a breath. She also taught me a great deal about irony. When you think of irony, you've got to think of an outside force looking in. Irony doesn't exist without a god of some kind. Irony is not a trait many kids learn. It's not just God sitting up there laughing at you; there's the whole universe sort of grinning wryly at you. The main point she taught me is how essential wonder is to a storyteller. The storyteller himself has to feel wonder in order to communicate it. Somehow I don't think that sense of mystery can be taught to you by your parents. It has to be taught by your grandparents or perhaps your aunts and uncles.

INTERVIEWER: Did Grandma Smith inspire you to become a writer?
KESEY: It was all part of doing magic shows when I was a kid. For one thing, you have to talk, explain things as you go along. I would go to farm producers' meetings with my dad and perform tricks for farmers and their kids. I always found a mean little redheaded kid in the audience. I would get him up on the stage and announce that I was going to tell a story about the pasteurization of milk. Chuck, my brother, helped me with an ice pick and a funnel. I pretended to bore a hole in the top of this kid's head with the ice pick, explaining that you had to use redheads because they are a whole lot more hotheaded than most people, and I poured the milk on top of his head, letting it run past his eyes, and explaining how when it comes down out your elbow, it's pure. Then I'd pump the milk out the elbow. A story went with each magic act, and the stories enhanced the act. This is what a shaman does: he has a little story and a few tricks along with it, a dance, some drumbeats, a painted set, and some beads strung together. Writing is just one of those parts. It has been elevated to the point that people think it is the "thing." It isn't. Shakespeare doesn't come alive until it's on stage. It's about performance.

INTERVIEWER: *Sailor Song* is your first novel in twenty-eight years. Do you consider it a comeback?
KESEY: Michael Douglas said to me when we were talking about doing a stage version of *Cuckoo's Nest*, Oh yeah, this would be a great comeback. I said, Good God, I didn't know I'd gone anywhere. I feel what I did with the bus, what I'm doing with my new play *Twister*, the political activity around here, reading these stories in children's hospitals, is all part of the same work. You put on a different costume. But you're always a shaman. The fire pit changes its shape. The fire gets more civilized when you're doing a reading back at the St. Mark's Church in the Bowery, but you're still a shaman. I haven't slacked off at all. But it has been really important and tremendously gratifying for me to finish a big book because no matter what you say, every writer knows that the novel is the bear and, as Faulkner says, every so often the dog has to go against the bear just to keep calling itself the dog. I set out to do this book in the early 1980s but got dragged away, mainly when my son Jed was killed. That really took the wind out of my sails. During that time I

did a lot of other things that were just ways of avoiding this book. I brought out *Demon Box*, a compilation of stories about the farm and the bus in what I think of as the comedown years—my gonzo time. But Viking wanted me to use my name and everybody's real names. *Demon Box* is fiction, although not many people would appreciate the fact that some of the stories happened and some of them didn't. *The Further Inquiry*, a screenplay about the bus, turned up in a box back at Viking. *Caverns*, a collaborative novel from a writing class I taught at the University of Oregon, was brought out. So these books came out as I was trying to avoid getting back to *Sailor Song*.

INTERVIEWER: What was the genesis of *Sailor Song*? You published *The Sea Lion*, the children's story which appears in *Sailor Song*, before the novel. Did one precede the other or did they evolve together?

KESEY: When I began *Sailor Song* I didn't have the story thought out, just the vision of what happens when a movie company comes to a little Alaskan town and takes it over. I needed a story within the story; I wanted it to be an ancient-seeming story, around which the larger tale could be folded. Then, as Larry McMurtry says, it was the job of the fiction writer to make stuff up, so I made up *The Sea Lion*. Although the two stories pretty much evolved together, the ideas behind *The Sea Lion* began when my brother and I went up to see an Indian storyteller in Washington up on the slopes of Mount Saint Helens. A family called Laluska makes masks up there. Those Northwest Indian images are tremendously powerful and as yet pretty much unused. They haven't been bled dry like many of the images from the Plains Indians and from the Ojibwa art back on the East Coast. I saw that there was a terrific power to these faces and masks, especially the eyes. You could see that it came from the way wood knotholes are worked by surf, giving them the look of leather. They have taken it and styled it beautifully so that you can see that surf-worn quality more clearly. This was in some way connected to the story. You can't really separate the mask and the look from the story and the performance. Just hanging a mask on the wall makes it a piece of art in the museum, but if you put it on and use it as part of a story, then the story comes alive; the mask comes alive. The look of these masks was the way I wanted my work to look in the reader's mind. Fiction is when you twist what's out in front of you and stylize it so it's more clearly seen by the reader—just the same way that the Indian carvers can create an eye that looks more like an eye than an eye—a fictional eye that enables you to see better than the true eye did. That's what good fiction is always about. Reading *Moby-Dick*, you see a whale more clearly than you could see him by going over to the coast and watching through a pair of binoculars. It's the stylization of the whales that lets you see inside and outside of them, their mythical as well as their mundane qualities.

INTERVIEWER: In the title essay of *Demon Box*, you express remorse about the intrusion of the filmmaker and the artist's eye into both private suffering and uncorrupted wilderness. The effect of Hollywood on an Alaskan town is the dramatic center of *Sailor Song*. Have you come to view the film industry as an evil?

KESEY: Well, writers have always had a real love-hate relationship with Hollywood. Even if your book sells really well, you don't make that much money out of it unless Hollywood picks it up. So you want Hollywood's attention, yet you don't want it. There's a saying, often attributed to Hemingway, that sums up my feeling about having your novel turned into a film: I don't like to see my bull turned into a bouillon cube. In *Sailor Song*, I'm not really trying to put Hollywood down. It's just another force moving on this earth. It has its benefits and it's a nuisance. We know movies better than novels. Most writers have seen more movies than they've read books. It is the common denominator, two hours of story. Sometimes you'll get something that will go well into a miniseries like Larry McMurtry's *Lonesome Dove*. The miniseries is not a bad form because the story can be developed in a leisurely way.

INTERVIEWER: Has the vanishing of the frontier and wilderness changed what it means to create an American hero?

KESEY: In Western novels, especially Zane Grey novels, there is a code of the West that the hero and most of the characters in the novels adhere to. It has to do with fairness, courage, but in a lot of ways I think it mostly has to do with forgiveness. A guy in a Zane Grey novel can be a real bad outlaw, running with the bad bunch, but he comes up against a woman who changes his heart and his ways and the good guys who have been after him accept him back into the fold. The code of the West is that you may have done a lot of bad stuff in the past but you can always turn over a new leaf at any point and change. The problem now is that the good guys aren't the good guys anymore. You don't want to turn over a new leaf and become part of society because you've seen society's dirty underwear and it isn't much better than the bad guys' dirty underwear. Then you drop out of the hero business.

INTERVIEWER: In *Sailor Song* there is a conflict about how to read the Indian story, "The Sea Lion." One character sees it as meaningless for

American audiences looking for symbols and plots. Do you believe stories should have a discernible meaning?

KESEY: I'm for mystery, not interpretive answers. When I was working on *Caverns*, I found out that one of the problems was that students kept looking for the answers to symbolic riddles and believed that modern fiction is supposed to supply you with the answer. The answer is never the answer. What's really interesting is the mystery. If you seek the mystery instead of the answer, you'll always be seeking. I've never seen anybody really find the answer, but they think they have. So they stop thinking. But the job is to seek mystery, evoke mystery, plant a garden in which strange plants grow and mysteries bloom. The need for mystery is greater than the need for an answer.

INTERVIEWER: How did the class show its desire to provide an answer?

KESEY: One student tried to tie *Caverns* up in a Buddhistic bag. There were thirteen of us contributing to the book. Without telling any of us, he introduced into the last chapter four pages of material that was pure Diamond Sutra; it came from the Rajneesh. He was a disciple all along and he had been keeping this in his mind. His answer was the same kind of dogma that people spout when they think the answer is Christ or environmental awareness. Anytime they do that they're already joining with the forces of ice-nine-hard mud.

INTERVIEWER: What was your response to the student writer?

KESEY: After his reading, the class was just ready to string him up. He had violated one of the most important taboos in writing fiction. What are you gonna do to him? someone asked. I said, We're not going to do anything. We're not gonna talk about it. We won't speak of it. We will not ever speak again of this to him at all. He came in the door and he said, What do you think of my new piece? So we didn't speak of it. The last week of class went on and he began to get a strange look in his eyes. We had sent him to some kind of literary Coventry. It had to be taken care of because what I had told the class in the beginning of the year was that I was going to try to teach them the job of the serious writer in modern America as best I could. It was my last day of class, and I was trying to give some kind of closing lecture to tie this up in a little package they could take home with them. I told them they had all read and studied, that they could all write. They knew fiction far better than I did. If there had been a test, they'd have just walked all over me because they knew the history of literature and the history of style better than I did. But I told them, So you guys can write, and well enough that one of these days you're going to have a visitation. You're going to be walking down the street and across the street you're going to look and see God standing over there on the street corner motioning to you, saying, Come to me, come to me. And you will know it's God, there will be no doubt in your mind—he has slitty little eyes like Buddha, and he's got a long nice beard and blood on his hands. He's got a big Charlton Heston jaw like Moses, he's stacked like Venus, and he has a great jeweled scimitar like Mohammed. And God will tell you to come to him and sing his praises. And he will promise that if you do, all of the muses that ever visited Shakespeare will fly in your ear and out of your mouth like golden pennies. It's the job of the writer in America to say, Fuck you, God, fuck you and the Old Testament that you rode in on, fuck you. The job of the writer is to kiss no ass, no matter how big and holy and white and tempting and powerful. Anytime anybody says come to me and says, Write my advertisement, be my ad manager, tell him, Fuck you. The job is always to be exposing God as the crook, as the sleazeball. Nelson Algren says the job of the writer in America is to pull the judge down into the docket, get the person who is high down where he's low, make him feel what it's like where it's low.

INTERVIEWER: Do you believe that an author imposes his own cultural vision on his readers in this way?

KESEY: I think that the artist should feel obligated to force whatever he can upon his audience and be the authority because if he doesn't, some advertising man will. Ronald McDonald will be out there telling people what to think. The cynic who says, Oh, none of this counts anymore, is wrong. I can remember when I thought that too. But the older you get, the more you see people in the past who have thoughts that last. Things you think you're saying for the first time ever, have been said better before by Shakespeare, though they may need saying again. As Faulkner says, there are the old verities. Revenge is about the same as it always was.

Ken Kesey: Still on the Bus

Robert K. Elder / 1999

A shorter version of this interview appeared on *Salon* magazine November 2001. © Robert K. Elder 1999. Reprinted by permission.

Time slows you down, even if it doesn't change you. That was what struck me most when I visited Ken Kesey for the last time in 1999. Though he had suffered a stroke eighteen months before, there were few outward indications. He couldn't handle a pen as well, but his eyes were bright and his head was full of new projects.

He was celebrating two thirty-fifth anniversary milestones, one for the publication of his novel *Sometimes a Great Notion* and the other for his first outing with the Merry Pranksters—but Kesey was looking to the future. "I've been more prolific than anybody imagines," he confided. "I just have piles and piles of stuff I've written."

Kesey was the kind of iconoclast who defined an entire era, inspiring artists and encouraging other writers—myself among them. I first met Kesey when I was a seventeen-year-old high school journalist and he was a traveling author, returning to the literary scene after a long hiatus. He had just published *Sailor's Song*, his first major work since the death of his son Jed and his first novel in twenty-eight years.

As I bumbled through that first interview, Kesey and his wife, Faye, couldn't have been more understanding. During our lunch, he gave me advice that had a powerful impact on my career. He said, "If you're going to be a journalist, just sink your teeth into it. Don't question it. It's not so important that you continue on the same line—it's that you commit yourself to something."

We spent much of that day together and Kesey astonished me later that evening when he bypassed an entire room of local literati and ditched his own book party to color with the children of patrons in the back room. But Kesey was like that—big-time generosity folded into gigantic nerve.

When I chose a college, my decision was influenced by Kesey, who told me about the University of Oregon and the green splendor of Eugene. He was an alumnus himself and had just finished teaching a course there. Over my time at the U of O, we became friends and I served as his archivist, annotating some of his personal papers at the Knight Library.

In 1999, I made one final visit to Kesey's Pleasant Hill farm. We sat outside and ate cashews on a splintered picnic table while we talked about his work, his health, and his family. A gifted, colorful raconteur, Kesey dodged as many questions as he answered and we kept chatting long after I ran out of tape.

The peacocks on Ken Kesey's Oregon farm sound like bawling babies. Their squawking drives Kesey nuts, but not half as much as when they climb on top of his writing sanctuary and pick fights with their reflections in the attic windows.

But it suits the literary renegade, the polychromatic birds fit in with the psychedelic décor of the place—even if they disturb its peace. With Faye, he lives in a fire engine red, converted barn nestled in the emerald countryside just outside Eugene, Oregon. Kesey's own wardrobe of tie-dyed work shirts and denim overalls make him look like the pit crew for Furthur, his blinding DayGlo colored bus, the Merry Prankster mobile, parked in the garage next to his computers and archived journals.

"When people ask me what my best work is, I always say the bus," Kesey says. "*Cuckoo's Nest* and *Great Notion*, they're good novels, but the bus is a living work, a work that is absolutely unique. That doesn't take away from the novels."

The original bus, the one driven by the amphetamine-fueled "fastest man alive" and Kerouac muse Neal Cassady, celebrates its thirty-fifth birthday rusting in a cow pasture. A plastic, science-class skeleton wearing sunglasses sits in the driver's seat, much as Cassady no doubt would, had he not died in Mexico of exposure and drugs decades earlier. Not only was Cassady Kerouac's Dean Moriarty in *On the Road*, but he could have doubled for Kesey's tragic hero Randall Patrick McMurphy in *One Flew Over the Cuckoo's Nest*.

That book, which launched Kesey's career in 1962, has had its share of attention. His much-ballyhooed fight with the producers of the 1975 movie version of *Cuckoo's Nest*, and subsequent refusal to see the Oscar-sweeping film, has received enough ink. But Kesey's career as a counterculture icon began after the 1964 publication of *Sometimes a Great Notion*, a sprawling family epic that Kesey contends outshines his freshman novel. That same year, he used his fame and his book advance to fund a trip across America turning people on to LSD (then a legal substance) and encouraging the populace to live life as a work of art. His psychedelic bus with his Merry Pranksters, and ensuing entanglements with the law, cemented Kesey as a true literary outlaw, a legend chronicled by Tom Wolfe in his book *The Electric Kool-Aid Acid Test.*

But that was thirty-five years ago. Sitting on his back porch, Kesey reflects on his double anniversaries, his life's work, and the friends not there to celebrate it with him. "I'm wiser, and I put more effort into trying to be thoughtful," Kesey says, watching his peacocks run at one another in the yard. "As you get older, you begin to see life itself as being more wonderful, and you're careful not to disturb it."

Kesey, sixty-four, still carries his barrel-chested wrestler's frame with grace, but he no longer sports the papa bear paunch of past years. In the years I've known Kesey, this is the best he's ever looked—trim, strong, and healthy. His eyes crackle with electricity as he discusses his plans for the future. Kamikaze hummingbirds swoop past our heads to nearby feeders as he talks about life as performance art.

It wasn't long ago that the curtain almost fell, prematurely, on his final act. A year and a half ago, Kesey suffered a mild stroke while going through some journals out in the garage. With immediate medical attention, and the use of an experimental drug tPA (or recombinant tissue plasminogen activator), Kesey has suffered few long-lasting effects normally associated with stroke victims. He still has trouble writing in longhand, but his typing skills haven't been affected much.

This was the second time Kesey has benefited from being a guinea pig for experimental drugs. (The first time: government-funded LSD experiments in Menlo Park, California, in the early '6os. Coupled with his work in a mental ward, the experiences inspired *Cuckoo's Nest.*) "It was more than the second time," Kesey says mischievously. He does not elaborate.

Faye half-jokes that she wishes the episode had scared him a little more, causing him to slow down. If anything, friends say, tasting his own mortality has made him work even harder. "He's gone balls to the wall now on everything we're doing," says Ken Babbs, Kesey's longtime friend and right-hand man.

"His energies are focused, really focused. When you get older, time speeds up. Through time, he's also grown more compassionate, loving and forgiving," Babbs says. "[He's] older and wiser and doing more things. He's not just a writer now; he's a complete artist, a performing artist."

Kesey, once the harbinger for change in pre-hippie America and leader of the consciousness-expansion revolution, hasn't let anything alter his course, although the velocity has changed. There have been endless court battles and police harassment, drug busts, jail, diabetes, and then the stroke. The death of his twenty-year-old son Jed in 1984 almost ended him, but he's survived it all. He's outlived most of his contemporaries and friends. Even Jerry Garcia, whose Grateful Dead provided the soundtrack for his Acid Test "happenings," is gone. Kesey sits relatively alone in the pantheon of '60s counterculture icons.

Earlier this year, this fact was illustrated when he was invited to the Sundance Film Festival for a screening of *The Source*, a new movie about the Beat Generation writers. An interview with Kesey appears as part of the documentary. "I don't have a large part in it; I was too young to be a beatnik, and too old to be a hippie," Kesey says. "But while I was there, I realized I was the only one of them left alive—Ginsberg was gone, Kerouac, Cassady, Burroughs."

Kesey attributes his longevity to his family and friends. "Those guys really didn't have a lot of family, and their circle was made up of literary professorial contemporaries," Kesey says. "I've always stuck pretty close to my family, and I think that's one of the reasons I've survived a lot of stuff that other people didn't."

And he's become more prolific. This year, Kesey has unearthed some of his jail manuscripts and journals, to be published as *Kesey's Jailbook* later this year. [The book was published posthumously in 2003 as *Kesey's Jail Journal*.] He's also started writing another book, tentatively called *Animals*, and in August finished with a Merry Prankster tour of England where the group performed the musical interactive play *The Search for King Arthur*.

Writing and performing are the same to him, although he's done more of the former in recent years. He quit writing for a while, announcing that he'd rather live his life like a work of art, but that stage was relatively short-lived.

His word processor was never really able to stay silent. Kesey continued magazine work, writing for *Rolling Stone* and starting his own literary magazine, *Spit in the Ocean*. The 1990s saw two new novels, *Sailor Song* and *Last Go Round*. Of his two children's books, *The Sea Lion* and *Tricker the Squirrel Meets Big Double the Bear*, the latter was included on the Library of Congress's list of suggested children's books in 1991. Then came *Twister*, a multimedia stage version of "The Wizard of Oz," with a dash of *The Rocky Horror Picture Show* thrown in for interactivity.

"*Twister* falls midway between a very modern publication, and a very, very ancient publication," Kesey says, feeling the cool of the evening and donning a sweater. "A publication is just that, when you put your work out in front of the public, that really opens it up . . . instead of saying publication is when you have something printed and distributed."

He continues: "I have a large body of work, that isn't published by the East Coast—like poetry festivals, and the Acid Tests. I'm grateful to New York for putting it out there, but I feel obligated to the sport of storytelling, to spread that out wherever I can."

Kesey works hard to preserve his standing as an accessible American icon. Fans can still find his number and address in the phone book. It can be an inconvenience from time to time, hosting strangers who show up on his lawn, but Kesey also understands the importance of legend, and he maintains it through constant contact with his audience. In addition to endless public appearances and support of community events, Kesey and Babbs also maintain a Website to communicate with their community and fans, IntrepidTrips.com.

"The idea of crawling off into your ivory tower and creating this thing that you slip out under the door, and then people publish it and you become famous, it's not healthy for the writer," Kesey says. "It's not really good for the public, because we're never really there.

"Writers are constantly complaining that they have to go to bookstores, etc. . . . but for me, that's part of the same job," Kesey continues. "You owe it to the work; you owe it to the reader. You owe it to all the storytellers that have come through history that have maintained that connection between audience and writer."

In part, the philosophy propelled Kesey's bus trip across America. In the pursuit of a new consciousness and life as art, the Merry Pranksters spread a message about drugs, peace, and love during a national identity crisis. Looking back on that time, Kesey says his association with psychedelic drugs wasn't overstated.

"I think drugs are tremendously important, and being high is important . . . but there are other ways to achieve enlightenment. Grief can do it. You can fast, you can pray," Kesey says. "LSD was the very serious thing. We were astronauts of interspace . . . it wasn't for the timid. But acid came along and we were trying to body forth a new consciousness, a completely new way to relate to your world."

Whether Kesey and company succeeded or not is up for generational debate, but his legacy remains forever tied to the '60s and a multicolored, technology hot-wired, suped-up bus with Cassady behind the wheel.

"I couldn't have done [the bus trips] without the writing," Kesey concedes. "I needed to have those type of publications under my belt before I could do something that outlandish. From that time on, I've never backed off from it," he says. "I write because I have to write. But I'm not writing to reveal my soul to the reader, I'm writing to reveal the reader's soul to the reader."

If he discovers something about himself along the way, then all the better.

"I still make loads of mistakes," Kesey says. "But I know now, when I'm so full of myself that it's not to my advantage or anyone else's."

What keeps Kesey going, keeps him writing, is what he describes as a single note. "If you've got that one true note ringing inside you, then whatever you do is going to be OK," Kesey says.

The note? "It's love, always love. If you've got love in your heart, whatever you do from that moment out is likely to be right."

Ken Kesey's Last Interview

Mike Finoia / 1999

A shorter version of this interview appeared in *Relix* magazine January 2002. © Mike Finoia 1999. Reprinted by permission.

I met Kesey at a Phish concert in upstate New York in the summer of '97. The Pranksters drove there in Furthur 2.0. I saw the bus from a distance and approached it in awe, like a child approaches a mall Santa Claus. And Kesey smiled and welcomed me in.

Fast-forward to senior year of college. I sold my advisor on a final project: I would interview concert goers on how the live music experience drives them to the road, and then I would interview Kesey about his experiences. She approved, but would Kesey? Would the lion allow me into the cage? He not only obliged but invited me to his home in Oregon. I jumped at the chance, and flew from Connecticut to the Pacific Northwest. I was twenty-one years old and scared out of my mind. But Kesey smiled and welcomed me in.

I stayed with him for a week. I wanted to know everything. I wanted to know what Garcia ate for breakfast. I wanted to understand the feeling of a cultural revolution. I needed to know how to trust my instincts and follow my heart and leave a mark on the world ahead of me. I wanted him to know how grateful I was for this unbelievable gift. And Kesey smiled and welcomed me in.

Mike Finoia: So that's the Thunder Machine?
Ken Kesey: Yeah, we've played that Thunder Machine with the Dead for decades, and they always hated it. (Laughs) In fact we'd go to a thing and ask, "Where should we put the Thunder Machine?" and they'd go "WHAT?" and I'd go "No, no, just kidding, just kidding."

MF: Describe a full Prankster practice.

KK: When we've got a full crew, Simon Babbs plays the bass banjo, Zane plays the Thunder Machine, I play the Theremin, George plays the AX-A-Phone, Babbs plays the trombone, Phil kind of waltzes around behind and plays all that stuff you were playing with. On the top of the Thunder Machine, you could blow air through it. CO_2 and an old factory whistle. We have two leads that come out it that work pretty good. And when it's all going, it all makes sound. Zane could really play it. It used to be impossible to take anywhere. And when we used to play it, we had no electricity hooked up to it at all. We'd wham this sucker.

MF: Where was your last Prankster performance?

KK: We played the week before last up at the Hemp Festival. Whammed it up there. We played—oh—forty-five minutes. And the longer we played, the more people came, which is a good sign. (Laughs) Apparently, we were playing a lot of Dead pieces, because Simon is in a band. He's always in a band. He could play just about anything. And Swan. So I always put them behind the machine so you see them back there playing with stuff before you actually see them step out with guitars. And so for a while it sounds like it's all coming from this thing. But the people that run the sound system didn't want to plug it in, because they were scared to death of it. Zane used to do it where you put a shotgun on top of here, a nice, old, double-barreled shotgun, and shoot off—kaboom! kaboom! And the shotgun shells filled with glitter and confetti and stuff would shoot out.

MF: Where did the AX-A-Phone come from?

KK: George Walker built that when he was the Tin Man in the play. And he could play it where people think he's playing. They don't know it is a kazoo going through a lot of effects.

MF: So The Pranksters and the Dead would play together?

KK: Yeah, all the time. The Acid Tests. We were equal. We'd slide out of our stuff and they'd slip into their stuff, back and forth. And the music had a real new level. We never knew whether it was good or not, but we would communicate.

MF: The Acid Tests drew the first real "Deadheads"—a beginning for both the Pranksters and the Dead civilization?

KK: Yes. When we first knew them, they were the Warlocks, and they used to come around and hang around Perry Lane before we were really big on rock music, which was an important thing, but we didn't realize it; we were grad students. And these longhaired younger kids were coming around for the first time. They were colorful, but we never really thought of them as being part of what we were doing until we began to split away from the university. We moved to La Honda and we started to have these things that would happen every Saturday night. We'd go out to the hill where we had the Thunder Machine in the earlier stages. We'd go out there, take acid, and plunk on that thing. And each weekend, there were more people and more people. And we'd plunk louder and play up there in the woods.

Finally, we had Rev. Anton LaVey and Kenneth Anger and that whole Satanic group come up to visit. By that time we were beginning to put on costumes and shows. I can remember when they were there; they were a serious bunch of people that believed in the devil—and we got on our most demonic outfits. At one point we led them up the hill to where the Thunder Machine was and sitting up there on a block was a birdcage—a nice big parrot cage sprayed golden—and in the cage was a chicken. We got up there and plunked and played and sang, worked ourselves up to a pitch, and went over and took that chicken out of the cage. Page Browning was at that time this character Z-Lot. Z-Lot was a pretty horrendous character. He took a lot of time putting on make-up, and that make-up looked like cracked granite. And he came up with an axe sprayed gold, everything was sprayed gold. And he reached in to take the chicken out of the cage and there was an egg, it laid an egg. And Herman saw that egg, oh, he was just delighted. He just ran up giggling and grabbed that egg, and he cracked it and ate it, all raw and warm and new. And, we stretched that chicken out over the block and chopped the chicken's head off, chanting these devilish songs. And all these Satanists began to get up and leave. (Laughs)

MF: You beat them at their own game.

KK: We got their attention. And we took that chicken and took it down and cooked it. And we played more music while we plucked and picked and cleaned the chicken and cooked it over the fire and, ritualistically, it was time to eat it. I think it was barely done in the middle. I think that was the last one we did in La Honda.

The next one we went off to Babbs's place down in Santa Cruz. We did a show down there the next Saturday night. The next Saturday we went to San Jose. But we went to that place in Santa Cruz and the Dead came with us. And by this time they were the full-out Dead. They moved Pigpen's huge,

huge organ in to Babbs's house. It just took all the effort in the world to carry it in there and set it up. They set the drums up in one room and the guitars in another room. So they were playing in a number of different places. We did the same thing the next weekend in San Jose at this place called Big Nig's, a very big 350-pound black guy. Again we had to set up in all these different rooms. Played for all these people in all these different rooms. And, when you're doing that it's hard for a band to just play numbers, especially when everybody's completely ripped. Just kinda plunkin' in and out.

The next thing we did was up in Palo Alto, at a place called The Big Beat. By then we had a big following, and the Dead were set up at one end and we were set up at the other end and we'd play and they'd come in and take over and play and soon it was just sound moving in and out of each other.

MF: Could you describe the scene there?

KK: I remember the scene there at Palo Alto. Late at night, at like three or four in the morning, there was this girl named Bubbles. She began to dance, and this big black friend of ours called Gaylord—we didn't know him well at that time—he sat down at the drums. He didn't know how to drum and she didn't know how to dance. Pretty soon she was watching her shadow and moving to the shadow and he was drumming to her and everybody completely got into it and she was entirely unaware that she was being watched where she was and everybody just watched this thing happen. It was meaningful for both of them. She was dancing with this black shadow and he was playing to this little, nubile nymphet and it went on for about a half-hour to forty-five minutes. It was just so good. I realized, man, this is art in a true form.

MF: Art?

KK: Given a chance, everybody has art in them and they're able to bring it out and give it an opening with a little bit of encouragement. So, from then on just whatever would begin to happen at these next Acid Tests, we'd just let it go and keep track of it. There's nothing like just taking a whole energy and putting it at the beck and call of somebody who's really high, who's not just out there trying to impress somebody. They're out there doing something with who they are and who these other people are and where they are and what they truly feel way down deep, what's really very important to them, and—I've just seen amazing things that people have done out there. Once they're accepted and they've got that light on them and they're accepted and comfortable with what they're doing and the musicians are playing to them—it's not like the dancers are dancing to the music—the dancers are creating the music. The music is responding to them. The Dead learned a tremendous amount from this. How to play music that was happening in the minds of the people before it was happening in their [own] minds. You could hear all of this early, early wonderful Dead stuff, the Fillmore Acid Test and the Trips Festival, where something is happening up there. You hear the Dead playing not just music but playing to the thing that's happening. And they were the best by far. They could read music off of anywhere, and they'd be watching for it and when it happened they'd begin to play it. The people in the audience would know, "Hey, they're playing this moment." It was a tremendously exciting thing for everybody. We could see, *this is different. This is music that is different from any music that is being played anywhere in the world. It's changing constantly and it's alert to what's going on.* If you'd see somebody really ripped and out of shape, we'd bring the lights down on them and let everybody back off of them. Pretty soon the Dead would be playing to them.

MF: So, there wasn't just a band on the stage and fans in the audience? It was more of a whole?

KK: It was a whole scene, very much a whole scene. And they only charged a buck, and everybody paid. It really made a great difference that it was cheap enough that everybody could get in. It was a wonderful thing. It meant everybody was equal, you know?

MF: Is it possible to obtain that type of feeling anymore?

KK: Oh, yeah. Everything is still happening, still important. When I begin to get depressed about something I'll go out and run into a bunch of kids, sixteen and seventeen, and they're as dedicated as you'd ever want anyone to be. They're smart, hard working, and they're in tune. It's always been important to spiritual causes and national causes, music. It happened, starting after WWII. It had a different feel to it: Jazz was no longer celebration music. Jazz dropped off of what it had been doing for a long time and it stopped being the real cutting edge. It dropped back and began to hone itself and work on itself as music. When you get to the '60s it's different. Things happened, and I think it's very old-fashioned kind of music that goes back to stuff that'd be played around fires at scenes where people would completely zone out to the music.

MF: It became more spiritual?

KK: And the drugs. Drugs are a part of this, going back thousands and thousands of years. People would get together, get high, play music, and the music turns into something else. It's traditional business that's been going on in music for a long time. But, I've been through stuff starting in the '60s that's still going on that's new. The one thing I think, the high that was happening at that time—the new high—various versions of LSD around, psilocybin, mescaline, and people played music on these things. But, somehow, at that time in the '60s—Kennedy having just been killed and the United States being recognized as a world power in art and military and just social thinking—it changed the style. And the people that got in on that style knew, "Hey, this is the most important and unique thing that I could ever remember." There'd be things happening that you knew never happened before in history. Even when there were other drugs and other musical things happening, this was the modern time. This was the time of electricity. Everything was faster. Things have changed very deeply in the core of America. And the people who were in on it knew that this was the most important thing that we'll ever have the chance to do. Everybody I knew that was in on it; they're very humble about it. You don't run into people who were in on this movement who are prideful and boastful. It includes all the religious faiths and it provides a buffer for everybody to be in. You could tell it was effective because suddenly a fear went through the world that, "Hey, this sort of thinking is detrimental to the great world economy. This means we won't sell near as many airplanes or bombs."

We began to come across opposition to it in the late '60s and early '70s. But, for a while there it got away with just murder. We weren't doing anything wrong, but we were doing something that was so against the grain of whatever else was going on. And we knew it and they knew it and they didn't realize there was as many of us as there were and that there was talent in these ranks. I mean, Jerry Garcia was a very, very smart man, and playing the guitar is one of the things he did, but that's not anywhere near what he's worth. It's something more than that. It didn't make any difference if you were a writer, painter, musician, whatever it was. You'd see each other across an airport, and eyes would connect—and you'd get a smile and a wink. And everybody'd know: this is far out. And the musicians who get involved in this are still very much devoted to this whole feeling.

MF: Even bands today?

KK: Yes. Even the very young musicians. They'll drop out of it. They don't get wrapped in the ritzy kind of new band look. But everybody knows that what happened with music and rock and roll in the '60s was historical and it's still going on. And it's full of youth as ever. You see some of the real heroes from this time are still playing music, and playing it really well. And the big eyes—the big New York and Hollywood—have looked away from them.

MF: Would you consider the music as the backbone to the counterculture movement?

KK: Musically, the most important expression of this revolution is it was a revolution that came with a changed mind, a mind that had been altered and it was trying to speak from where it was as well as it could. And there were a lot of silly songs that came out, but for the most part, it was very, very righteous and it still is.

MF: As the scene grew, venues grew, and crowds grew. Was there ever a serious clash of interests due to experience?

KK: There were different chemicals that hit it, and you could feel them. When cocaine hit the music scene, it was nowhere near as important or as exciting as when LSD hit the music scene. People have been doing speed and coke and playing music for years and years, and you can really crank it out and get a good, fast beat. But, that's different from what we were doing and the Dead were doing back then. We played stuff, old stuff from the Dead, in which they were playing along and suddenly it occurs to them they're playing too slow and they'll just suddenly begin to speed it up and move it up to another beat. And you hear them doing it and you can feel them thinking it. And in all of these things, Garcia was so strong. His mind was so strong and he was so into spirit that you know that this was a guy, whether he was a musician or an artist or he was making jet engines or whatever it was, he was going to be a success at it. A smart man. Every time I'd discuss books with Garcia, he would have read everything I'd read. He was tremendously well read. He slept very little. He sat up at night in a chair. He didn't lie down much. He would just sit and read, fall asleep and wake up again, read, and fall asleep.

MF: How did your appearance on stage with Phish come about?

KK: Well, we were coming back from the Rock and Roll Hall of Fame, that's what it was. The guy we were traveling with was the main guy from the Hall of Fame, that's the way it happened. I've been in contact with him and they invited us.

MF: On stage, in the beginning of your performance, you announced, "For two years, nobody has heard from the Bozos. Where are the Bozos?" Who are the Bozos?

KK: The Bozos were—there was an old record put out, *No Bozos on This Bus.* Did they ever show up on stage, do you know?

MF: Yes, dressed as ten-foot ghost-like clowns. Came right out of the crowd.

KK: (Laughs) The Bozos are good. They're a product of this Prankster we know in San Francisco. He just carries these costumes, and once you put on a costume, you're a Bozo, and you do what you're told. (Laughs) We're all Bozos on this bus. It's when the Bozos and the bus connected.

MF: Your appearance definitely gapped two generations. Phish has been compared to the Grateful Dead for years, but it's apples and oranges.

KK: More like apples and grapes.

MF: Did you know it was important? That you were bridging a gap?

KK: Oh yeah. When you hear them play—they're out there. The end of a long strand. I didn't know they were broken up. That's too bad. Hope it's not the last we see of them, though.

MF: They're all doing separate things. Supposedly, it's just a break, like the Dead's. (Laughs)

KK: The real mistake the Dead made was when Garcia died, they stopped being the Grateful Dead . . . But there was a thing that would happen with Garcia. You'd be listening to his music, your eyes closed, following it. Following each little movement he was doing and suddenly like, "He's listening to me. He's following my music." And this is the startling thing that would happen with the Dead. It was when you realized they weren't just playing with each other. They were playing with you. Every so often it would become real obvious. After Jed died, we had tickets to go see the Dead over at the local opera house. It was still quite new at the time, and it was a big event. Jed had been dead about a month, if that. We had our tickets come in and everybody said, "You don't have to go," and I said, "Well, it's the sort of a time when you lost somebody and they're dead and you got tickets to the Grateful Dead and if you don't go see them you're missing a great opportunity."

At the end of the program, there was great applause. It was a wonderful show. And we were applauding and applauding and they finally came out. And they played "Brokedown Palace," and as they were playing, Garcia begins to look up into the audience where I was sitting. And soon all the Dead were looking up at me and my family. Then, pretty soon, everybody was turning and looking at us. Everybody in the audience knew that I'd lost a son. And it was as touching and wonderful a thing as you'd ever imagine. They played that with no applause. Afterwards, people began to leave and as they came by they nodded to me and told me how sorry they were. It was as powerful a thing as you could ever hope for from as powerful a group. Whenever I hear that song, tears will jump into my eyes.

MF: That is beautiful.

KK: So much of this has to do with Cassady. Cassady was the main antenna that brought in all this energy that was being used in art, music, literature, revolution. He was never a great Dead fan. He was never a great rock and roll fan. He'd go with them, but the whole rock and roll thing—it was too juvenile for Cassady. He liked jazz. He liked to get into it and follow it. Follow the movement of Coltrane or Miles Davis. You'd see him off somewhere standing with his eyes closed playing a record player in the house. You think he's completely into it. He's moving to every movement, every beat. He's *be bap boom bing ba boom boom boom.* Then he'd be over talking about stuff and then suddenly he'd say something that'd make you realize he's completely aware of every conversation going on in the room and he'd be making comments about them. This meant that he not only had to be really perceptive and alert, but he had to have good ears. So much of this stuff goes back to Neal Cassady, and I think that anybody in the Dead, if they were asked, knows that so much of the power that came out of the music and the whole revolutionary vibration set about in that time came from Neal. He had the ability to make everything within beat. He'd always be moving all the time, doing stuff, twitching—wonderful scene to watch.

MF: Is that why he was dubbed "The Fastest Man Alive"?

KK: Yup, the fastest man alive. (Laughs) But, we were fast, too. Me and Garcia and Bob Weir were on the Tom Snyder Show. (Laughing) Have you seen that?

MF: Yeah. He asked you about the Acid Tests.

KK: Yes. And the whole thing was going and somebody would start to answer a question and the other guy would pick it up and the other guy would pick it up and pretty soon, we were going way too fast for Tom Snyder to do anything but laugh. (Imitating Snyder) Ha, Ha, Ha, Ha. Laugh and Laugh. He started off thinking he was interviewing some three somebodies but he ended up realizing that he was interviewing Huey, Dewey, and Louie. (Laughs) And that's one of the sad things about Garcia dying. He just had one of the best raps out of anybody ever. He talked very high and talked very fast and very clear. He was so well read. It was great to talk literature with him, he really knew his stuff. Not just the Hemingway and Faulkner bunch, but Russian literature. He read all that Russian stuff. He'd get really into it and really excited about it.

MF: What main differences do you see now from the '60s?
KK: Well, the world had been turned on its ear by musicians of that time. It's like ragtime. When ragtime happened, a door opened that'll never be closed. That's really kind of the beginning of jazz. Once it occurred, you just have to factor it into the equation from now on. Whether you're listening to classical or jazz or be-bop or rock, it has a bit of that ragtime piano.

We used to go to the jazz places up in San Francisco and see Coltrane, Miles Davis, Gardner, all these people. All those people were downers. You went to these shows and you sit there with a frown on your face nodding your head following these downers on smack, singing really good stuff about bad things that'd happened. I remember when I first heard Billie Holiday sing "Strange Fruit." Have you ever heard that song?

MF: Sure have.
KK: God damn, what a song! It's a tremendous, powerful song. But, as philosophy, it's nothing you want to be left with. It's great that she did it and somebody had to do it. But I wouldn't have wanted to have been that person. Most of the people I knew that came through Stanford, they were all very comfortable with jazz, all the grad students. They had figured out every so often they'd go up to San Francisco, listen to some guy stoned to the gills, playing slow music. People listening and nodding and sometimes it'd get a little faster.

MF: Kerouac captured this scene well in *On the Road*. Running up and down the strip with Cassady.
KK: Oh yes. Very much. That's a great feeling, running up and down, watching Cassady listen to these guys. With the introduction of the Beatles and that whole new feeling, that really avenging feeling of rock and roll, in its first times in the '60s—it was exciting and thrilling, but very few

people thought it was important musically because too many kids were screaming.

We took the bus once to see the Beatles at the Cow Palace in 1965, and it was scary it was so powerful. It was scary to us, it was scary to the people putting it on, and it was scary to the Beatles. The only people that weren't scared were the audience, the kids. Every time they'd start singing, the audience would press toward them. And they'd try to stop singing and tell people to please back up and stop pushing forward. And everybody'd be quiet for a minute. As soon as they started singing, there would be just screams and people'd be out of their seats pushing toward them. And the Dead were on the bus with us when we went up there to this thing. And they saw it too and they were very affected. Everybody was. It meant to the Dead to avoid that, to get into a situation where you are in contact with people, and they are in contact with you. And you are singing back and forth to each other, between the audience and the Dead on stage. And, so when something happened, instead of the Dead not looking at it, they would turn to it and be into it and they would play to it. So, there was never any threat to the audience. You never see the Dead under any huge, pressing, forward threat, although they had as big an audience, as devoted an audience. They didn't just come in and sing "She's Got a Ticket to Ride" and end it. They came in, sang their pieces, and when they went into their solos, they were really aware of the audience. Like these films we have of Garcia when he's playing in 1972 and 1982. In the scene in 1972, you could see him watching the audience; he's not paying attention to his hands or the tune. He's watching the audience, doing the best he can with what he's got to work with. And the audience becomes his music. I've seen him turn and pick out a person and play the dance the person is dancing. This is nothing that ever happened in jazz or classical music. This is completely personal to rock and roll, especially personal to the Grateful Dead. The Beatles never did get into it. They backed right off of playing live.

MF: So it's all about spontaneity?
KK: Yes. When you see the Rolling Stones, they have learned how to do it with lots of effects that spread one side of the stadium to the other and stuff that goes up very high and large, large pictures of themselves so you don't have to press close to see them. You could stay back—

MF: And Mick Jagger jumps all around the stage.
KK: Yeah, and not just on stage. They have these walkways that run all the

way out to the edge of the stage area and clear up into the audience and around the other side. Jumping and twisting and carrying on.

MF: Is there as much spontaneity and improvisation in music today?
KK: Oh, I think a lot of people do it continually now. They have groups get together and they play a song and in the midst of the song they—it's not like a jazz break—it's like them finding themselves earning their space and they know people will listen to them and they could really get out there and experiment. Just about all the groups I listen to now have this quality, unless they're a real old kind of Roy Orbison group that plays the same stuff and just gets it better and better each time.

MF: What bands do you listen to now?
KK: Well, most of the ones connected to the Dead. Vince Welnick. Bobby Weir, and the whole crew that has splintered out from them. And, I'll go see big time old time bands like the Who and Dylan. But I don't get to see, like, Phish unless someone invites me and tells me about it and we go there and learn about it and after that we might really listen to their stuff, which is very nice, but it's diminutive. Nimble and clever.

MF: Maybe sometimes a little more playful than the Dead?
KK: Yeah.

MF: A lot of the old Dead jams are sharp, almost scary.
KK: Oh, yeah. A lot of times. They would wander into scary waters, and they didn't back out of it. They work their way through it. You could go to a Dead concert and be there for five, six hours, waiting, doing stuff, listening to music, just for this one moment when it happens. When whatever it is happens and everybody knows it happened and the Dead knows it happened and cops who've never heard of the Dead, they could feel it happen.

We were up once in Bellingham, Washington, and we've gone up there to do some readings. We took the bus. Ginsberg was along. Cassady was driving. Hell of a scene. And we drove up there, and got there on Tuesday, I guess. I had to teach classes until Saturday night, when everything began to come in from everywhere. The Jefferson Airplane was the big time lead band. This is 19 . . . I'd say '68, maybe '67. And the bus was parked out there full of people having a wonderful time. They didn't have to get up or do anything. Cassady was just having the greatest time of his life. And finally we decided, "It's Saturday. The Jefferson Airplane was coming. We better take some acid." And we all took a good jolt of acid and we wandered into the gymnasium where it was supposed to take place, we got off the bus and the world was tipping, the cement slabs were doing this (he gestures with his hand). We went, dragging, stumbling in there. It was one of these gymnasiums with an outside ring where they have popcorn for sale and then you go through the doors to the inside where the ball games are played. We got to that outside arena, and we just couldn't figure out where we were, what was happening.

Finally, we all just kind of collapsed there on the floor, and we're sitting in the great segment there and finally, the door opened up and this guy who at that time was the lead roadie for the Dead, can't remember his name, great friend of ours. He came swirling in there and he saw us and we looked up at him and he says, "Uh-Oh!" And we nodded at him. He dragged us on in and made us a place where we could pile up there on the floor in front of the first seats. And it was completely crowded and all the lights were on. Wonderful scene. And Cassady looked out and found that audience.

"Man," he said, "There's this audience. All I need is a little hallucination."

He had on this DayGlo driver's vest. That's all he had from the waist up. Every so often he'd bend the top of it down and put it back up and he's just twisting and having the best time. He played that audience for a good twenty minutes, and he would look at them and dance to them and he couldn't be heard—it was noisy in there.

Finally, the Airplane came out and the audience quieted down enough so they could turn off the lights and get going. The first song they played was "Somebody to Love." And, man, everything just began to happen. All these people and all the unanswered questions about what was going to happen, they changed and everything was different. Wonderful scene. Just an absolutely wonderful thing and it was spreading up. I could feel, "This is where it starts. This is where the actual millennium begins. From here on out, it will just go from one bunch of people to the next bunch of people and it will continue and it will expand and it will be understood in history. People will look back on it and all agree. Yeah, this is where it happened. This is the beginning."

At the end of the first song, Marty Ballad hollered over to the guy running the soundboard and he says, "Hey! Next time you start fiddling with those dials, you'd better wait 'till we give you the say so." Bring this up and that up, and suddenly; his voice was so harsh and strange. And all I could think was, "Wait now. I mean, everything is about to go good on earth for a thousand years and you're arguing with this little guy about a microphone?"

I sat there and they sang another piece, and couldn't get this off my mind. And they stopped the second piece. I said from the edge of the stage, "Hey, Marty. You ought to apologize to that guy for getting on his case so bad."

Suddenly, Cassady was all over me. Whamming me. WHOMP! WHOMP! WHOMP! And I tripped out.

Suddenly I wasn't there anymore. I was up on the top of a hill outside Babbs's place in La Honda, after the Acid Test Finale. The big Acid Test Graduation. I'd gone through a tough scene there at that thing. Just barely escaped with my brain. This was the one where I told everyone we had to stop taking acid because I'd been surrounded by reporters and cops. Besides, the Hells Angels kept coming around, sticking stuff in my mouth. Ripped to the top. And, finally, we had a get together and worked it out. Everybody got out and sat down. Worked it out. Talked it through. There was this little guy, an amazing little guy of about eighteen, and nobody ever seen him before or ever again. And, I'd talk and he'd make these little poetic statements at the end of everything I'd say. This guy was good. He was way out beyond himself. Doubt he even remembers. I know I'll never forget it. But anyway, Babbs took me back and he put me in this suit of clothes he had for me because I was in bad shape and he straightened me up. He put me in this suit, a thing that Gretchen made for him—a really sharp green and orange outfit. And he showed me how to tuck the shirt in as a Marine and how to tag it around so it was straight up and down. And he said, "Now, walk back out there."

And I strolled out there. Man, I looked good. And I remember driving home when we finally got everything packed up. It was a nice sunny Sunday morning in San Francisco. At one point, I began to talk again and my mind began to unravel, and George said, "There's a sign up there that says 'Wrong Way.' Go back!" So I said, "Oh. OK."

So we got on back to Babbs's. I couldn't sleep, so I headed up above Babbs's place into the hills above Santa Cruz. As I headed up, his two big old hound dogs, Curly and Joe, or something else, they went up in the hills with me. And we walked and walked and finally I began to come down. I laid down and looked at Babbs's house down there. And I could see Zane, he's probably seven. He came out earlier than everyone else. He came out to Babbs's rabbit cage and crawled on top of the rabbit cage. And he's fiddling with the rabbits. I was so pleased to be there with these dogs on either side of me, so mellow and nice. I thought I'd holler at him. And I went, "Ugghrruggaah!!"

This voice just came out of me and these dogs looked at me and began to pound me with their feet, and they're pounding me and beating me, and suddenly it's Cassady beating me and I was back at the Jefferson Airplane concert. And I realized I'd been through this trip, and something has taken me through and shown me, "Hey, you don't want to make these noises at this time. You want to keep quiet."

And I did. I quieted down and we sat there and watched the rest of the concert, which was a great concert, but it no longer had the chance of being the greatest concert in the history of the world. It had the door open for a second, but things got a little messy.

MF: Well, after all you've been through, what words of advice would you give to young music fans today?
KK: I think you always want to go to a scene that has an opening for you to play in, not to where you just go and sit there and listen. I get bored real easy. I want to play a little.

Index

www.ingramcontent.com/pod-product-compliance
Lightning Source LLC
Chambersburg PA
CBHW030309060726
47498CB00002BB/552